# THE COMPLETE IDIOT'S GUIDE® TO

# PC Basics

## Windows 7 Edition

by Joe Kraynak

ALPHA

*To my "kids," Nick and Ali, who constantly inspire me to keep up with the latest technology.*

## ALPHA BOOKS

Published by the Penguin Group

Penguin Group (USA) Inc., 375 Hudson Street, New York, New York 10014, USA

Penguin Group (Canada), 90 Eglinton Avenue East, Suite 700, Toronto, Ontario M4P 2Y3, Canada (a division of Pearson Penguin Canada Inc.)

Penguin Books Ltd., 80 Strand, London WC2R 0RL, England

Penguin Ireland, 25 St. Stephen's Green, Dublin 2, Ireland (a division of Penguin Books Ltd.)

Penguin Group (Australia), 250 Camberwell Road, Camberwell, Victoria 3124, Australia (a division of Pearson Australia Group Pty. Ltd.)

Penguin Books India Pvt. Ltd., 11 Community Centre, Panchsheel Park, New Delhi—110 017, India

Penguin Group (NZ), 67 Apollo Drive, Rosedale, North Shore, Auckland 1311, New Zealand (a division of Pearson New Zealand Ltd.)

Penguin Books (South Africa) (Pty.) Ltd., 24 Sturdee Avenue, Rosebank, Johannesburg 2196, South Africa

Penguin Books Ltd., Registered Offices: 80 Strand, London WC2R 0RL, England

International Standard Book Number: 978-1-61564-067-6
Library of Congress Catalog Card Number: 2010912366

13  12          8  7  6  5  4  3  2

Interpretation of the printing code: The rightmost number of the first series of numbers is the year of the book's printing; the rightmost number of the second series of numbers is the number of the book's printing. For example, a printing code of 11-1 shows that the first printing occurred in 2011.

*Printed in the United States of America*

**Publisher:** *Marie Butler-Knight*
**Associate Publisher/Acquiring Editor:** *Mike Sanders*
**Senior Managing Editor:** *Billy Fields*
**Development Editor:** *Michael Thomas*
**Production Editor:** *Kayla Dugger*
**Copy Editor:** *Krista Hansing Editorial Services, Inc.*

**Cover Designer:** *Kurt Owens*
**Book Designers:** *William Thomas, Rebecca Batchelor*
**Indexer:** *Angie Bess*
**Layout:** *Brian Massey*
**Proofreader:** *John Etchison*

# Contents

# Introduction

A funny thing happened on the way to the twenty-first century. Computers became more human. By "human," I don't mean "humanoid." I only mean that the computer has evolved from being a stodgy office tool to a revolutionary home appliance and entertainment system, a device designed to help us manage and enjoy our lives more fully.

Sure, you can still use a computer to type and print a letter, but the latest computer technology can completely revolutionize your professional and personal life. Here's just a glimpse of what you can do with a computer, an Internet connection, and some additional equipment:

- Compose letters.

- Create custom publications.

- Decorate your documents with professional clip art and other graphics.

- Shop at mega-malls and specialty shops without leaving your home—and save money, too!

- Send and receive mail electronically—no postage, and same-day delivery.

- Carry on conversations with friends, relatives, and complete strangers anywhere in the world—without paying long-distance charges.

- Plan your vacation, get medical advice, and find maps to nearly any location.

- Copy music clips from the Internet and from your CD collection and burn your own custom CDs.

- Take photos with a digital camera, transfer them to your computer, make prints, and e-mail them to your friends and family.

- Create your own websites or blogs (web logs) to express your views, communicate with family and friends, or market your products and services or yourself.

- Edit your home videos, create movies using photos and videos, and burn your movies to DVDs.

- Find a date or a mate. (I do recommend meeting in person before you make any commitments.)

xviii     The Complete Idiot's Guide to PC Basics, Windows 7 Edition

Sounds pretty cool, huh? Well, it is—assuming, of course, that you know what you're doing. To master the high-tech world of computers and electronic gadgets, you must first master the basics. You need to know your way around a computer, how to point and click with a mouse, how to run programs in Windows, and how to enter commands. After you've mastered a few basics, as explained in the first few chapters of this book, you'll be well prepared to explore and exploit the full power of your computer and the Internet as you proceed through later chapters.

## What You Learn in This Book

You don't have to read this book from cover to cover (although you might miss some savvy tidbits if you skip around). If you just purchased a computer, start with Chapter 1 to learn how to get your computer up and running. If you need a quick lesson on using Windows, skip ahead to Chapter 4. If you need to get wired to the Internet, check out Chapter 18.

To provide some structure for this hodgepodge of computer skills and techniques, I've divided this book into the following six parts:

**Part 1, Getting Started,** covers the bare minimum: buying a PC, setting it up and turning it on, using your mouse and keyboard to make it respond to your every command, and getting around in Windows. I also show you how to get help when you run into trouble.

**Part 2, Taking Control of Your PC,** shows you how to take control of the Windows desktop (a virtual desktop on which you create documents and play games), install and run programs, upgrade your PC with new hardware, share your computer peacefully with others, manage your files and documents, and network your computers so they can share valuable and often expensive resources.

**Part 3, Getting Down to Business,** teaches you everything you need to know to type a letter and other documents, add clip art and other graphics to your documents, and print documents and mailing labels. You also learn your way around spreadsheet and personal finance programs.

**Part 4, Tapping the Power of the Internet,** launches you into the world of telecommunications. In this part, you find out how to connect to the Internet, surf the World Wide Web, find just about anything on Google, send and receive e-mail, connect with friends and family on Facebook and Twitter, share videos on YouTube, shop online, chat and videoconference with others, create your own website or blog, and much more.

**Part 5, Going Digital with Music, Photos, and Video,** takes you on a tour of the wonderful world of digital audio, imaging, and video. Here you learn how to copy music clips from CDs and from the Internet to burn your own custom CDs and transfer music clips to a portable music player, buy a digital camera and use it to snap and print photos and e-mail them to your friends and family, and use video-editing software to splice your home movie clips into a full-length motion picture and burn it to a DVD you can watch on TV.

**Part 6, Maintaining and Troubleshooting Your Computer,** acts as your PC maintenance and repair guide. Here you learn how and when to clean your PC, give it regular tune-ups to keep it running like new, troubleshoot common problems, and find additional technical support when all else fails.

## Conventions Used in This Book

I use several conventions in this book to make it easier to understand. For example, when you need to type something, it appears in **bold**.

Likewise, if I tell you to select or click a command, the command also appears in **bold**. This enables you to quickly scan a series of steps without having to reread all the text.

## Extras

A plethora of sidebars offer additional information about what you've just read. Here's what to look for:

**DEFINITION**

In the computer industry, jargon and cryptic acronyms rule. When a computer term baffles you or an acronym annoys you, look here for a plain-English definition.

**NOTE**

For nonessential but usually very useful information, look for the Note icon. Think of Notes as bonus material.

**WHOA!**

Before you even think about clicking that button, check out these sidebars for precautionary advice. Chances are, I've made the same mistake myself, so let me tell you how to avoid the same blunder.

**INSIDE TIP**

When you've been in the computer business for as long as I have, you learn better ways to perform the same tasks and pick up information that helps you avoid common pitfalls. To share in my wealth of knowledge, check out my Inside Tips.

## Acknowledgments

Several people had to don hard hats and get their hands dirty to build a better book. I owe special thanks to Mike Sanders for choosing me to author this book and for handling the assorted details to get this book in gear. Thanks to Mike Thomas and Krista Hansing for guiding the content of this book, keeping it focused on new users, ferreting out all my typos, and fine-tuning my sentences. Kayla Dugger deserves a free trip to Aruba for shepherding the manuscript (and art) through production. The Alpha Books production team merits a round of applause for transforming a collection of electronic files into such an attractive book. I also owe special thanks to my agent, Neil Salkind, and the rest of the staff at Studio B for expertly managing the minor details (like paying me).

## Special Thanks to the Technical Reviewer

*The Complete Idiot's Guide to PC Basics, Windows 7 Edition*, was reviewed by an expert who double-checked the accuracy of what you'll learn here, to help us ensure that this book gives you everything you need to know about understanding and using your Windows 7 PC. Special thanks are extended to Meryl K. Evans, who not only checked for accuracy but also contributed her own technical expertise, insights, and tips.

Meryl earned her B.A. in education from American University and her Internet Technology certificate from New York University. Little did she know when she came home from summer camp in 1981 that she would connect with life-changing technology in the Apple ][+, which came without lowercase letters. Computers not only allowed her to connect with the world as a profoundly deaf person, but also allowed her to meet her husband before online dating was cool and start meryl.net, her freelance writing and editing business.

Meryl is the author of *Brilliant Outlook Pocketbook*, co-author of *Adapting to Web Standards: CSS and Ajax for Big Sites*, and contributor to other books on business, blogging, writing, and technology. She has served as tech reviewer for books on HTML, CSS, and software. The native Texan lives with her husband and three kid-dos in Plano, a heartbeat north of Dallas, where many of the stories about the city's people are tall tales.

## Trademarks

All terms mentioned in this book that are known to be or are suspected of being trademarks or service marks have been appropriately capitalized. Alpha Books and Penguin Group (USA) Inc. cannot attest to the accuracy of this information. Use of a term in this book should not be regarded as affecting the validity of any trademark or service mark.

# Getting Started

When you purchase a car, the salesperson sits you down behind the wheel and shows you how to work the controls. You learn how to tune the radio, activate cruise control, adjust the seat, and work the headlights and windshield wipers. When you purchase a PC—a much more complicated piece of machinery—you're on your own. You get several boxes containing various gadgets and cables, and it's up to you to figure out how to connect everything, turn it on, and start using it.

To make up for this lack of guidance, Part 1 acts as your personal driving instructor, leading you step by step through the process of buying, setting up, starting, and shutting down your PC and using the controls (the keyboard and mouse) to navigate Windows 7, run programs, and enter commands. You also discover where to look for help when you run into trouble or just don't know what to do.

# Buying the Right Computer for You

### In This Chapter

- Evaluating your computing needs
- Choosing between a desktop PC and portable models
- Knowing what to look for in specific hardware components
- Researching makes and models, and finding the best price

When buying a PC, you have much more to consider than simply whether you want a desktop PC, notebook, or netbook. You need to think not only about portability, but also processor type and speed, disk storage capacity, memory, CD/DVD drives, audio, video, operating system, and a whole lot more. In addition, you want to find the right PC at the best price.

Well, you've come to the right place. This chapter explains key considerations, provides guidance on making the right choices for your needs, and shows you how to shop for great deals on PCs.

## Assessing Your Computing Needs

Your choice of *PC* hinges on the reasons you're getting a new PC and how you plan to use it. Complete the following checklist to identify your computing needs. Check all items that apply.

## Focusing on Mobility

If you need or want to travel with your PC, mobility is the first and most important consideration. You can rule out entire categories of computers based solely on how portable you need your PC to be. The following sections describe your options from least to most mobile/portable.

**DEFINITION**

What is a **PC,** anyway? PC stands for *personal computer,* but in this book, we use it to refer to any computer that's not a Macintosh (Mac).

## Desktop PC

Desktop PCs are the largest, sturdiest, heaviest, and least portable of the bunch, but they offer three major advantages:

- **More bang for your buck:** A comparably equipped portable PC costs several hundred dollars more.

- **More suitable for meeting advanced needs:** A top-of-the-line desktop model can do things a top-of-the-line portable PC may not, such as play the latest video games at warp speed and produce theater-quality video and sound.

- **More room to grow:** Desktop models typically offer more upgrade options to meet future needs.

Desktop models also come as space-saving all-in-one PCs that look like a monitor with a mouse and keyboard attached (with cables or without). All-in-one models often have touch-screens to make them even easier to use.

## Notebook (Laptop)

Notebook PCs, also called laptops, include everything most users need in a single, compact unit that typically weighs less than 5 pounds.

## Tablet PC

A tablet PC is like a notebook with a screen that pivots, folds back, and allows you to write on it. (See Figure 1.1.) It's perfect for people who need to jot down handwritten notes, sign digital documents, or pivot the screen to show something to clients. Real estate agents, financial planners, investment brokers, and others who must travel, present information to clients, and have them sign documents often find a tablet PC the ideal solution.

**Figure 1.1**
*Dell Latitude tablet PC.*
(Photo courtesy of Dell Inc.)

## Netbook

Netbooks are streamlined notebooks designed primarily to use the Internet and perform basic tasks. They typically have smaller screens and keyboards, weigh about 3 pounds or less, and are very affordable. The biggest drawback may be the lack of an internal CD or DVD drive. You can add an external CD or DVD drive, but it just isn't quite the same.

## Recommendation

I'm a big fan of portable PCs and almost always recommend notebooks, tablet PCs, or larger netbooks over desktop models. Why? Because you can connect a mouse and a full-size keyboard and monitor to a portable computer to make it more like a desktop model, but you can't make a desktop model any smaller or lighter. Some portable PCs even have optional docking stations to enable you to quickly and easily connect the PC to any and all external devices.

# Focusing on Key PC Components

A PC is a collection of components designed to work as a unit. When you start shopping, you'll encounter lists of components along with specifications for each component. The following sections describe the most important components and what to look for based on your needs.

## Central Processing Unit (CPU)

The central processing unit (CPU) or processor is the computer's brain; it performs all the calculations for the computer. When choosing a CPU, consider the following factors:

- **Architecture:** This is the overall design of the CPU. One of the most important design considerations is the number of cores the CPU has. Multi-core processors, including dual- and quad-core processors, are like having two, three, or four processors built into a single CPU.

- **Clock speed:** Measured in gigahertz (GHz), clock speed indicates how fast the CPU processes instructions.

- **L2 cache:** Also known simply as cache, L2 cache is temporary storage built into the chip for recently or frequently used data and instructions. It helps the CPU function at top speed.

- **Front side bus:** This is the path that connects the CPU to other key components, including memory. Front side bus speed is measured in gigabytes—the faster, the better.

## Operating System

You can tell a lot about a computer by checking the version of Windows 7 that's installed on it. First, check whether the PC has a 32- or 64-bit version of Windows 7. The 32-bit version is fine for most needs and may be best if you have older 32-bit hardware or software you want to use. If you're looking for a performance boost or starting from scratch, lean toward a PC that runs the 64-bit version of Windows. The 64-bit PCs and software handle larger amounts of memory (4GB and higher). All computers that have the Windows 7 Compatible logo can run either the 32- or 64-bit version.

After choosing between the 32- and 64-bit version, you have another choice to make: Windows Starter, Home Premium, Professional, or Ultimate edition.

- **Windows Starter:** This is a streamlined version exclusively for netbooks.

- **Home Premium:** Windows 7 Home Premium can handle all your basic needs, simplify the process of setting up a home network, and manage all your media and entertainment needs, including managing and sharing photos, videos, and music; watching, recording, and copying DVDs; listening to, recording, and copying CDs; and watching and recording TV shows (with the addition of a TV tuner).

- **Professional:** Windows Professional has everything Home Premium has, plus a few features typical for businesses: Running Windows XP productivity programs in Windows XP Mode, automatically backing up files to your home or business network, and connecting easily and securely to your company network from remote locations.

- **Ultimate:** Windows Ultimate has everything included in the Professional edition, plus the ability to encrypt data on a portable PC or portable storage device, features for IT professionals, and support for 35 different languages.

## Random Access Memory (RAM)

Random access memory (RAM), often referred to simply as memory, stores all the data and instructions the PC requires to perform its job while it's on. When you turn off your PC, everything is erased from memory. When shopping for RAM, consider the following:

- **Amount:** 1GB will get you by. I recommend at least 2GB for most users and 4GB for serious media, entertainment, and gaming junkies. If the PC comes with the 32-bit version of Windows, don't bother with more than 4GB.

- **Type and speed:** Look for DDR2 or DDR3 SDRAM and compare speeds, measured in gigabytes. DDR stands for "double data rate," and SDRAM stands for "synchronous dynamic random access memory." Just remember that DDR2 is good, DDR3 is better, and higher speed translates into better performance and higher cost.

- **Upgradeability:** Make sure you can add more RAM later to meet your future needs. See "Shopping for a PC with Room to Grow" later in this chapter for details.

## Hard Drive

The computer's hard drive is a disk inside the computer that stores data permanently; when you turn the computer off, the data remains on the disk. When comparing hard drives in different PCs, consider the following factors:

- **Storage capacity:** Size or storage capacity is measured in gigabytes. 250GB is usually more than enough. Photographers, videographers, serious gamers, and game designers require more space—at least 500GB.

- **Speed:** Speed is measured in revolutions per minute (RPMs) and is directly related to the rate at which the drive can read data from the disk. A speed of 5400 RPMs is standard and sufficient for most needs. High-end users should consider speeds of at least 7200 RPMs.

- **Interface:** The Serial ATA (SATA) interface is standard and sufficient for most needs. A SATA drive coupled with motherboard that supports it can transfer data at up to 300MB per second. Steer clear of the older ATA (also called IDE) interface. SCSI is another high-performance option.

- **Buffer:** A buffer is memory built into the drive to store data temporarily so the system doesn't need to wait for the relatively slow-spinning disk to read frequently accessed data and instructions. Most hard drives have an 8MB buffer, which is sufficient for most needs; 16MB or more is better.

## Optical Drive for CDs and DVDs

Optical drive is another name for CD or DVD drive. When comparing optical drives, consider the following features:

- **Multi-format:** Most optical drives are multi-format, meaning you can use them to store computer data and play or record CDs or DVDs. Opt for a multi-format DVD+RW—a single drive that can handle all of these tasks.

- **Speed:** Speed is expressed as X (times), which describes how fast the drive can write data to the disc. 8X is standard, but I recommend 16X or faster. Recording with an 8X drive is pretty slow, even if you don't burn discs all that often.

- **Interface:** You have the same choices here as you do with hard drives: ATA (IDE) or SATA. Again, I recommend going with a SATA interface, but in the case of optical drives, ATA (IDE) is sufficient and very common.

- **Slot or tray load:** With a slot-load drive, you insert the disc like a quarter in a pop machine, which is cool, easy, and efficient. Traditional drives require you to eject a tray, place a disc on it, and then load the tray.

- **Dual-layer support:** Some optical drives can read from and write to both sides of a dual-layer disc, essentially doubling its storage capacity. If you plan to back up files, dual-layer DVD+RW are great; otherwise, this feature isn't all that important.

- **Laser disc labeling:** Many optical drives (often referred to as LightScribe burners) can print labels on discs designed to have labels printed on them, which is pretty cool but not all that important.

- **Blu-ray support:** Planning to watch high-definition movies on your computer? Then consider a Blu-ray drive. In addition to being able to play Blu-ray video, these drives can store up to 50GB on a single disc.

If you're planning to copy a lot of CDs or DVDs, having two drives makes the job much easier.

## Video Adapter

A video adapter processes the data required to display images on a monitor. Many computers include integrated video (part of the motherboard) supporting one or more of the following standards:

- **Digital Visual Interface (DVI):** DVI enables you to play high-definition video.

- **High-Definition Media Interface (HDMI):** Like DVI, HDMI is designed for high-definition video. The only difference is that HDMI carries both video and sound, whereas DVI carries only video. Computers typically support one or the other.

- **Blu-ray support:** Blu-ray discs are copy-protected by AACS technology, so if you're planning to watch high-definition video, make sure the PC supports High-Bandwidth Digital Content Protection (HDCP) decoding.

Most important is that the PC you buy have the right port (DVI or HDMI) for the monitor you choose. You may encounter some older PCs and monitors that support the VGA standard, but this is obsolete.

Top-line PCs have a separate video card (or two). If you're a hardcore video game player, look for a PC that has a separate video card and consider the following video card specifications:

- **Video Standard:** PCIe (Peripheral Component Interconnect Express) is a big step up in speed and performance from the older Accelerated Graphics Port (AGP) standard.

- **Memory:** Graphics cards have their own memory to improve display quality and performance. 256MB is standard; 1GB is better for serious game players, photographers, or videographers.

- **Dual display support:** Look for a PC that allows you to connect two monitors so you have the option of a dual-display configuration. This allows you to expand your desktop, as explained in Chapter 6, so you can, for example, have your e-mail displayed in one window while you're working on a document in the other.

- **Multiple display support:** Hardcore game players often opt for systems with multiple video cards (as many as four) linked together for optimum display quality and performance. If this is what you have in mind, look for systems that support the nVidia Scalable Link Interface (SLI) or ATI Crossfire technology.

- **DirectX 10:** Newer graphics cards support DirectX 10 (DX10), Microsoft's multimedia technology for displaying realistic images with complex lighting and shading effects.

- **DVI or HDMI support with HDPC decoding:** DVI or HDMI is essential for playing Blu-ray DVDs and taking advantage of advanced graphics and animation in video games.

## Monitor

A monitor displays everything so you can see what you're doing. Make sure the monitor you're getting is large enough for your needs and clear enough for your eyes. The following list describes the most important characteristics to consider:

- **Size:** Size is the most important consideration. Don't settle for anything smaller than 15 inches, unless you're shopping for a netbook PC. A 19- or 21-inch monitor is usually sufficient for working and for watching TV or DVDs, as long as you sit really close. You may also want to consider a widescreen monitor to work on two documents side by side.

- **Interface:** Newer monitors support DVI or HDMI, both of which send a digital signal directly to the monitor for better performance and quality.

- **Aspect ratio:** Aspect ratio is the ratio of width to height. For standard monitors, the aspect ratio is 4-to-3. Newer, wide-screen monitors have an aspect ratio of 16-to-9, which is ideal for viewing documents side by side and watching HDTV and DVD movies in wide-screen format.

- **Maximum resolution:** Maximum resolution is a measure of the number of colored dots (pixels) that comprise the screen. Generally, the more dots, the clearer the picture. Typical resolution for a 17- or 19-inch flat-panel LCD is 1280×1024 dpi (dots per inch). Comparable wide-screen models have a resolution of 1440×900 dpi. Unless you're in the market for a small portable PC, don't settle for anything less than 1280×960 dpi.

- **Contrast ratio:** The contrast ratio is the difference in brightness between white and black. Look for a contrast ratio of at least 500-to-1 for a clearer, crisper display.

- **Response time:** Response time, measured in milliseconds (ms), expresses the time it takes a pixel to change colors. For most purposes, a response time of 8ms is sufficient. Game players should look for response times of 5ms or less.

- **Ergonomics:** If you plan to sit in front of the computer for several hours a day, make sure you can adjust the monitor's height and angle for maximum comfort. Some monitors also swivel from side to side, which comes in handy if you need to show something to a colleague, client, or family member sitting beside you.

- **Gloss:** Some portable PCs come with glossy screens designed to produce a sharper display, but some users don't like the reflective nature of these screens.

- **Touch-screen:** Touch-screens, available for both desktop and portable PCs, are a standard option on tablet PCs. A touch-screen enables you to interact with your computer by pointing and tapping the screen with your finger, as shown in Figure 1.2, instead of or in addition to using a mouse. If you're in the market for a touch-screen, look for a *multi-touch* model or ask the dealer whether the PC supports Windows Touch.

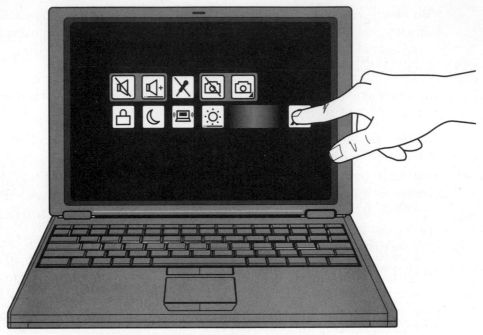

**Figure 1.2**
*Lenovo T400 ThinkPad with Simple Tap touch-screen.*
(Photo courtesy of Lenovo.)

## Sound Card

Sound goes hand in hand with video. Standard models come with integrated audio, which often produces high-quality surround sound output—5.1, meaning five speakers plus a subwoofer. If you can't settle for less than bone-rattling, theater-quality sound or you're using your PC to record and mix audio, you'll need to step up to a midlevel or high-end dedicated sound card. When comparing sound cards, consider the following characteristics:

- **Surround sound:** Midlevel sound cards support 5.1 surround sound. High-end sound cards support 7.1 surround sound—seven speakers plus a subwoofer, to really immerse you in sound.

- **Interface:** Newer sound cards are built with a PCI interface for improved performance. Steer clear of older IDE versions.

- **Sampling rate:** Sampling rate determines how fast the sound card pulls data from an analog (sound wave) signal to convert it into a digital signal. The higher the sampling rate, the clearer the digital recording.

- **Bit depth:** Bit depth is the amount of data recorded for each sample and directly corresponds to the resolution or richness of the sound. All you really need to know is that CD-quality audio is 16-bit, whereas higher-quality DVD audio is 24-bit.

- **Number of voices:** When reading specs, you're likely to encounter the numbers 32 and 64, as in AWE32 or AWE64. This has nothing to do with bit depth. It refers to the number of distinct "voices," or sounds, the card can play simultaneously.

- **Signal-to-noise ratio:** This is the ratio of the power of the signal to the power of undesirable background noise. The higher the ratio, measured in decibels (dB), the less noticeable the background noise. Look for this number to be 105dB or higher.

- **Blu-ray support:** Blu-ray discs are copy-protected by AACS technology, so if you're planning to watch high-definition video, make sure the computer is equipped with a sound card that has a decoder for Dolby Digital and DTS surround sound formats. Without the appropriate decoder, the soundtrack still plays, but not in theater quality.

Some sound cards are specifically designed for home theater, gaming, or recording and mixing music. If you have any of these high-end needs, be sure to ask the dealer about available sound card upgrades.

## Ports and Jacks

All PCs have ports and jacks into which you plug your peripheral devices, including a monitor, printer, mouse, keyboard, digital camera, webcam, phone line, networking cable, and scanner. Any PC you choose should have the following ports and jacks:

- **Universal Serial Bus (USB):** USB ports enable you to easily connect all sorts of external devices (over 100) to a single port, including external hard drives, CD and DVD drives, mouse, keyboard, webcam, and so on. Make sure the PC has at least two, and preferably four, USB 2.0 ports.

- **Graphics port:** A DVI or HDMI port that's suitable for the monitor you plan to use is essential.

- **Audio input (microphone):** Almost all PCs include a microphone jack, for voice communications over the Internet and speech recognition—you talk, it types.

- **Audio output:** Even if you purchase a portable PC with built-in speakers, make sure it includes an audio output and headphone jack so you can connect external speakers and headphones.

- **Modem (optional):** An internal dial-up modem enables you to connect to the Internet over a standard phone line. As broadband Internet (via cable, satellite, or Wi-Fi) becomes more popular and accessible, dial-up modems are becoming obsolete, but a dial-up modem is useful if broadband options are not available or as a backup if you lose your broadband connection.

To take advantage of cutting-edge technologies, I also recommend that you purchase a PC with the following ports:

- **eSATA:** An eSATA port is a nice addition if you're planning to use high-speed external storage devices, but USB 2.0 is plenty fast enough for most users' needs.

- **ExpressCard:** An ExpressCard slot is particularly beneficial on portable PCs because it enables you to easily add and remove devices, including a TV tuner, memory card reader (for cards like those used in digital cameras), wireless broadband Internet device, Wi-Fi, an eSATA port, and even extra RAM or a hard drive. Standard ExpressCards are 54mm wide and can accept 34mm cards. The 34mm slots are often used on smaller portable PCs, to save space and consume less battery power.

## Networking, Wi-Fi, and Wireless Broadband

Almost all computers include the following networking options, but make sure both are available:

- **Local area network (LAN) port:** Also called an Ethernet port, a LAN port enables you to connect the computer via cable to a network. The port looks like an oversized phone jack.

- **Wi-Fi:** Wi-Fi is for wireless networking either in your home or business or in Wi-Fi hotspots, including some hotels, coffee shops, airports, and Internet cafes and kiosks. Opt for the latest Wi-Fi standard (802.11n as I was writing this book), which is typically backward compatible with earlier standards, including 802.11b and 802.11g.

Many portable PCs also come equipped with support for wireless broadband Internet, but you can add it later with a wireless broadband USB or ExpressCard modem.

## Bluetooth Wireless Connectivity

Bluetooth is a wireless technology that enables any two Bluetooth-enabled devices within range to communicate without cables. For example, you can connect a Bluetooth keyboard, mouse, webcam, and headset to the computer or exchange data between your cellphone and PC. I recommend purchasing a computer with Bluetooth support.

## Webcam

A webcam is a small (sometimes tiny) camera that can capture a photo or video of you as you sit in front of your computer. Many computers come with a built-in webcam, which I consider an essential component of any portable PC. If you purchase a desktop model, it may not include a webcam, but a quality webcam is inexpensive and very easy to add later. When comparing webcams, consider the following:

- **Resolution:** Resolution determines image size and quality. A resolution of 640×480 is sufficient for most uses; 960×720 is better, especially if you're going to be video recording yourself to share with others.

- **Autofocus:** An autofocus lens keeps you in focus as you move around.

- **Frame rate:** Frame rate is a measure of the number of frames in each second of video. For smooth video, look for a webcam that supports at least 30 frames per second (fps).

- **Low-light support:** Low-light conditions can negatively affect frame rates and quality, so make sure the webcam has built-in technology to correct for this.

- **Built-in microphone:** Webcam microphones are great for videoconferencing because they're directional and noise-cancelling.

- **Skype support:** Skype is a popular service that enables you to make free PC-to-PC "phone" calls, make affordable PC-to-phone calls, and videoconference using your PC, as discussed in Chapter 25. Make sure the webcam wears the Skype logo, for optimum quality and performance.

- **Connection:** For portable PCs, built-in is best. For desktop models, look for a Bluetooth or USB webcam.

- **Size:** Generally, the smaller the better. The camera need not be large to produce high-quality images.

- **Design and adjustments:** Some webcams are designed to sit on a desk; others clip onto the monitor. This is pretty much a personal preference, but if the webcam is not built in, make sure you can adjust it easily up and down and side to side.

## Keyboard

A keyboard enables you to type and enter commands. You don't have much choice here unless you purchase a keyboard separately. Two features I recommend are wireless (Bluetooth), so you have one less cable to deal with, and full size, so you don't have to type on a dinky keyboard.

## Mouse or Touchpad

A mouse or touchpad enables you to enter commands simply by pointing to what you want and clicking a button or tapping the touchpad. A mouse is a fairly standard piece of equipment, so you don't have much choice here. However, if the computer you choose supports Bluetooth, get a wireless mouse.

Almost all portable PCs have a built-in touchpad instead of a mouse, although you can disable the touchpad and connect a mouse. A touchpad translates finger motion into pointer position on the screen. Unfortunately, I can't provide any guidelines here. Try before you buy, if possible, and read reviews to see if any users have had trouble using a particular PC's touchpad.

## Additional Portable PC Considerations

Portable PCs are a different species entirely. As you shop, keep the following factors in mind:

- **Battery life:** How long do you need the PC to operate on battery power alone? Some portable PCs are designed to run for eight hours or more on a single charge.

- **Weight:** Some portable PCs are lighter than others. How heavy of a PC are you willing to lug around—3 pounds, 5 pounds, 7 pounds? Expect to pay a premium or surrender features and functionality for the lightest of the bunch.

## Printer

Printers are usually sold separately. Following are key considerations:

- **Laser or inkjet?** Laser printers are typically faster, pricier, and a better choice for business use. Inkjet printers tend to be slower, more affordable, and more versatile, making them better for home use. If you're planning to print photos, opt for an inkjet.

- **Printer only or multi-function?** Choose a multi-function printer that can print, copy, fax, and scan documents and images. You may not think you need all these functions now, but you'll miss them later if you choose a printer that doesn't have them.

- **Print quality:** Print quality is typically measured in dots per inch (dpi). 600dpi is sufficient for most users, but if you think you'll need higher-quality output, choose a printer with a resolution of 1200dpi or higher. These can print in lower resolutions, to conserve ink or toner.

- **Speed:** Print speed is measured in pages per minute (ppm). If you're buying the printer to share among multiple network users, you may need something that's superfast (more than 20ppm). For home use, 10ppm is usually fast enough.

- **Connection:** Printers can connect to PCs in a variety of ways. Most connect via a USB port, but some connect wirelessly via Bluetooth or via Wi-Fi access points with built-in print servers. If you plan to share the PC on a network, Wi-Fi is best, but you can still share a USB printer by connecting it to a wireless router.

- **Consumables:** Paper and ink can get very expensive. Consider paying extra for a printer designed to use less ink. Also check the prices and capacity of the replacement ink or toner cartridges the printer uses.

- **Memory card slots:** Many newer printers have memory card slots on the front that provide a convenient way to transfer photos from a digital camera to your printer. Some printers also include a USB port for transferring images directly from the camera.

## Shopping for a PC with Room to Grow

Most computers are not all they can be. They're fine for now, but as technology and your individual needs change, they may not keep up. Fortunately, you can upgrade most computers by installing a bigger hard drive or a second hard drive, adding RAM, or installing a faster and more powerful video card.

If you're shopping for a desktop model, check for the following:

- **Two open drive bays:** These enable you to add a hard disk, DVD, or backup drive to your computer later.

- **Two or three open PCI expansion slots:** If you want to plug in extras later (a sound card, external drive, scanner, or TV tuner card), you'll need some open expansion slots.

- **Two to four USB 2.0 ports:** You can string together over 100 devices on one USB port, making upgrades a snap.

- **Expandable memory:** Make sure you can add memory modules without removing the existing modules. If the computer has a 1GB RAM module in each of its two RAM slots, you'll have to remove one of the modules to add more memory. It's better if one slot has a 2GB RAM module and the other is open.

Portable PCs are more difficult and expensive to upgrade, so you're better off buying a portable PC that has more than what you need right now. You can forget about expansion slots, because portable PCs don't have any, but USB ports and an ExpressCard slot provide you with many upgrade options.

## Warranty and Technical Support

Almost all computers come with a limited warranty, and many include limited tech support for a set amount of time. For the rank beginner, I recommend paying extra for an extended warranty, preferably with onsite service, so you don't have to take the computer "into the shop" or ship it to the dealer. I also recommend paying extra for technical support so you have someone on call if anything goes wrong. While you're at it, check the dealer's return policy.

If you take a pass on paying extra for tech support, Chapter 35 shows you how to obtain plenty of free tech support on the Internet.

# Going Shopping

Shopping for a computer is a process of narrowing your choices down to one computer. The following sections lead you through the process I follow when shopping for a new computer.

## Finding a Manufacturer and Line of PCs You Like

After deciding on a type of computer (desktop, notebook, tablet, or netbook), narrow your selection by manufacturer. Top PC manufacturers include HP/Compaq (www. hp.com), Dell (www.dell.com), Acer (www.acer.com), Lenovo (www.lenovo.com), Toshiba (www.toshiba.com), Sony (www.sony.com), and Gateway (www.gateway.com). Visit a few of these manufacturers' websites to check out the products they offer. (Use a friend's computer or a computer at your local library to visit the websites mentioned here.) Also visit your local electronics or office supply store so you can see and touch a few makes and models.

What you're shopping for at this point is a computer that has the desired look and feel. Jot down the manufacturer and line of products for three or four computers that catch your eye—for example, Dell Vostro or Sony Vaio or Acer Aspire. In the following section, you'll be looking at different models in each line.

## Exploring Different Models and Packages

Within every product line, PC manufacturers offer several models and packages that typically range from low-budget, bare-bones versions to top-of-the-line models that are the most powerful, the fastest, and the most feature packed.

Check out the different models and packages to see what the pricier models have that the lower-cost models are missing. Pricier models typically have a faster CPU, more RAM, a larger and faster hard drive, a better video card, and sometimes a larger monitor or more and/or better software, but you may not need all those extras. Look for a model/package that meets your needs with room to grow, as explained in the following section.

When shopping online, you typically choose a model and then have the option to customize it; for example, you may want additional memory, a larger monitor, more hard drive space, and a better sound system.

## Researching Your Options

After narrowing your selection to a few candidates, research each of them on the web. If you don't have a computer with Internet access, borrow one. A manufacturer can claim anything it wants about a product, but only a product's reviews and ratings provide an unbiased view, and the best place to find these ratings and reviews is the web.

Visit Google at www.google.com and search for the make and model followed by the phrase "rating review" (without the quotation marks). (See Chapter 20 for details on how to use Google.) The search results provide links you can click to obtain ratings and reviews of the product. You may also find valuable ratings and reviews at the following websites:

- Manufacturer's website

- Websites of any stores that sell the specific make and model

- CNET, at reviews.cnet.com

- *PC Magazine*, at www.pcmag.com (click **Reviews** in the menu)

- *PC World*, at www.pcworld.com/reviews.html

- Computer Shopper, at computershopper.com

## Shopping for the Best Price

Fortunately for you, competition in the PC market keeps profit margins slim, but it's still a good idea to shop around for the best price. Following are some tips:

- Check with your school, the company you work for, and any organizations you belong to, to determine whether they receive any special deals on PCs or have a PC purchase program in place to help cover the cost.

- Shop online. Head to Google at www.google.com and search for the make and model. You'll find plenty of dealers online, along with comparison-shopping sites that can help you track down the best price. If you don't have a computer connected to the Internet, borrow one.

- Shop offline. Visit local electronics and office supply stores and even Walmart and Target to see whether they're offering any special deals. It's not likely, but you may find a better deal offline than online.

## The Least You Need to Know

- Minimum requirements netbook PC: 1GHz CPU; 1GB RAM with room for one additional GB; 80GB hard drive; 10-inch display; full-size keyboard; built-in microphone, speakers, and 480×640 webcam; two USB 2.0 ports; 802.11 b/g wireless card; Bluetooth support; Windows 7 Starter.

- Minimum requirements basic PC: 1.6GHz CPU, 1–2GB RAM with room for more, 120MB hard drive, 8X DVD+RW drive, integrated audio and video, 802.11 b/g wireless networking, 15- or 17-inch flat-panel monitor, two USB 2.0 ports, Windows 7 32-bit Home Premium.

- Minimum requirements intermediate PC: Dual-core CPU a step or two down from the highest speed available, at least 2GB RAM with room for more, 250GB hard drive, 16X DVD+RW drive, 5.1 surround sound audio, 802.11 b/g wireless networking, 17- or 19-inch flat-panel monitor, four USB 2.0 ports, Bluetooth support, Windows 7 32-bit Professional or Ultimate.

- Minimum requirements advanced PC: Quad-core CPU, 4GB RAM with room for more, 500GB hard drive, 16X Double-Layer DVD+RW drive, high-definition audio card, 512MB or more PCI video card with DVI or HDMI support, 802.11 b/g/n wireless networking, 20-inch flat-panel monitor or larger, four USB 2.0 ports, two FireWire ports, Bluetooth support, Windows 7 64-bit Professional or Ultimate.

# Setting Up, Starting, and Turning Off Your PC

## In This Chapter

- Safely unpacking the parts of your PC
- Setting up your PC in a healthy environment
- Connecting a monitor, keyboard, mouse, and other add-ons
- Turning your PC on and off the right way

Bringing home your first PC is nearly as exhilarating and worrisome as adopting a new puppy. You're excited, but you really don't know what to expect or how to get started. How do you connect everything? What's the proper sequence for turning on the parts? How do you respond to your PC the first time you start it?

This chapter shows you what to expect. Here you learn how to prepare a space for your PC, set it up, and turn on everything in the correct sequence. This chapter also provides plenty of tips and tricks to deal with the unexpected the first time you start your PC.

## Unpacking Your Equipment

You don't need detailed instructions to know how to open boxes, but be careful and be aware of the following precautions:

- Take your time.
- Clear all drinks from your work area.
- Unpack on the floor, to avoid dropping anything.
- Don't cut open the boxes. You can easily scratch something inside or hack through a cable.

- For any large part, such as a system unit or monitor, check the box for guidance on how to unpack it. The box usually includes some indication of which side is up and whether to lift the part out of the box or slide it out from the side.

- Save all the packing material. Many manufacturers accept returns only in the original packing. The packing material is also useful if you ever need to move.

- Read the packing list(s) thoroughly to be sure you received everything you ordered. If something is missing, contact the manufacturer or dealer *immediately*.

- Inspect the cables for cuts and check for bent pins on the connectors. If you find a bent or damaged pin, call the manufacturer instead of trying to fix it yourself, which could void the warranty. (You'll find out more about connectors and pins later in this chapter.)

- Let the computer sit for two or three hours to adjust to the room temperature and humidity.

- Don't turn on *anything* until *everything* is connected. On some PCs, you can safely plug in devices when the power is on, but check the manual to be sure.

- Remove any spacers or packing materials from the disk drives and printer. These materials are commonly used to keep parts from shifting during shipping.

- Complete and submit any registration or warranty forms. This can save you hundreds of dollars down the road.

**INSIDE TIP**

Store your PC instructions, warranty, and other paperwork in a folder or gallon-size sealable plastic bag, and store it in a safe place for future reference.

# Finding a Comfortable Home for Your PC

Choose a place for your PC that's convenient and comfortable. To keep your PC healthy, make sure the location meets the following criteria:

- A cool, dry, well-ventilated area away from direct sunlight.

- As free of dust, smoke, and pet hair as possible.

- Near a properly grounded outlet that's not on the same circuit as an appliance that draws a lot of electricity, such as an air conditioner. You can buy an inexpensive three-prong outlet tester at your local hardware store to determine whether outlets are properly grounded.

- Near a phone jack or cable-Internet outlet, depending on how you plan to connect to the Internet.

- On a sturdy surface.

# Connecting Everything

If you purchased a desktop PC, you may have several components you need to connect to the system unit—the box that contains the CPU and other central components. Before you start connecting anything, set all the parts where you want them to be. (Moving the parts around after you connect them tends to tangle the cables.)

Fortunately, many PCs come with illustrated instructions on how to connect the various components and/or use color-coded plugs and ports. Otherwise, simply match the plug on the cable with the size, shape, and pin configuration of its corresponding port, as shown in Table 2.1.

**Table 2.1   Matching Plugs with Ports**

| Device | Connector Type | Plug | Port | Color |
|--------|----------------|------|------|-------|
| USB keyboard, mouse, etc. | USB Type A | | | Black |
| Printer, etc. | USB Type B | | | N/A |

*continues*

*continued*

| Device | Connector Type | Plug | Port | Color |
|---|---|---|---|---|
| Camera, etc. | USB Mini-B (5-pin) | | | N/A |
| High-Definition monitor | DVI | | | White |
| High-Definition monitor | HDMI | | | N/A |
| Main speakers, head-phones | 3.5mm audio | | OUT | Lime green |
| Micro-phone | 3.5mm audio | | | Pink |

| Device | Connector Type | Plug | Port | Color |
|--------|----------------|------|------|-------|
| Audio input | 3.5mm audio | | (•) IN | Light blue |
| Network router | LAN (RJ-45) | | | N/A |
| Modem | RJ11 | | | N/A |
| PC power | PC Power Supply | | | N/A |
| Power source | Power cable | | | N/A |
| Portable power | Power adapter | | POWER | N/A |

> **WHOA!**
>
> Don't force anything. Plugs should slide easily into ports or outlets. If you have to force something, the plug is probably not properly aligned with the port or it's the wrong port. Forcing the plug may bend or break the pins. Also, plug all power cords into a surge protector or uninterruptible power supply (UPS) to prevent damage from power fluctuations.

# Turning It On

Turning on a laptop or an all-in-one desktop model is a snap. All you do is press and release the power button, and your PC comes to life. Starting a standard desktop PC is a little more involved because you have more than one component to power up. Here's standard operating procedure for starting a desktop PC:

1. Press and release the power button on your monitor.

2. If your PC is connected to a cable modem for Internet service, turn it on and wait for the indicator lights to show that a connection with the Internet service provider (ISP) is established.

3. If your PC is connected to a router, turn on the router.

4. Turn on any other devices connected to your PC that you plan to use this session, such as a printer or scanner.

5. Turn on your speaker system. If it has an audio control, turn it to about quarter volume so you don't burst your eardrums when the PC comes to life.

6. Press and release the power button on the system unit. At this point, the monitor may display some startup messages as it reads its startup instructions and performs its preflight checks.

# Dealing with the First-Time Startup Ritual

When you start your PC for the first time, it leads you through several preliminary tasks. Just follow the onscreen clues and instructions. The usual routine includes the following:

- **Activate and register Windows.** Assuming that your PC is connected to the Internet, Windows contacts Microsoft's website and leads you through the process of activating and registering Windows. Activation is required. Registration is optional.

If your PC is not connected to the Internet, you can still use it prior to activating and registering Windows, but you should activate and register it soon. See Chapter 18 for details on how to connect your PC to the Internet.

- **Adjust your regional settings.** Windows asks you a series of questions so it can properly set the date and time.

- **Install or configure new hardware.** If you connected any peripheral devices to your PC, Windows identifies the devices and installs the drivers required to use those devices. You may be asked to insert a disc that came with the device.

- **Install Windows updates.** Microsoft is constantly improving Windows. If your PC is connected to the Internet, Windows may download and install the latest updates to make it more reliable and secure. This may take a long time depending on the number of updates and the speed of your Internet connection.

It's likely that your PC came with a trial version of an antivirus program, and you may be prompted to register for the free trial. You can proceed or skip ahead to Chapter 29, where I show you where to go for a free antivirus program and install it.

From now on, when you start Windows, you won't be bothered with all of these preliminary tasks. However, if you connect new hardware or Windows requires an update, you may need to address these issues on future startups.

On subsequent startups Windows may prompt you to log on. If you're not prompted to log on, your PC is set up for a single user. If a log-on screen does appear, click your username and then, if requested, enter the password that has been assigned to this user account. (For more about user accounts and logging on and off in Windows, see Chapter 7.)

Eventually, you should see the Microsoft Windows desktop, as shown in Figure 2.1. If you have a touch-screen monitor, you may see several icons you can tap to perform various tasks.

**Figure 2.1**

*The Windows 7 desktop greets you on startup.*

# Turning It Off, Shutting It Down

When you're done using your PC, you may want to shut it down to reduce wear and tear and conserve electricity. Although you can shut down most components, including the printer and monitor, by pressing and releasing or holding down the power button for a second or two, you should never do this with the system unit. Instead, let Windows power it down for you:

1. Click the **Start** button, in the lower-left corner of the screen, as shown in Figure 2.2.

2. Click **Shut down**. Windows logs you off and powers down your PC.

3. Turn off everything else.

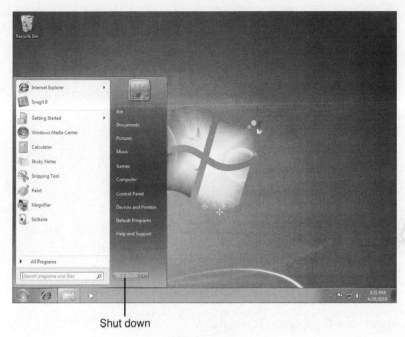

Shut down

**Figure 2.2**
*Shut down Windows.*

Windows features several other options for logging off your PC or shutting it down. To access these options, click the arrow to the right of the Shut down button:

- **Log off:** If Windows is set up for more than one user (see Chapter 7), you can log off the current user so another user can log on. Logging off clears everything from your desktop and displays the Windows log-on screen so that you or another user can log on. (It's a good idea to save whatever you're currently working on before logging off so you don't lose some or all of your work.)

- **Switch user:** Switch user allows a different user to log on while keeping the current user's applications running. The current user can then log on later and pick up where he or she left off.

- **Sleep:** Click **Sleep**, press and release the power button on your PC, or close the lid of a portable PC, and Windows puts the PC to sleep—a power-saving mode similar to pressing pause on a DVD player. You can wake up your PC by pressing and releasing your PC's power button.

- **Hibernate:** Hibernate saves what you're doing to the hard disk and then turns off the PC. When you turn it back on, Windows restores what you were doing so you can resume. Hibernation uses the least amount of power of all the power-saving modes.

- **Restart:** Restart exits and starts Windows. You may need to restart your PC after you install a new program or device, change a Windows setting, or fix a problem.

- **Lock:** Lock returns you to the log-on screen. If you password-protect your PC (see Chapter 7), you can lock it whenever you step away from it, to prevent other people from using it.

Windows automatically powers down newer PCs after a certain period of inactivity, to conserve power. You can adjust the power-saving settings to suit your preferences. See Chapter 6 for details.

## The Least You Need to Know

- Be careful unpacking your PC and peripheral devices.
- Put all your equipment in place before connecting anything.
- To figure out where to plug in all the cables, check the manual or setup instructions that came with your PC and match the shape and configuration of the connectors with the ports.
- When starting your PC, turn on all the peripheral devices before turning on power to the system unit.
- To turn off your PC, click the Windows **Start** button, click **Shut down**, and then turn off anything that's connected to the system unit, including the monitor.

# Taking Control with Input Devices

## In This Chapter

- Pointing and clicking with your mouse or touchpad
- Typing and entering commands using your keyboard
- Pointing, selecting, and dragging on a touch-screen
- Brushing up on voice and speech recognition
- Configuring your input devices for comfort and efficiency

To get your PC to do anything, you need to be able to communicate with it in a way it understands. Traditionally, this has meant using a mouse to choose commands onscreen or pressing key combinations associated with specific commands.

Fortunately, PCs are becoming friendlier and better able to communicate like people do. Assuming that your PC is properly equipped, you can now point and "click" with a touchpad, use your hands to perform tasks on a touch-screen monitor, or even bark out commands and type text via speech recognition.

In this chapter, you learn how to use standard input devices, along with a few other technologies to "talk" to your computer.

## Mastering Basic Mouse Moves

A mouse is a two-button device (sometimes with a wheel between the two buttons or other variations with more buttons) that allows you to point and click commands and options, and drag and drop items on the screen. To use a mouse effectively, master the following basic mouse moves.

- **Moving the mouse:** Hold the mouse gently with your index finger on the main mouse button (left for righties and right for lefties). Slide the mouse over a clean, smooth surface slowly in the direction you want the onscreen pointer to move. If you run out of room, lift the mouse, move it in the direction opposite of where you need to go, and then set it down and continue sliding the mouse in the direction you want the mouse pointer to go.

- **Point:** Move the tip of the mouse pointer over an object or command. The mouse pointer may change appearance when it's over an object. If it's over an object you can click, the pointer may appear as a pointing hand. If it's over text, it appears as an I-beam, which indicates where the insertion point will be moved if you click the left mouse button.

- **Rest (Hover):** Rest the tip of the mouse pointer over a menu item to open a submenu or over an object to view information about it.

- **Click:** Press and release the left mouse button, typically to select an object or command.

- **Double-click:** Press and release the left mouse button twice in quick succession, typically to execute a command or run a program.

- **Right-click:** Press and release the right mouse button once, typically to open a *context-sensitive* menu—a menu that contains commands exclusively for this particular object.

- **Drag:** Hold down the left mouse button while moving the mouse. You may drag to move something, draw something, select text, or change the size or shape of an object.

- **Drag and drop:** Click the left mouse button on an object to select it and keep it down while dragging an object from one location to another, and then release the button to drop it in place.

If your mouse has a wheel between the two buttons, you can use the wheel to perform some additional maneuvers.

- **Scroll:** Rotate the wheel forward to scroll down or backward to scroll up.

- **Pan:** Click and hold the wheel while moving the mouse forward or back. (Panning is sort of like scrolling, but smoother.)

- **Autoscroll:** Click the wheel and then move the mouse forward or back. This is sort of like panning, except that you don't have to hold down the wheel. When you're done autoscrolling, click the wheel again to disable it.

- **Zoom in or out:** Hold down the **Ctrl** key while rotating the wheel forward to zoom in or backward to zoom out.

# Navigating with a Touchpad

The purpose of a touchpad, a standard feature on mobile PCs, is the same as that of a mouse, but instead of moving the mouse to move the onscreen pointer, you slide your finger across the touchpad. The touchpad has left and right buttons that correspond to the left and right mouse buttons. However, most touchpads also let you use the touchpad itself to click, double-click, and drag:

- **Click:** Tap the touchpad once to select an object.

- **Double-click:** Tap the touchpad twice in quick succession to execute a command or run a program.

- **Drag:** Tap the touchpad twice, as if you're double-clicking, but keep your finger on the touchpad the second time down and slide your finger across the touchpad. (This move can be tough to execute.)

# Pecking Away at the Keyboard

Computer keyboards are populated with more than just the standard letter and number keys required for typing:

- **Function keys:** The 10 or 12 "F" keys at the top of the keyboard (F1, F2, F3, and so on) enable you to quickly enter common commands without moving your hands from the keyboard.

- **Arrow keys:** The arrow keys—Page Up, Page Down, Home, and End—move the cursor or insertion point in a document to wherever you want to type or enter a correction.

- **Numeric keypad:** The numeric keypad contains a group of number keys positioned like the keys on an adding machine. With NumLock off, they function as arrow keys.

- **Ctrl and Alt:** The Ctrl (Control) and Alt (Alternate) keys make the other keys on the keyboard act differently from the way they normally act. For example, you can press **Ctrl+C** (hold down the Ctrl key while pressing C) to copy a selection.

- **Esc:** The Esc (Escape) key in most programs backs you out of or quits whatever you're currently doing.

- **PrtSc:** PrtSc (Print Screen) sends the screen image to the Windows Clipboard so you can paste it into a document.

- **Scroll Lock:** Scroll Lock (ScrLk) is a rarely used key left over from older PCs. It locks scrolling up or down.

- **Volume controls:** Many newer keyboards feature controls to adjust speaker and microphone volume and other common computer settings.

- **Programmable buttons:** Most keyboards include special programmable buttons that enable you to quickly open your Internet home page, navigate the Internet, check e-mail, and put your computer in sleep mode. If you don't use one of the buttons for its designated function, you can reprogram it to perform some other frequent task.

## Pressing Key+Key Combinations

Many keys can perform additional tasks when used in tandem with other keys. For example, you can press **Alt+F4** to close the currently active window. To execute a key combination, hold down the first key(s) while pressing and releasing the last key, and then release the first key(s).

## Cutting Corners with the Windows Key

Inspect your keyboard carefully to see whether it has a Windows key—a key with the Windows logo, typically near the lower-left corner of the keyboard. The Windows key provides quick access to commonly entered commands, as presented in Table 3.1.

**Table 3.1  Windows Key Shortcuts**

| Press ... | To ... |
| --- | --- |
| Windows | Open the Start menu |
| Windows+Tab | Cycle through running programs in the taskbar |
| Windows+F | Find a file |
| Ctrl+Windows+F | Find a computer on a network |
| Windows+F1 | Display the Windows Help window |
| Windows+R | Display the Run dialog box (for running programs) |
| Windows+Pause/Break | Display the System Properties dialog box |
| Windows+E | Run Windows Explorer for managing folders and files |
| Windows+D or Windows+M | Minimize or restore all program windows |
| Shift+Windows+M | Undo minimize all program windows |

## Using Dual-Function Keys on Portable PCs

Portable computers, especially netbooks, may lack the space for a full set of keys plus buttons to turn on the computer, adjust the display, and move the mouse pointer. To fit all the keys and buttons into this limited space, many keys are assigned double-duty. For example, a key may be used with another key to adjust the speaker volume.

In most cases, the keyboard includes a key labeled Fn, as shown in Figure 3.1. Keys that perform double-duty have their primary functions displayed in black or white, and their secondary functions displayed in the color that matches the Fn key (typically blue). To take advantage of the secondary function of the key, hold down the Fn key while pressing the key labeled with the desired function; for example, on my netbook PC, Fn+Up Arrow cranks up the volume.

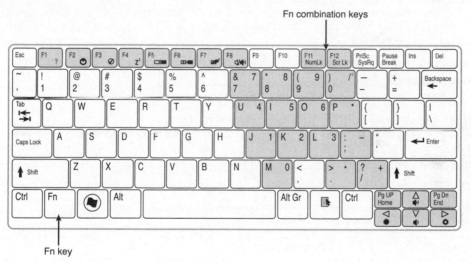

**Figure 3.1**

*The Fn key enables other keys to perform specialized tasks.*

# Getting in Touch with Your Touch-Screen

Thanks to the iPhone, touch-screens have become the latest fad in the world of personal computers. With a touch-screen and Windows 7, you can now navigate your computer, its resources, and just about everything the Internet has to offer by touching, tapping, and flicking the screen:

- **Tap:** Tapping an object is like clicking it.

- **Grab:** Press your finger against an object, slide your finger to drag the object, and then release to drop it in place.

- **Scroll:** Scroll a document up or down by sliding your finger up or down over the contents of the document. Scroll left or right using two fingers.

- **Flick:** Slide your finger quickly left or right over a page to "flip" to the next or previous page as you would do in a book or newspaper.

- **Select text:** Select text in a document by dragging your finger over the text from lower right to upper left or vice versa. You can then grab the text and drag it wherever you like.

- **Right-click:** To right-click an object, hold one finger against it and tap the screen with a second finger. You can also press and hold the object until a circle appears around your finger and then release.

- **Zoom in or out:** Press one finger against the upper-left corner of the area, press a second finger against the lower-right corner, and then slide your fingers apart to zoom in or closer together to zoom out.

- **Two-finger tap:** Tap with two fingers, one on either side of the object you want to work with, to expand that section of the screen.

# Customizing Your Mouse, Touchpad, and Keyboard

Windows gives you some control over the way your mouse, keyboard, and touchpad behave. The following sections show you how to access these settings.

## Adjusting Your Mouse Settings

If you're a lefty or you have trouble clicking fast enough to execute a double-click, you can customize your mouse to accommodate the way you work. Click the **Start** button (in the lower-left corner of the screen) and then click **Control Panel**, **Hardware and Sound**, **Mouse** (under Devices and Printers). This opens the Mouse Properties dialog box. If your PC has a touchpad, Your Mouse Properties dialog box may look a little different.

**INSIDE TIP**

If your PC is equipped with a touchpad, touch-screen, or other pointing device, check the Mouse Properties dialog box for additional settings that control its special features. You may also have an icon in the Windows notification area (lower-right corner of your screen) that you can right-click or double-click to access the device settings or disable the device. Rest the mouse pointer over any icon in the notification area to view its name.

## Adjusting Your Keyboard Settings

If you hold down a key on your keyboard, Windows automatically "types" the character repeatedly. You can adjust the key repeat delay (how long you have to hold down the key before it starts to repeat), the repeat speed (how fast the characters are repeated), and the cursor blink rate (how fast the insertion point blinks):

1. Click **Start**, **Control Panel**.

2. Click the **View by Category** option (upper right) and click **Large Icons**.

3. Click **Keyboard**.

4. Enter your preferences and click **OK**.

# Enabling Windows Accessibility Features

If you have a physical, vision, or hearing impairment that makes your mouse, keyboard, or monitor difficult to use, click **Start**, **Control Panel**, **Ease of Access**, **Ease of Access Center**. Click the following options to enable one or more of the ease of access features.

- **Start Magnifier** zooms in on an area of the screen. After starting Magnifier, open its **Views** menu and choose the desired option: **Full screen** magnifies the entire screen, pushing some of the contents off-screen; move the mouse pointer to the edge of the screen to scroll off-screen content into view. **Lens** displays a rectangle that magnifies the area of the screen the mouse is over. **Docked** allocates the top of the screen to display the magnified area.

- **Start Narrator** activates a narrator who describes what's displayed onscreen and any actions you perform using the keyboard so you can hear what you're doing. After clicking **Start Narrator**, enter your preferences and then click the minimize button to shrink the window. You can exit Narrator at any time by clicking its icon in the taskbar and clicking **Exit**.

- **Start On-Screen Keyboard** displays a picture of a keyboard so you can type by clicking keys with your mouse, touchpad, or other pointing device.

- **Set Up High Contrast** allows you to turn on a high-contrast display to ease eyestrain and improve readability. To turn high contrast on or off, press **Left Shift+Left Alt+Print Screen**.

Below these four main options is a section called "Explore all settings," with additional options for making your PC easier to use. Each of these options enables you to activate and configure several accessibility options to achieve the desired goal. For example, if you click **Make the computer easier to see**, you can enable high contrast, Magnifier, and Narrator; turn off unnecessary animations; and hide background images.

# Barking Out Commands with Speech Recognition

With a good microphone (preferably a headset microphone) and Windows Speech Recognition, you can literally tell your computer what to do. To enable Speech Recognition, click **Start**, **Control Panel**, **Ease of Access**, **Speech Recognition**. The first time you run Speech Recognition, Windows leads you through a process of setting up your microphone and tuning the feature to recognize your voice. Simply follow the onscreen instructions.

After setting up Speech Recognition, Windows enables you to take an onscreen tutorial on how to use it and provides a list of commands the feature is set up to recognize, such as Start Listening (turn on Speech Recognition), Start Notepad, Scroll Up, Scroll Down, and Stop Listening (turn off Speech Recognition).

## The Least You Need to Know

- Click an object to select it; double-click to open or run it.
- Key+Key means you press and hold the first key while pressing and releasing the second key.
- To adjust the mouse settings, click **Start**, **Control Panel**, **Hardware and Sound**, **Mouse**; enter your preferences; and click **OK**.
- To enable any of Windows' accessibility features, click **Start**, **Control Panel**, **Ease of Access**, **Ease of Access Center**.
- To enable Speech Recognition, click **Start**, **Control Panel**, **Ease of Access**, **Speech Recognition**.

# Getting Around in Windows 7

## In This Chapter

- Touring the Windows desktop
- Running programs from the Windows Start menu
- Performing essential Windows maneuvers
- Checking out applications and games included with Windows

To accomplish anything with your PC, you need to master some essential Windows maneuvers, including running programs, selecting menu commands, and switching between open windows. This chapter takes you on a tour of Windows, reveals its most important features, and shows you how to communicate with your computer through Windows.

## Exploring the Windows Desktop, Start Menu, and Taskbar

After you start your PC and log on, Windows appears. The opening screen consists of four main components—the Windows desktop, Start button, taskbar, and notification area, shown in Figure 4.1.

> **NOTE**
>
> The appearance and functionality of your Windows desktop depend on whether your computer supports the Aero desktop experience. If it does, any windows on the desktop feature a translucent glass design so you can see what's behind each open window.

Windows desktop

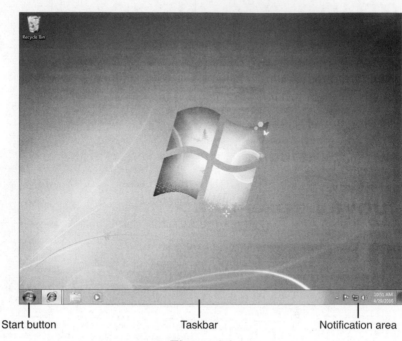

Start button            Taskbar            Notification area

**Figure 4.1**
*Windows 7 opening screen.*

## Windows Desktop

The Windows desktop is your designated area for work and play. Whenever you run a program, it appears in a separate window on your desktop. Like the actual top of a desk, the Windows desktop can become very cluttered with all sorts of stuff: desktop icons to run programs you frequently use; gadgets to tell you what time it is and report the weather; files, folders, and programs; and even desktop accessories— Notepad, Calculator, and so on. (For more about gadgets, see Chapter 6.)

Initially, the desktop contains only one item—the Recycle Bin icon. Whenever you delete anything, Windows places it in the Recycle Bin so you can restore something if you accidentally delete it. For details, check out Chapter 8.

## Start Button

Whenever you need to start doing anything, click the **Start** button to open the Start menu, as shown in Figure 4.2. The Start menu is divided into three sections: Search box (just above the Start button); left pane for running programs; and right pane for accessing folders, the Control Panel, Windows Help, and Shut down options.

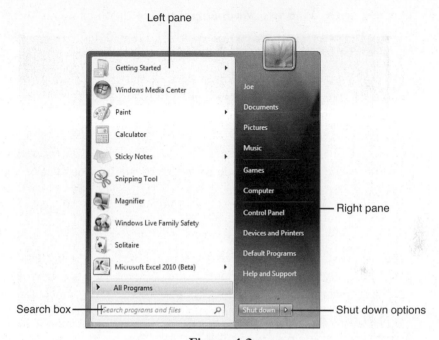

**Figure 4.2**
*The Windows Start menu.*

From the Start menu, you can perform any of the following common activities:

- **Start a program:** Click the **Start** button and click the program you want to run. If you don't see the program, rest the mouse pointer on **All Programs** to view more programs and program folders. (Windows adds frequently used programs to the Start menu's left pane so you don't need to open All Programs to find them.)

- **Search for files, folders, and programs:** Just above the Start button is a search box. Simply type a word or two describing what you're looking for and press **Enter** to have Windows help you find it.

- **Open frequently used folders:** The right side of the Start menu contains a list of frequently used folders, including your personal folder (at the top), Documents, Pictures, Music, Games, and Computer (providing access to all the disks on your computer).

- **Access the Control Panel:** The Windows Control Panel gives you access to all of your computer's settings and enables you to install and remove programs.

- **Get help with Windows:** On the right side of the Start menu, near the bottom, is an option to access the Windows Help system called Help and Support. See Chapter 5 for details.

- **Shut down or log off:** In the lower-right corner of the Start menu is the Shut down button, for turning off your PC. You can click the arrow to the right of the Shut down button to access additional options.

If you click **Start**, **All Programs** and then click a folder, a Back button replaces All Programs. You can click the **Back** button to return to the previous list of Start menu options.

## Taskbar

The taskbar is the horizontal bar at the bottom of the screen. It contains the Start button (on the left), Quick Launch buttons (to the right of the Start button), and notification area (on the right). (See Figure 4.3.) Unlike the desktop, which can be hidden by open windows, the taskbar always remains in front.

Whenever you run a program or open a file, a button for it appears in the taskbar. The button for the currently active program is darker than buttons for inactive windows, which appear faded. You can quickly access an open program or file by clicking its button. If you rest the mouse pointer on a button, a thumbnail image of the window appears above the button to remind you what's going on in that window. (Thumbnails appear only if your computer supports Aero desktop features. If your computer does not support Aero, you'll see a tooltip with a brief description of the item.)

You can add toolbars and buttons to the taskbar to place frequently used programs and other items within easy reach. For details, see Chapter 6.

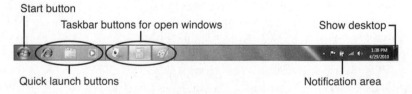

Figure 4.3
*The Windows taskbar.*

## Notification Area

The notification area (at the right end of the taskbar) includes the time, the date, and icons that indicate the status of programs and services running in the background. For example, your notification area may have icons for an antivirus program, your network connection, battery power for a portable PC, or USB devices connected to your PC.

Rest the mouse pointer on an icon to view its name or status. Right-clicking most icons in the notification area displays a context menu with additional options. Double-clicking usually opens a dialog box or window you can use to enter preferences for the program or device. Some icons may display notifications occasionally to call your attention to something important.

If the notification area contains more icons than can fit in its limited space, click the arrow pointing up (the **Show hidden icons** button to the left of the navigation area) to access the additional icons.

# Managing Windows on Your Desktop

Each time you run a program or open a file in Windows, a new window appears on your desktop, as shown in Figure 4.4. After several hours of work, your desktop can become very cluttered, making it difficult to find what you need. Fortunately, Windows provides several methods to control open windows, as described in the following sections.

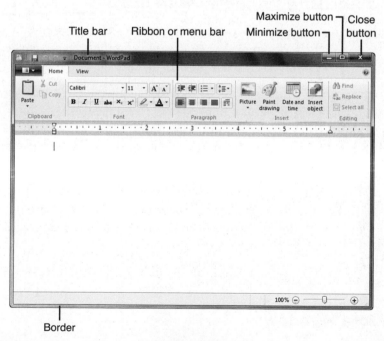

**Figure 4.4**
*Parts of a window.*

## Resizing a Window

Windows provides several methods for resizing Windows:

- Click the **Maximize** button or double-click the title bar to display the window full screen.

- Click the **Restore** button or double-click the title bar to return a maximized window to its former size.

- Click the **Minimize** button or the window's taskbar button to clear the window from the desktop. You'll still see the window's button in the taskbar.

- Rest the mouse pointer over the window's border or corner so the mouse appears as a double-headed arrow, and then drag to make the window larger or smaller.

## Moving a Window

To move a window, drag its title bar. (For more about dragging, see Chapter 3.)

## Moving and Resizing Windows with Snap

The Windows Snap feature enables you to move and resize windows by snapping them to the edges of the desktop. (When dragging to the edge of the desktop, you must drag all the way until the mouse pointer hits the edge.)

- **Arrange two windows side by side:** Drag a window's title bar so the mouse pointer touches the left or right edge of the screen. An outline appears displaying the future position and dimensions of the window. Release the mouse button, and the window is resized to consume the left or right half of the desktop.

- **Expand a window vertically:** Drag the window's top border up or bottom border down to the edge of the screen and release the mouse button to expand the window to the full height of the desktop without changing its width.

- **Maximize a window:** Drag the window's title bar to the top of the desktop and release the mouse button to expand it to fill the entire desktop.

## Switching to a Window

The easiest way to switch to a specific window is to click its taskbar button. This moves the window to the front of the stack. If a program has more than one document open, rest the mouse pointer on the button to display thumbnails of the documents and then click the one you want. (Your computer displays thumbnails only if it supports the Aero desktop features.)

If you can see any portion of the window you want to change to, click it to move the window to the front of the stack.

## Arranging Windows on the Desktop

To quickly arrange windows on the desktop, right-click a blank area of the taskbar and, from the shortcut menu that appears, choose the desired arrangement: **Cascade windows** (layered so you can see each window's title bar), **Show windows stacked** (from top to bottom), **Show windows side by side**, **Show the desktop** (hide all windows), or **Show open windows** (display all windows that were on the desktop before you chose Show the desktop). (You'll see either **Show the desktop** or **Show open windows**, never both.)

If your PC supports the Aero desktop features, you can use a three-dimensional arrangement with Aero Flip 3D to choose the desired window. Hold down the **Windows** key and press **Tab** repeatedly or rotate the mouse wheel to flip through the open windows in 3D, as shown in Figure 4.5. You can hold down the **Tab** key to cycle continuously. When the window you want is in the front, release the **Windows** key to display it.

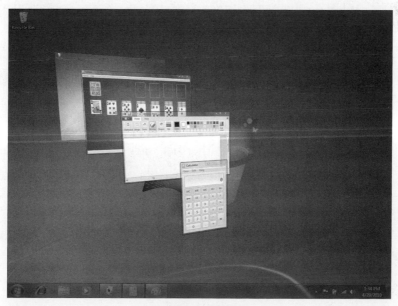

**Figure 4.5**
*Flip through windows in 3D.*

## Closing a Window

If you're done with a program or document, click its **Close** button or right-click its taskbar button and click **Close window**. This closes the document and/or exits the program and removes the window from the desktop. If you close a document you haven't saved, Windows prompts you to save the document first.

## Clearing the Desktop

At the far right end of the taskbar is a long rectangular box, which is the Show desktop button. When you click the button, Windows clears everything off the desktop. When you click it again, Windows restores all open windows. Hover the mouse over the button, and all open windows turn transparent to reveal the desktop.

## Shaking a Window into Focus

If your computer supports the Aero desktop features, you can shake a window to make it the center of attention and clear any other open windows off the desktop (minimize them). To shake a window, quickly drag its title bar left and right.

## Seeing More with Scrollbars

If a window cannot display everything it contains, a scrollbar appears along the right side and/or bottom of the window. The scrollbar on the right enables you to scroll up and down; the scrollbar at the bottom lets you scroll left and right. You can use the scrollbar to bring the hidden contents of the window into view, as follows:

- Drag the scroll box (inside the bar) to the area of the window you want to view. For example, to view the middle of the window's contents, drag the scroll box to the middle of the bar.

- Click inside the scrollbar on either side of the scroll box, to move the view one window at a time. For example, if you click once below the scroll box, you'll see the next window of information.

- Click a scroll arrow (at each end of the scrollbar) to scroll incrementally in the direction of the arrow. You can hold down the left mouse button to scroll continuously.

# Ordering from Menus and Dialog Boxes

Windows provides several ways for you to "talk" to your computer by clicking buttons, selecting menu commands, and responding to dialog boxes (onscreen fill-in-the-blank forms).

## Clicking Menu Options

The Windows Start menu isn't the only menu you'll encounter in Windows. You'll find menus everywhere—in menu bars near the top of most program windows, in toolbars, and even hidden inside objects (context menus). You click a menu's name to open it and then click the desired option or command.

If a double-headed, downward-pointing arrow appears at the bottom of a menu, you can click it to view more options. As you choose options, Windows may move them closer to the top of the menu so the options you use most frequently are within easy reach.

## Using Context Menus

Context menus provide convenient access to commands and options available only for a specific object. You right-click the object to display the context menu and then click the desired option.

## Talking with a Dialog Box

If you choose a menu command that's followed by a series of dots (...), the program displays a dialog box requesting additional information, as shown in Figure 4.6. You must then enter your preferences and give your okay.

**Figure 4.6**
*A dialog box asks you to enter additional information and settings.*

# Bypassing Menus by Using Toolbar Buttons

Although menus contain a comprehensive list of available options, they can be a bit clunky. To help you bypass the menu system, most programs include a ribbon or toolbars with buttons for the most frequently used commands. (See Figure 4.7.) To perform a task, you simply click the desired button.

**Figure 4.7**
*A ribbon or toolbar provides quick access to commonly used commands.*

# Checking Out Windows Accessories and Games

Chances are good that your computer came loaded with all sorts of software. If you purchased a home PC, it probably includes Microsoft Works or some other program suite (package) and a couple of computer games. But even if your computer wasn't garnished with additional programs, Windows has several desktop accessories, including Calculator, WordPad, Paint, and Sound Recorder. To run any of these programs, click **Start**, **All Programs**, **Accessories**, and then click the program you want to run.

Windows also features several games you can play to limber up your mouse fingers and have some fun, including Chess Titans, FreeCell (very addictive), Hearts, Mahjong Titans, Minesweeper, and Solitaire. Click **Start**, **All Programs**, **Games**, and click the game you want to play.

## The Least You Need to Know

- The Start menu provides you with access to all of your programs, PC settings, documents, and Windows Help, and enables you to log off Windows or shut down your PC.
- Use the buttons in the taskbar to switch to the program or document window you want.
- You can quickly maximize, minimize, restore, and close windows by using the three buttons in the upper-right corner of every window.
- Drag a window's title bar to move it.
- Drag a window's border or corner to resize it.

# Getting Help

## In This Chapter

- Getting help when using Windows
- Accessing help specifically for what you're currently doing
- Enlisting the assistance of other people
- Getting help when using applications and games

Although this book provides everything you need to know to use your Windows 7 PC, you may need a quick refresher when this book isn't nearby or help using programs or Windows features not covered in this book. In this chapter, my goal is to make you self-sufficient by showing you where to go to get the guidance and instructions you need.

## Using the Windows Help System

Windows features a comprehensive help system that can teach you everything you need to know about its features. To get help, click the **Start** button and click **Help and Support**. You can use the Windows help system in the following ways:

- Search for help on a specific topic
- Browse help topics
- Learn how to get started with your PC
- Brush up on Windows basics
- Ask other people for help

Figure 5.1 shows a typical help screen for a specific topic and provides some guidance on how to navigate Windows Help and Support.

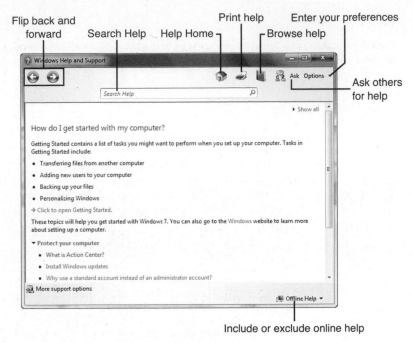

**Figure 5.1**
*Windows Help and Support.*

## Turning Online Help On and Off

If your PC is connected to the Internet (see Chapter 18), make sure Online Help is on so that when you search for a topic, Windows includes any new help topics and the latest versions of existing topics in the search results. Check the lower-right corner of the Windows Help and Support window. If Offline Help is displayed and your PC is connected to the Internet, click **Offline Help** and then click **Get online help**.

## Searching for Specific Help

The easiest and fastest way to get help with a specific task is to search the help system:

1. Click in the **Search Help** box.

2. Type one or more words to describe what you need help with.

3. Press **Enter** or click the magnifying glass to the right of the box. This displays a list of help topics that match the description you typed.

4. Click the desired help topic.

**INSIDE TIP**

Click the **Home** button (upper right) to head to the help system's opening page regardless of where you are in the help system.

## Browsing the Help System

You can browse the help system's table of contents for the assistance you need:

1.  Click the **Browse Help** button (the book icon in the upper right) to display the help system's equivalent of a table of contents.

2.  Click a heading to display a list of topics related to that heading.

3.  Follow the trail of links to the answer or instructions you need. (Links appear as blue text that's underlined when you rest the mouse pointer on them.)

## Learning How to Get Started with a New PC

On the Help and Support window's Home page (the page that appears when you first run Help and Support), click **How to get started with your computer** to learn common tasks for the first few weeks you begin using a new computer, including protecting your computer and installing new hardware and programs.

## Brushing Up on Windows Basics

On the Help and Support window's Home page (the page that appears when you first run Help and Support), click **Learn about Windows Basics** to get up to speed on the basic Windows maneuvers covered in Chapter 4.

# Getting Context-Sensitive Help

Windows knows what you're doing at any given time and is always ready to lend a hand. When you need assistance, simply head to the desktop and press the **F1** key. (If you press **F1** when one of your application windows is active, you'll get context-sensitive help for that application.) The Windows Help and Support window pops up, offering information and instructions related to the activity in which you're currently engaged. If this isn't quite the help you were looking for, you can use the Help and Support window to search or browse for additional help.

In many dialog boxes and some windows, you'll see a question mark icon, shown in Figure 5.2. Click the icon for help with this particular dialog box or window.

Click the question mark for help

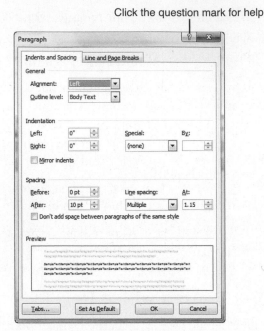

**Figure 5.2**
*Get help with a dialog box.*

# Getting Help from Other People

If you can't find the help you need *inside* Windows, you may need to consult a resource *outside* Windows. Click **Ask** (upper right) or **More support options** (lower left) to learn how to get help from other people over the Internet. In the following sections, I cover these additional support options.

## Getting Remote Assistance from a Friend

Most people have a computer-whiz friend or family member they can call on when they run into trouble. Unfortunately, your personal PC guru may live across town or in another state, but you may be able to use Remote Assistance to enlist that person's assistance. With Remote Assistance, your assistant can connect to your computer, view your computer screen, chat with you about what you're both looking at, and even take control of your PC (with your permission, of course) to show you how to perform a task or to troubleshoot a problem.

If you're both using Windows 7, you can use Easy Connect to establish a connection. If not, you first need e-mail access (see Chapter 21) or an instant messaging program (see Chapter 25) to send an invitation to your remote assistant. When you're ready to obtain assistance, here's what you do:

1. Click **Start**, **All Programs**, **Maintenance**, **Windows Remote Assistance**.

2. Follow instructions as Windows leads you through the process. If you choose to send an invitation via e-mail, Remote Assistance e-mails the recipient a file and generates a password you can send to the person in a separate e-mail message, via a chat session, or over the phone. The recipient runs the attached file and enters the password, and then can view your computer.

3. You can talk with your assistant over the phone or use the resulting chat box to type and exchange messages with one another during the session.

4. If the person attempts to take control of your computer, a message pops up on your screen asking for your permission, as shown in Figure 5.3. Click **Allow [So-and-So] to respond to User Account Control prompts** and click **Yes**.

When either of you exits Remote Assistance, the connection is terminated and a dialog box appears on the other person's screen, indicating that the session has ended.

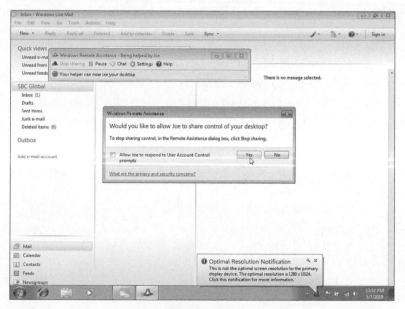

**Figure 5.3**
*A remote assistant can see your computer and take it over, with your permission.*

## Exploring Microsoft Answers

Microsoft Answers is an online community of Microsoft tech support personnel and users helping other users. If you're connected to the Internet, you can use your web browser, as explained in Chapter 19, to go to answers.microsoft.com and then browse answers by topic or search for help on a specific feature or problem.

You can also access Microsoft Answers directly from the Windows Help and Support window. Search the help system as you normally would. If it doesn't have the answer you're looking for, click **Ask** or **More support options** and then click **Microsoft Answers**. This runs your web browser, which accesses the Microsoft Answers site and searches for the word or phrase you typed in the Search Help box.

## Contacting Your Computer Manufacturer or Microsoft Support

For solving more mystifying problems, you may need to call in the big guns— Microsoft Customer Support or your computer manufacturer. Most manufacturers have very useful sites for troubleshooting hardware and software issues and obtaining any software updates your PC may need.

To connect with Microsoft Customer Support or your computer manufacturer, run Windows Help and Support, click **More support options** (lower left), and then, under Contact technical support, click **computer manufacturer** or **Microsoft Customer Support** and follow the onscreen cues and clues to find what you're looking for. If you choose **computer manufacturer**, Microsoft provides links and phone numbers for all major PC manufacturers.

## Getting More Windows Help on the Web

Microsoft offers much more help with Windows via its website. If your computer is connected to the Internet, head to windows.microsoft.com/en-us/windows7/help for how-to videos, tutorials, and more.

For assistance with a technical issue, search Microsoft's Knowledge Base at support. microsoft.com/search/. When you get there, click **Show more search options** (below the Search box) so you can narrow the search to a specific Microsoft product, such as Windows 7.

# Getting Help with Applications and Games

Most applications and games don't include printed instructions on how to use them. Software developers provide instructions via help systems, in much the same way

Windows does. To obtain help with a particular application or game, use its Help menu, as shown in Figure 5.4, or press **F1** while in the application.

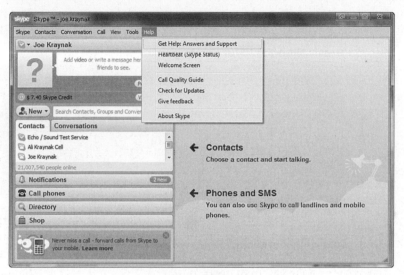

**Figure 5.4**
*Get help via the application's Help menu.*

## The Least You Need to Know

- To get help with using Windows, click **Start**, **Help and Support**.
- The quickest way to get help is to display the Help and Support window and use the Search Help box to find what you're looking for.
- To obtain context-sensitive help (for what you're currently doing), press the **F1** key.
- To obtain help from other people, click **Start**, **Help and Support**, **More support options** (lower left), and then click the link for the desired option and follow the onscreen cues.
- Almost every program and game has a Help menu.

# Taking Control of Your PC

A PC is like a newborn baby. It's packed with potential, but until it has operating system software that provides it with the instructions it needs to function, it's relatively unproductive. Fortunately, your PC comes equipped with an operating system called *Windows* that enables the PC to communicate with its various components and run application software you can use to perform specific tasks and play games.

The chapters in Part 2 show you how to personalize Windows 7 to look and behave the way you want it to, manage other PC resources (including the files you create) through Windows, install and uninstall programs, upgrade your PC with new hardware, and network your PCs so they can share files, a printer, an Internet connection, and other valuable resources.

# Changing the Look and Feel of Windows

## In This Chapter

- Giving Windows a makeover with themes
- Adding desktop icons to place programs and files within easy reach
- Accessorizing windows with gadgets
- Revamping the taskbar and Start menu
- Adjusting the Windows power-saving settings

If you're like most people, you enjoy decorating your home or office to add your own personal touch. You might paint the walls a different color, hang a few photos of friends or family members, or populate your shelves with knickknacks and family photos. In similar ways, you can customize and decorate the Windows desktop. This chapter shows you how.

## Personalizing Windows

Microsoft ships Windows with default settings that control its appearance, but eventually, every user's version of Windows starts to look a little different as the individual personalizes it to suit his or her tastes. Here you discover several adjustments for injecting a little of your personality into Windows (see Figure 6.1):

1. Click **Start**, **Control Panel**, **Appearance and Personalization**, **Personalization** or right-click a blank area of the Windows desktop and click **Personalize**.

2. Scroll through the collection of themes and click the one you want.

3. Click **Desktop Background** (below the themes).

4. Scroll through the collection of background pictures and click the one you want. If you click more than one, Windows will cycle through them as a slide show.

5. Click the **Picture position** button and choose the desired position. For example, you can choose to have the picture centered or fill the entire desktop.

6. If you chose more than one background picture, click the **Change picture every** button and choose how often you want Windows to change background pictures. You can also choose to shuffle the pictures for random display and/or pause the slide show when the PC is running on battery power, to conserve power.

7. Click **Save changes**.

8. Click **Window Color**.

9. Click the desired color or click **Show color mixer** (near the bottom of the window) and mix your own custom color.

10. If your PC supports Aero, you can click **Enable transparency** to enable (checked) or disable (unchecked) the window transparency feature.

11. Drag the **Color intensity** slider left or right to set the desired brightness of the selected color.

12. Click **Save changes**.

13. Click **Sounds**.

14. Click the button directly below **Sound Scheme** and click the desired scheme.

15. Under **Program events**, you can double-click an event to play the sound assigned to that event.

16. When you've settled on a scheme you like, click **OK**.

17. Click **Screen Saver**.

18. Click the **Screen Saver** button and click the screen saver you want to use. Windows displays a preview of the screen saver in action.

19. Enter your preferences to specify the amount of time your PC is inactive before the screen saver kicks in and whether you want Windows to display the log-on screen when you resume use.

20. For some screen savers, you can click the **Settings** button and enter additional preferences, such as how fast the design moves across the screen.

21. Click **Save changes**.

22. When you're done making changes, scroll to the top of the theme gallery, click **Save theme** at the bottom of **My Themes**, type a name for your theme, and click **Save**. Your theme is now part of your theme gallery.

You can now close the Control Panel or leave it open to customize Windows even more. Click **Appearance and Personalization** in the top bar to return to this screen.

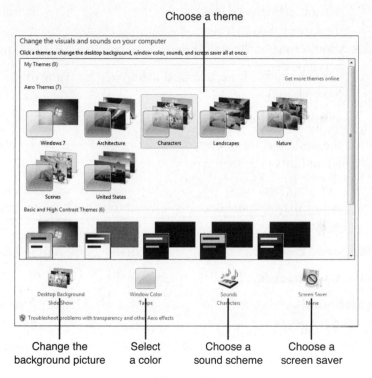

**Figure 6.1**
*Personalize Windows.*

**INSIDE TIP**

If you see a photo or other image on your computer or on a web page that you'd like to use as your background image, right-click it and click **Set as desktop background** or **Set as Background**.

# Adjusting the Display Settings

You can adjust display settings in Windows to fit more on the screen, make text more readable, or connect to a projector or external display, as explained in the following sections.

## Changing Text and Object Size

You can make everything on your desktop smaller (to fit more) or larger (to see it better):

1. Click **Start, Control Panel, Appearance and Personalization**.

2. Under Display, click **Make text and other items larger or smaller**.

3. Click the desired size.

4. Click **Apply**.

## Adjusting the Screen Resolution

In Windows 7, you can adjust size and screen resolution to fit more stuff on the screen or display larger objects and text:

1. Click **Start, Control Panel, Appearance and Personalization**.

2. Under Display, click **Adjust screen resolution**.

3. If more than one monitor is connected, click the **Display** button and select the monitor you want to adjust.

4. Click the **Resolution** button and drag the slider up or down to the setting marked **(recommended)**.

5. Click **Apply**.

## Managing a Dual-Display Configuration

If you have a PC with two video ports or a portable PC with one video port, you have everything you need for a dual-display configuration, so you can look at two programs or documents in separate windows at the same time. Connect your two monitors to your PC and turn them on. Windows will detect both monitors and display the same thing on both of them. If Windows fails to detect the second monitor or you want to change the dual-display configuration, here's what you do:

1. Click **Start, Control Panel, Appearance and Personalization**, and then, below Display, click **Connect to an external display**. Windows displays controls for managing your dual-display configuration. (See Figure 6.2.)

2. If Windows did not detect the second monitor, click **Detect**.

3. Click **Identify** to see which monitors Windows has designated as 1 and 2. Windows briefly displays the number 1 on one screen and 2 on the other.

4. To rearrange the displays, drag and drop one of the monitor images to the far side of the other image.

5. Open the Multiple displays box and choose how you want Windows to configure your dual display:

   • **Duplicate these displays:** Displays the same thing on both monitors, which is useful if you're giving a presentation.

   • **Extend these displays:** Extends the desktop across both screens so you have more room to spread out.

   • **Show desktop only on 1:** Shows Windows only on display 1.

   • **Show desktop only on 2:** Shows Windows only on display 2.

6. You can use the **Display** and **Resolution** drop-down lists to set the resolution for each display independently.

7. Click **Apply**.

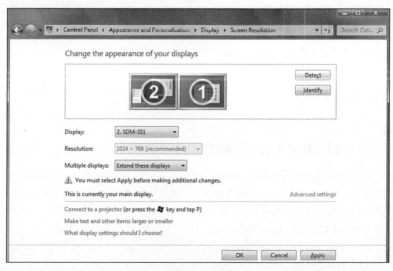

**Figure 6.2**
*Manage your dual-display configuration.*

> **INSIDE TIP**
>
> On most portable PCs, you can press **Fn+F5** to switch between using the display screen, the external monitor, or both.

## Connecting a Projector to Your PC

When giving a presentation, you may need or want to connect a projector to your PC to display the presentation on a larger screen:

1. Turn on the projector and plug it into a VGA, DVI, or USB port on your computer.

2. Click **Start**, **Control Panel**, **Appearance and Personalization**.

3. Under Display, click **Connect to a projector**.

4. Click the option that best describes how you want your desktop to be displayed: **Computer Only**, **Duplicate**, **Extend**, or **Projector only**.

# Taking Control of Desktop Icons

Initially, Windows displays only one desktop icon—the Recycle Bin. For easy access to the programs, games, files, and folders you use most frequently, you can create additional desktop icons. The following sections show you how to add icons to the desktop and manage them.

## Adding Desktop Icons

You can add desktop icons for programs, files, pictures, and other items. Find the item you want to create a desktop icon for. This can be a program on the Start, All Programs menu; a disk, file, or folder icon (see Chapter 8); or an icon for a specific hardware device. Right-click the item, point to **Send to**, and click **Desktop (create shortcut)**, as shown in Figure 6.3.

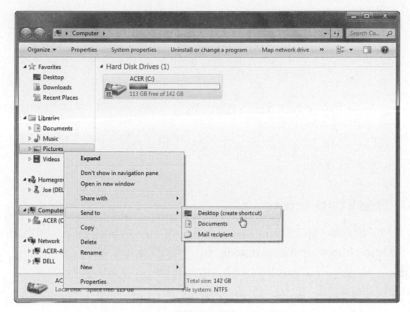

**Figure 6.3**
*Create a desktop icon.*

You can quickly add some standard icons to your desktop so you don't have to go hunting for them on the Start, All Programs menu: Right-click the desktop and click **Personalize**, **Change desktop icons**. Click the check box next to each icon you want placed on the desktop: Computer, your personal folder, Network, Recycle Bin, and Control Panel; then click **OK**.

You can also click an icon and click **Change icon** to choose an icon with a different appearance. (If you mess up, you can always click the icon and click the **Restore Default** button to go back to the original icon.)

## Deleting Desktop Icons

Most desktop icons are shortcuts, small images that merely link to the items they represent. Deleting the shortcut doesn't delete the file or other item it's linked to. If you delete a file's original icon, however, Windows deletes the file by moving it to the Recycle Bin. To flag an icon as a shortcut, Windows displays the icon with an arrow in its lower-left corner, as shown in Figure 6.4.

**Figure 6.4**
*A shortcut icon.*

To delete a desktop icon, right-click the icon, click **Delete**, and, when prompted for confirmation, click **Yes**.

## Hiding All Desktop Icons

To toggle the display of desktop icons on or off, right-click the desktop, point to **View**, and click **Show desktop icons**.

## Renaming Icons

To rename an icon, right-click it and click **Rename** (or click the icon twice slowly, not a double-click), type the new name, and press **Enter**.

## Rearranging Icons

If your desktop gets too cluttered or unmanageable, Windows has several tools to help you control the size and arrangement of the desktop icons. To move an icon, drag and drop it to the desired location.

To change the appearance or position of all icons on the desktop, right-click a blank area of the desktop and point to **View** or **Sort by**, and choose the desired option. For example, you can choose **View**, **Large Icons** and **View**, **Auto Arrange** to bump up the icon size and have Windows arrange the icons on the desktop for you.

# Adding Gadgets to Your Desktop

Windows provides quick access to customizable mini-applications called *gadgets*, which include a calendar, clock, news headlines (from the Internet), weather updates, and more. To turn on a gadget, right-click the desktop, click **Gadgets**, and double-click the gadget you want to use, as shown in Figure 6.5.

**Figure 6.5**
*Add a gadget to the desktop.*

Windows provides several controls for manipulating your gadgets. Rest the mouse pointer on the gadget to display its controls. Then, depending on the gadget, you can do the following:

- Drag the gadget to move it. (You can simply drag the gadget or use the drag handle that appears when you mouse over the gadget.)

- Click **X** to close the gadget.

- Click the size icon and choose the desired size.

- Click the wrench to enter gadget preferences. For example, the weather gadget enables you to enter a location to get your local weather updates.

To toggle the display of all gadgets on or off, right-click the desktop, point to **View**, and click **Show desktop gadgets**.

**INSIDE TIP**

If your PC is connected to the Internet, you can add more gadgets to your gadget gallery. In the lower-right corner of the gadget gallery, click **Get more gadgets online**. Be careful, however—gadgets can be memory hogs.

# Configuring the Taskbar

Your taskbar may not look like much, but it has a lot of potential. In the following sections, I show you how to customize the toolbar to fully tap its power.

## Adjusting the Taskbar Properties

Right-click a blank area of the taskbar, click **Properties**, and use the resulting dialog box to enter your preferences, as shown in Figure 6.6. Most of the properties are self-explanatory, but a couple are a little vague:

- **Lock the taskbar** prevents you from accidentally moving or resizing the taskbar.

- **Auto-hide the taskbar** minimizes the taskbar when you're not using it. To bring the hidden taskbar back into view, move the mouse pointer to the edge of the screen where the taskbar usually hangs out.

**Figure 6.6**
*Adjust the taskbar properties.*

## Moving and Resizing the Taskbar

The taskbar is not an immovable object. To move it, right-click a blank area of the taskbar and, if **Lock the taskbar** is checked, click it to remove the check mark and unlock the taskbar. Now you can use your mouse to drag the taskbar to any edge of your screen.

To resize the taskbar, rest the mouse pointer over the edge that's closest to the desktop so that the mouse pointer appears as a double-headed arrow. Then drag the edge toward the middle of the desktop to make the taskbar bigger. You can always make it smaller by dragging in the opposite direction.

## Adding Icons

Just as you can add icons to the desktop, you can add icons to the taskbar. Simply drag an icon over the place on the taskbar where you want it to appear and drop it in place. You can also right-click an icon and click **Pin to taskbar**. To remove an icon, right-click it and click **Unpin from taskbar**.

## Adding a Toolbar

You can add an entire collection of buttons and other controls to the taskbar by adding a toolbar.

Right-click a blank area of the toolbar, point to **Toolbars**, and click the toolbar you want to use. You can move a toolbar by dragging it to the other side of another toolbar. To resize a toolbar, drag its handle, as shown in Figure 6.7. You can remove a toolbar by right-clicking it and choosing **Close toolbar**.

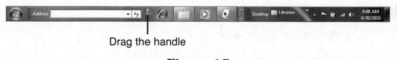

Drag the handle

**Figure 6.7**
*Drag the toolbar's handle to resize it.*

## Changing the Date and Time

At the right end of the taskbar, Windows displays the current date and time. To change the date or time, click the date or time, click **Change date and time settings**, **Change date and time**, and then use the resulting dialog box to enter your changes.

To change the date, click the arrow button on either side of the month to display the current month, and then click today's date. To change the time, click the hour, minute, or second you want to change and then click the up or down arrow to the right of the time to make your change. When you're done, click **OK**.

# Personalizing Your Start Menu

The Start menu is designed to put everything within easy reach, but it doesn't always succeed. Fortunately, you can step in and optimize the Start menu for the way you work.

## Pin a Program to the Start Menu

Pinning an item places it at the top of the Start menu so it's always within easy reach. To pin an item, right-click its icon and click **Pin to Start Menu**. Another way to pin something to the Start menu is to drag it over the Start button and then, when the menu opens, drag it up into the menu area and drop it in place.

You can change the order of pinned items by dragging them up or down. To remove a pinned item from the Start menu, right-click it and choose **Unpin from Start Menu**.

## Removing Programs from the Start Menu

To remove a program from the Start menu, right-click it and click **Remove from this list**. Removing the program from the Start menu does not remove it from the All Programs list or from your computer. To learn how to uninstall a program, see Chapter 9.

## Clear Recently Opened Files

Windows keeps track of your recently opened programs and documents and displays a list of them in the Start menu's left pane for easy access. To clear this list and prevent Windows from keeping track of recently opened items in the future, follow these steps:

1. Right-click a blank area of the taskbar and click **Properties**.
2. Click the **Start Menu** tab.
3. Click the following options to uncheck them: **Store and display recently opened programs in the Start menu** and **Store and display recently opened items in the Start menu and taskbar**.
4. Click **OK**.

## Customize the Appearance of Start Menu Items

You can further customize the Start menu to include or exclude certain items, change their appearance, and change the size of the Start menu to display more or fewer recent programs and items. Right-click the taskbar, click **Properties**, click the **Start Menu** tab, enter your preferences, and click **OK**.

You can restore the Start menu to its original state by clicking the Use Default Settings button at the bottom of the dialog box.

# Configuring Power-Saving Features

Windows conscientiously helps you conserve energy (and battery power if you're using a portable PC). Unless you adjust the settings, Windows places your PC on a balanced plan—balancing performance with energy. If you want to be more or less aggressive in cutting back on energy consumption, you can change plans and/or adjust specific settings:

1. Click **Start**, **Control Panel**, **Hardware and Sound**, **Power Options**.

2. Click the power plan you want to use. (Power plan availability depends on what your PC supports.)

3. Next to the selected power plan, click **Change plan settings**.

4. Use the resulting options to specify the number of minutes or hours of inactivity that must pass before Windows dims the display, turns off the display, and puts the computer to sleep, as shown in Figure 6.8.

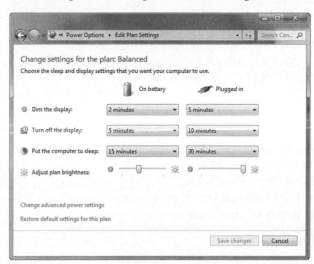

**Figure 6.8**
*Adjust your power plan settings.*

5. Drag the **Adjust plan brightness** slider (if it has one) to increase or decrease your display's brightness. (Different PCs may have different options.)

6. (Optional) Click **Change advanced power settings**, use the Power Options dialog box to enter more detailed power settings, and click **OK**.

7. Click **Save changes**.

# Adjusting Your PC's Speaker Volume

The trick to adjusting the volume on a computer is to start with the obvious controls first: any volume dials on the computer, sound card, or speakers. Set these controls to the desired level. If you're not sure which way to turn them, set them at the halfway point so that when your computer starts to play audio, it won't burst your eardrums.

> **NOTE**
>
> If you're working on a notebook PC or have a newfangled keyboard, you may have volume controls for both the speaker and the microphone within easy reach of the keys. Look around the periphery of the keyboard area for volume controls. You may also have a volume control in the notification area that allows you to drag a slider.

Next, check the volume control in Windows. Click **Start**, **Control Panel**, **Hardware and Sound**, **Adjust system volume**. Windows displays a Volume Mixer with one or more sliders that control volume for different components. Drag the **Device** slider to the desired volume level. To mute a device, click the speaker icon below its slider.

## The Least You Need to Know

- To personalize Windows, right-click a blank area of the desktop, click **Personalize**, and use the resulting dialog box to enter your preferences.

- To add an icon to the desktop, right-click the icon, point to **Send to**, and click **Desktop (create shortcut)**.

- To pin an item to the Start menu, right-click the item and click **Pin to Start Menu**.

- To access settings for your taskbar and Start menu, right-click the taskbar and click **Properties**.

- To access the Windows power-saving settings, click **Start**, **Control Panel**, **Hardware and Sound**, **Power Options**.

# Creating and Managing User Accounts

## In This Chapter

- Creating user accounts
- Securing your computer with passwords
- Restricting PC and Internet access for children and teens
- Logging off and back onto Windows

Sharing a computer is like sharing a car. When you share a car, each driver adjusts the seat and steering wheel for individual comfort, adjusts the mirrors to see out the back, and stores the garage door opener in a unique hiding place. Likewise, some computer users like a plain, uncluttered desktop, whereas others prefer to populate their desktops with dozens of icons, a sidebar, and other accessories.

Fortunately, Windows enables you to set up a separate user account for each person so that each person can customize Windows without affecting the appearance and function of Windows for other users. In addition, user accounts enable each user to keep a separate e-mail account, which means the messages for all users don't get mixed up in the same mailbox. User account passwords also provide privacy in a shared environment.

## Adding a New User to Your PC

When you or your computer's manufacturer installed Windows, the setup program automatically created a user account so Windows could greet you on startup.

To add a user account, click **Start**, **Control Panel**, **Add or remove user accounts** (under User Accounts and Family Safety), and then **Create a new account**. Use the resulting dialog box to name the new account and specify the account type: Standard user or Administrator. (See Figure 7.1.) When you click **Create Account**, Windows takes you to the Manage Accounts window, where you'll see a new icon for the account you created.

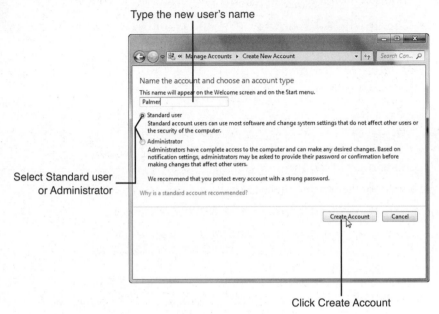

Type the new user's name

Select Standard user or Administrator

Click Create Account

**Figure 7.1**
*You can create a new user account.*

# Making Changes to a User Account

You can edit a user account to change its name, protect the account with a password, change the picture that represents your account, and more. To get started, click **Start**, **Control Panel**, **Add or remove user accounts**, and then click the account you want to configure. Windows displays several options for configuring the account, as shown in Figure 7.2:

- **Change the account name:** Simply click this option, type a new name, and click **Change Name**.

- **Create a password or Change the password:** To prevent unauthorized access to a user account, password-protect it. Click this option, type your password in the two designated boxes, enter a password hint (optional), and click **Create password**.

- **Remove the password:** An administrator can remove user account passwords.

- **Change the picture:** This option enables you to change the picture that represents you. You can even use the **Browse for more pictures...** option to choose a digital image, such as a photo, stored on your PC.

- **Change the account type:** An administrator can change an account type from Standard user to Administrator.

- **Delete the account:** This option enables an administrator to remove an account that is no longer in use.

**WHOA!**

Don't delete an account unless you're absolutely sure you won't ever use it again. Deleting an account permanently removes any passwords you've chosen to save and any e-mail messages.

**Figure 7.2**

*You can change a user account's settings or delete the account.*

# Enabling or Disabling the Guest Account

If you have guests who occasionally use your computer to check their e-mail, browse the web, or play games, you can enable the Guest Accounts feature to let them log on as guests without having to enter a password. They can then run programs and perform other tasks, but they cannot install new software or change any account settings. In short, guest users can use your PC without messing it up.

To enable or disable the guest account, click **Start**, **Control Panel**, **Add or remove user accounts**, and then click either **Turn On** or **Turn off the guest account**.

# Setting Parental Controls for a User

If you're setting up a user account for a child or teenager, consider activating Windows Parental Controls. You can prohibit computer use during certain days or times of day, and limit or block access to certain games or programs. With the addition of Windows Live Family Safety (a free add-on), you can also monitor and restrict a child's activity on the web.

Before activating Windows Parental Controls, perform the following tasks to prevent users from signing on using an unprotected user account:

- Make sure the guest account is off.

- Make your account a password-protected administrator account. Always password-protect administrator accounts; otherwise, it's easy for anyone to log on as an administrator and change settings, possibly locking you out of your own PC!

- Make sure the child's user account is set to Standard user.

## Activating and Configuring Windows Parental Controls

To activate Windows Parental controls and enter your preferences, follow these steps:

1. Click **Start**, **Control Panel**. Then below User Accounts and Family Safety, click **Set up parental controls for any user**.

2. Click the user account you want to control.

3. If you're prompted to sign in to set up Family Safety, close the window for now. You'll deal with this option in the following section.

4. Click **On**, **enforce current settings** to activate Parental Controls.

5. Under Windows Settings, click **Time Limits**, drag over the time blocks that indicate the days and times this user is prohibited from using the PC, and click **OK**. (See Figure 7.3.)

6. Click **Games**, enter your preferences to restrict this user from playing certain games, and click **OK**.

7. Click **Allow and block specific programs**, and then do one of the following:

   - Click **User can use all programs** and click **OK**.

   - Click **User can only use the programs I allow**, select any programs you want blocked for this user, and click **OK**.

8. Click **OK** to close the Parental Controls window and then exit the Control Panel.

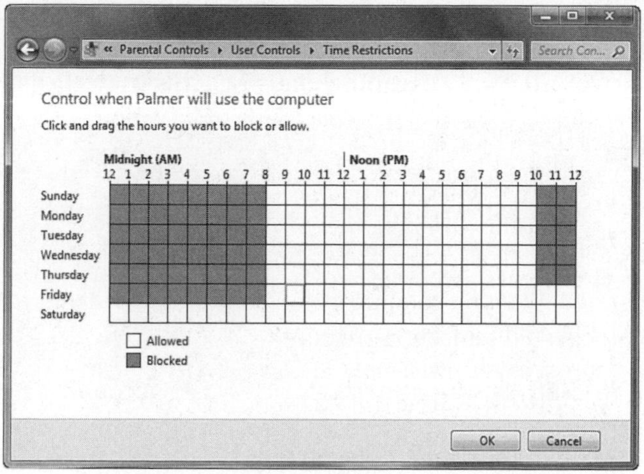

**Figure 7.3**
*Restrict PC use to certain hours.*

## Using Windows Live Family Safety

Windows Live Family Safety is a part of the free Windows Live add-on. If your PC is connected to the Internet, go to Windows Live Family Safety (at explore.live.com/ windows-live-family-safety), click the **Download** button, and follow the onscreen instructions to download (copy to your PC) and install Windows Live and create a free Windows Live account. (Chapter 18 shows you how to connect your PC to the Internet.)

After installing Windows Live, click **Start**, **Control Panel**, and then **Set up parental controls for any user**. Near the bottom, open the Select a provider list and click **Windows Live Family Safety**. The first time you choose this option, Windows prompts you for the e-mail address and password you use for your Windows Live account. After you log in, Windows prompts you to choose which user accounts to monitor. Click the check box next to each user account you want to monitor, click **Save**, and click **OK** when Windows indicates the setup is complete.

From this point on, you use the Windows Live Family Safety website to monitor and configure the safety settings for all of your user accounts. Go to home.live.com, log in, click **More** (in the top menu bar), and click **Family Safety**. Windows displays icons for all user accounts on your PC. For each user, you can click **Edit settings** to bring up the following options.

- **Web filtering** displays options to turn web filtering on or off, set the level of filtering, block specific websites, and allow or prevent this user from downloading files.

- **Activity reporting** displays options for turning activity reporting on or off and obtaining information about what this user's been doing on the PC, Internet, and web during the specified range of dates.

- **Contact management** enables you to control who your child can e-mail or chat with on Windows Live Hotmail, Messenger, and Spaces. (Your child needs a Windows Live ID, as discussed in Chapter 21.)

- **Requests** enables you to approve or deny requests from family members to access blocked content or contacts.

- **Remove** deactivates monitoring for this user account.

# Logging Off Windows

On weekends, when my kids and their friends are hanging out, they circle my computer like hungry hyenas, just waiting for me to head to the kitchen for a cup of coffee. Then they descend to play games, chat with friends, and do other things that don't require them to work or play outside. When I return to the computer, I usually find a couple of new programs installed on "my" account and several changes to my desktop.

The moral of the story is this: always log off or lock your computer when you step away from it. This prevents other users from changing your settings, snooping in your e-mail account, and performing other sinister or careless acts. For more about logging in and logging off and locking your PC, check out Chapter 2.

## The Least You Need to Know

- To add or remove a user account, click **Start**, **Control Panel**, **Add or remove user accounts**, and use the resulting screen to make your changes.

- To prevent others from logging on to your Windows account, add a password to your account.

- To enable Windows Parental Controls for a user, click **Start**, **Control Panel**, **Set up parental controls for any user**, and use the resulting screen to make your changes.

- If you share your PC with other users, be sure to log off or lock your PC before you step away from it to prevent others from messing with your stuff.

# Managing Disks, Files, and Folders

**In This Chapter**

- Identifying disk drives, easy as A-B-C
- Cutting, copying, moving, and deleting files and folders
- Tracking down lost and misplaced files
- Burning computer files to a CD or DVD
- Sharing files among users and networked PCs

Every computer has one or more disk drives for permanent storage of programs, documents, music, video, and content. These disk drives can read content from disks and write (record) content to disks, assuming that the disks are recordable. This chapter introduces you to the types of disks and disk drives you're likely to encounter and shows you how to access and manage everything stored on the various disks inside your PC.

## Disk Drives: Easy as A-B-C

Your computer assigns a letter to each disk drive to identify it. Most new PCs come with two drives: C for the hard drive inside the PC, and D for the CD or DVD drive. A and B are reserved for floppy drives, which are relics of the past. The important thing to remember is that disk drives are identified by letters, as shown in Figure 8.1.

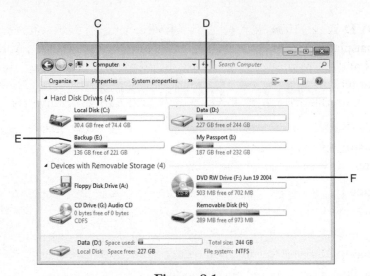

**Figure 8.1**
*Your PC uses letters from the alphabet to name its disk drives.*

## The Hard Disk Drive: C

The drive inside the computer is the internal hard disk drive (hard drive for short), usually called drive C. With hard drives, you don't handle the disk; it's hermetically sealed inside the drive, which is inside the PC.

> **INSIDE TIP**
>
> A hard disk drive can be partitioned (divided) into one or more drives that the computer refers to as C, D, E, and so on.

## The CD or DVD Drive: Usually D

A CD (compact disc) or DVD (digital video disc) drive is standard equipment on every new computer. It's usually located on the front of the system unit on a desktop PC or on the right side of a portable PC. The computer usually refers to it as D.

Be sure you purchase the right discs for the drive and your intended purpose (see Chapter 2 for more about the various types of CD and DVD drives):

- **CD-R:** Use CD-R (CD-Recordable) discs to make music CDs so you can play the CD not only on your PC, but also on most audio CD players.

- **CD-RW:** Use CD-RW (CD-ReWritable) if you plan to store computer files on the discs and perhaps erase files and add other files later.

- **DVD-R or DVD+R:** Use -R or +R (Recordable) discs to make video DVDs that play not only on your PC, but also on most standard TV DVD players. -R and +R work the same but use different symbols because they are competing technologies. Check the front of the disc drive or its documentation or look up the drive on the web to see which formats it supports.

- **DVD-RW or DVD+RW:** Use -RW or +RW (ReWritable) discs if you plan to store computer files on the discs and perhaps erase files and add other files later. RW discs can be rewritten a thousand times.

- **Speed:** Recordable discs and drives are rated by speed, so make sure the maximum speed of the disc is equal to or greater than that of the drive.

- **Printable:** The latest craze is to print labels right on the disc. If your drive supports this feature, you may want to buy printable discs compatible with the labeling technology—for example, LightScribe.

- **Dual-layer:** If your drive supports dual-layer discs, it can store double the amount of data on each disc, which is especially useful for backing up large amounts of data.

- **Blu-ray:** Most newer optical drives can play Blu-ray DVDs but aren't built to record to them. However, if you have a drive that can record Blu-ray discs and you're planning to make your own Blu-ray DVDs, make sure the discs support Blu-ray, too.

## External Drives and Other Anomalies

Although internal hard drives and optical drives are standard fare on PCs, other types of drives are very popular for use in backing up files or taking files on the road:

- **External hard drives:** These drives sit outside the computer and connect to the system unit by a data cable, typically a USB cable.

- **USB flash drives:** Commonly referred to as *thumb drives*, these drives are small enough to fit on a keychain and plug right into your computer's USB port.

- **Memory cards:** These cards are primarily used in digital cameras and printers designed to print digital photos.

- **PC card drives:** Many portable PCs come with a PC card slot into which you can plug various devices, including a disk drive.

## Loading and Unloading CDs and DVDs

If you've ever loaded a CD into your audio CD player or a DVD into your DVD player, you have all the technical expertise required to load discs into your PC's CD or DVD drive. Just be sure to handle the disc only by its edges so you don't scratch the surface or get any dirt or fingerprints on it. The technique for loading a disc into a CD or DVD drive differs depending on the drive:

- If the drive has an open slot on the front, slide the disc, shiny side down or left, into the slot, just as you would insert a coin into a pop machine.

- If the drive has a drive tray, press the load/eject button on the front of the drive to open it; then lay the disc in the tray, shiny side down, and press the load/ eject button. (Don't push in the tray to close it, as this may damage the loading mechanism.)

> **INSIDE TIP**
>
> If you ever have trouble playing a CD or DVD, the disc might be dirty. To clean the disc, wipe it off with a soft, lint-free cloth from the center of the disc out to its edges, never in a circular motion. (Wipe the side without the picture or printing on it, because this is the side that the drive reads; some discs are two-sided.) If something sticky gets on the disc, dampen the cloth with a little distilled water and wipe it dry. Let the disc dry thoroughly before inserting it into the drive.

The Windows AutoPlay feature attempts to identify the contents of the disc and find the right program to play it. Windows does a pretty good job of matching disc contents to programs, but if it needs help, it prompts you to select an AutoPlay option, as shown in Figure 8.2. You can select one of the options Windows suggests or click **View more AutoPlay options in Control Panel** to select a program from a more comprehensive list.

**Figure 8.2**
*Windows prompts you to choose an AutoPlay action.*

If Windows automatically performs the wrong action on this type of disc, you can specify a different action by clicking **Start**, **Control Panel**, **Hardware and Sound**, **AutoPlay**. Next to the type of disc whose AutoPlay setting you want to change, open the drop-down list and click the action you want Windows to perform whenever a disc of this type is inserted.

To eject a disc, you usually have two options. You can either press the eject button on the drive itself or save wear and tear on the button by having Windows eject the disc for you. Click **Start**, **Computer**, right-click the drive's icon, and click **Eject**.

### Using an External USB or Flash Drive

To use a USB drive, simply plug it into one of your PC's USB ports. What happens next varies depending on what's on the drive:

- Windows may identify the drive as a storage device and assign it a letter so you can use it as any other drive on your PC.

- Windows may prompt you to choose an AutoPlay option, as it does sometimes when you load a CD or DVD.

- The drive may come with its own software that launches as soon as you connect the device.

Follow the onscreen prompts and clues to determine how best to proceed.

The only drawback of a USB drive is that it's easier to lose data by removing the drive before Windows is done writing to it. Before unplugging the drive from the USB port, click the **Safely Remove Hardware and Eject Media** icon in the notification area, click the **Eject** option for the device, and wait for Windows to display the Safe To Remove Hardware notification.

# Exploring Your Disks, Folders, and Files

All the programs, documents, and other data on your PC is stored on disks as files organized (grouped) into various folders. To see what's on one of your PC's disks, click **Start**, **Computer**, and then double-click one of the disk icons. Windows displays the contents of the selected disk drive, as shown in Figure 8.3.

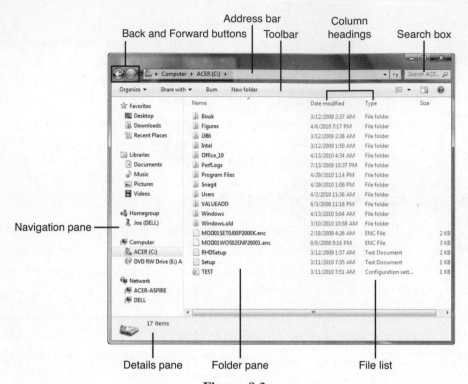

**Figure 8.3**
*Windows helps you navigate disk contents.*

You can tell a great deal about the items stored on your computer by glancing at their icons.

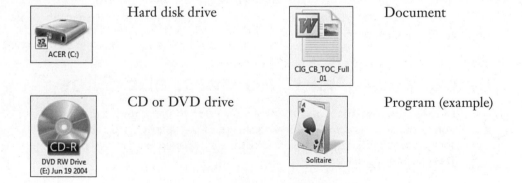

Hard disk drive

Document

CD or DVD drive

Program (example)

Empty folder

 Music

 Folder with documents

 Picture

 Folder with subfolder(s) and documents

 Video

To navigate your disks and folders, double-click the disk on which the file or folder is stored and then double-click folder after folder to follow the trail to the folder or file you're looking for. (You can double-click folders in the navigation or library pane.) You can always use the **Back** button to go back to the previous folder or click **Forward** if you go back and then want to return to a folder. To open a file or run a program, double-click its icon.

The trail to a file is actually called a *directory path* that starts with the drive letter (sometimes called the *root directory*) and ends with whatever folder or file name you're looking for—for example:

```
c:\Users\Public\Public Pictures\Sample Pictures\Koala
```

Figure 8.4 shows the directory path as it appears near the top of every Windows Explorer Window. You can click a folder in the path to change to that folder or click the **Back** button to back up to the previous folder.

**INSIDE TIP**

You can make a disk, folder, file, or program more accessible by placing an icon for it on the Windows desktop. Right-click the icon, point to **Send To**, and click **Desktop (create shortcut)**.

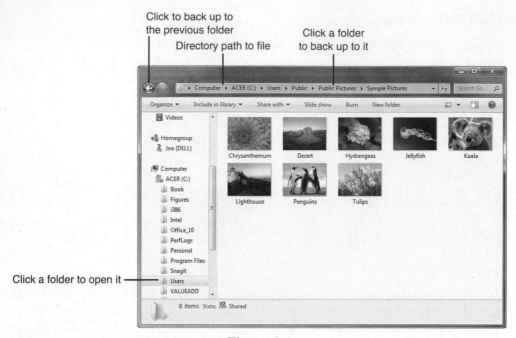

**Figure 8.4**
*Follow the directory path to the file or folder.*

## Using the Navigation Bar

You can also use the navigation bar to follow the path to a folder or file. Notice in the navigation bar that certain folders have a hollow triangle/arrow to the left of them. This indicates that the folder has subfolders that are not being shown. Click the arrow to display the subfolders. The hollow arrow changes into a black triangle to indicate that the folder's subfolders are now displayed.

## Changing Icon Size

To change the way Windows displays files and folders, right-click a blank area in the folder pane (above, below, or between items), point to **View**, and click the desired option. The first four options are pretty obvious: **Extra large**, **Large**, **Medium**, or **Small icons**. **List** displays tiny icons in a newspaper-column format; **Details** displays additional information about each file, including, size, type, and date modified; **Tiles** is sort of like List, but with larger icons; and **Content** displays tile-size icons followed by larger names and date modified.

## Rearranging Items

Windows arranges icons by name from A to Z. To sort by some other criterion, right-click a blank area in the folder pane, point to **Sort by**, and click the desired sort order: **Name**, **Date Modified**, **Type**, or **Size**. You can also choose to sort items in **Ascending** order (A to Z or 1 to 10) or **Descending** order (Z to A or 10 to 1).

To display items in groups, right-click a blank area in the folder pane, point to Group by, and click **Name**, **Date Modified**, **Type**, or **Size**. You can also choose to display groups in **Ascending** or **Descending** order.

## Applying View Preferences to All Folders

Changing the view settings and sort order for one folder does not change the settings for all folders. To change the view settings and sort order for all folders of the same type (for example, all picture folders), follow these steps:

1. Enter your view and sort order preferences for a folder, as explained in the previous two sections.

2. Click **Organize** (left end of the toolbar, as shown in Figure 8.3) and click **Folder and search options**.

3. Click the **View** tab.

4. Click **Apply to Folders** and click **OK**.

## Choosing Single-Click or Double-Click Navigation

Unless you choose otherwise, Windows has you click files or folders to select them and double-click to open files or run programs. That's a lot of clicking.

To reduce the amount of clicking, click **Organize** (left end of the toolbar) and click **Folder and search options**. Click **Single-click to open an item (point to select)** and click **OK**. Now you just have to get used to it.

## Adjusting More Folder Options

You can change numerous settings to control the appearance and behavior of folders, but this book doesn't really have the space to cover all the options. To explore on your own, click **Organize** (left end of the toolbar) and then click **Folder and search options**.

You should be aware of two advanced settings on the View tab. Under Hidden files and folders, consider turning on **Show hidden files, folders and drives**. Windows hides some files to protect them, but this can cause problems when you're trouble-shooting and need to find a particular Windows file.

Also consider turning off **Hide extensions for known file types**. Almost all file names have a period at the end, followed by a three-character extension that indicates the file type—.doc (file created in Microsoft Word), .jpg (a special type of graphic file), .exe (an executable program file), and so on. These can come in mighty handy when you're instructed to look for a file with a certain file extension.

# Managing Your Files Using Windows Libraries

Windows 7 is designed to help you track down files wherever they happen to be stored on your PC. If you're obsessively organized like me, you probably need to know where everything is and you're likely to carefully construct your own filing system that makes sense to you. If you're not well organized, you can stick files and folders anywhere and use the Windows Libraries and its Search feature to find the needles in your haystack.

## Understanding Windows Libraries

Initially, every user has four libraries: Documents, Music, Pictures, and Videos. You can see your libraries in the navigation pane. Libraries are folders with a twist. The twist is that each library acts more as an index of files and folders stored anywhere on your PC, so the actual files and folder don't have to actually be stored inside the library folder. For example, your Pictures library might include digital photos stored inside the library itself, in a different folder (such as C:\Photos), or even in a folder on an external hard drive (such as D:\VacationPhotos).

## Browsing a Library's Contents

To browse a library's contents, click **Start**, **Computer**, and then click the library you want to browse. For convenience, Windows lists a few libraries on the right pane of the Start menu, so you can click **Start**, **Documents** (for example) to access the Documents library directly. You can then open folders and documents stored in the library as described earlier in this chapter.

## Adding Folders to a Library

You can add folders to any library, regardless of where those folders are stored. Simply select the folder you want to share and then click **Include in library** (in the toolbar) and click the desired library. (See Figure 8.5.) The folder and its contents remain in place, and an icon for the folder is added to the chosen library. (The folder must be under Computer or one of its folders or subfolders. Choosing a folder under Libraries/Documents, for example, won't work—Include in library will not appear in the toolbar.)

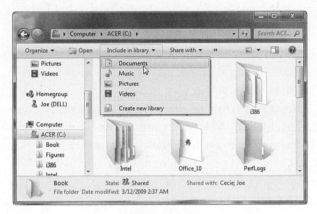

**Figure 8.5**
*Add a folder to the library.*

## Creating a New Library

To create your own library, select the folder you want to share, and then click **Include in library** (in the toolbar) and click **Create new library**. Windows creates a new library and assigns it the same name as the folder you selected.

To rename the library, right-click it in the navigation bar, click **Rename**, type the new name, and press **Enter**.

## Arranging a Library's Contents

In addition to being able to sort items in the library as you sort items in a folder, you can arrange a library's contents. Open the library or a folder inside a library and then click the button next to **Arrange by:** (upper right) and click the desired arrangement.

You can also rearrange the library locations. When you're in one of the libraries, click the **locations** link below the library's name (in the upper left of the folder pane, not in the navigation pane). Click a location and then right-click it and choose **Move up** or **Move down**. Click **OK**.

## Changing the Default Save Location

When you begin using programs to create documents and other types of files, you eventually save your work to disk for safekeeping. When you choose the **File**, **Save** command to save a document, the program displays a dialog box asking you to name the file and choose the folder in which you want it saved.

Most Windows programs are set up to save files in the Documents folder (also called My Documents in some programs) or in one of the other standard Windows libraries, such as Pictures. You can choose a different drive and folder to save this particular file, but the next time you create and save a file, Windows will default to the Documents folder again. In some programs, you can choose a different default location, usually through the Tools, Options command.

Here's an easier way to change the default save location through Windows: When you're in one of the libraries, click the **locations** link below the library's name. Click the location you want to use as the default save location, and then right-click it and choose **Set as default save location**. Click **OK**.

# Finding Files and Folders

The more files and folders you store on your PC, the more likely you'll lose or misplace something. Fortunately, Windows can help you find just about anything in about the time it takes to type a description of what you're looking for. The following sections show you how to perform different types of searches in Windows.

## Searching Your Entire PC

To perform the easiest and broadest search, click **Start** and type a word or two describing the item you're looking for. As you type, Windows displays a list of items that match the description you typed so far, as shown in Figure 8.6. Keep typing to narrow your search. Type less to broaden your search.

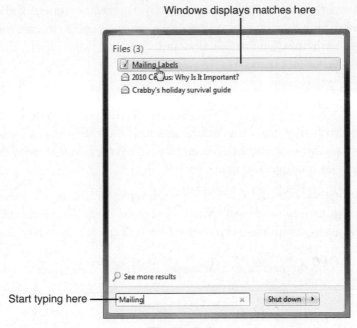

**Figure 8.6**
*Search from the Start menu.*

## Searching a Library or Folder

To perform a more targeted search, search the library or folder where you think the item is likely to be. Windows will search all locations in that library or folder:

1.  Open the library or folder you want to search. For example, click **Start, Documents**. (To search all libraries, click **Start, Computer, Libraries**.)

2.  Click in the **Search** box (upper-right corner) and start typing one or more words to describe the file or folder. As you type, Windows searches and displays all the items that have the entry you typed in their names or content. The more you type, the fewer items you see as Windows narrows the search. For each item in the list, Windows highlights the text that matches what you've typed.

3.  If you see a file that may be the one you're looking for, click it and then click the **Show preview pane** button (the middle button below the Search box). Windows opens the preview pane on the right. If your PC has a program that can open the file, a portion of the file's contents appears in the preview pane.

4.  To open the file, double-click it.

If you don't see the file you're looking for, scroll to the bottom of the search results and click one of the **Search again** in options. For example, you can perform the same search in Libraries or Computer.

## Using Search Filters

Regardless of whether you search for a specific word, you can narrow the list of files displayed in the folder pane by selecting a search filter. For example, you can choose to filter by date and then limit the results to files modified yesterday, last week, earlier this week, or on a specific date.

Click in the **Search** box to display the Search menu, and then click one of the search filters at the bottom of the Search menu: **Authors**, **Type**, **Date modified**, or **Size**. Use the resulting options to specify your filter criteria, as shown in Figure 8.7.

**Figure 8.7**
*Use a search filter.*

# Managing Files and Folders

You have complete control over the folders and files stored on your PC. The following sections show you how to select items and copy, move, or delete the items from a disk. You also learn how to create new folders and copy (burn) files to a recordable CD or DVD.

## Selecting Files and Folders

Before you can do anything with a file or folder, you must select it:

- Click a file or folder to select it. (Remember, if single-click access is on, you select the file by resting the tip of the mouse pointer on it.) Selected items appear highlighted, as shown in Figure 8.8.

- To select non-neighboring (noncontiguous) items, select one item and then hold down the **Ctrl** key and select each additional item. (You can deselect a selected item by selecting it again.)

- To select neighboring (contiguous) files and folders, select the first file or folder and hold down the **Shift** key while selecting the last one in the group.

- You also can select a group of items by dragging a box around them. Point to a blank area above and to the left of the block of items you want to select, and then hold down the left mouse button while dragging down and to the right until the box surrounds all the items you want. When you release the mouse button, all the items within the box's borders are highlighted.

**Figure 8.8**
*Selected items appear highlighted.*

## Tagging and Rating Files

Tagging and/or rating certain files, including music and photos but not documents, can make finding them much easier later and help you recall a file's contents. To rate a file, select it in Windows File Manager; then, at the bottom of the window, click the desired rating star. To tag the file, click **Add a tag** and type one or more descriptive words or phrases separated by semicolons.

## Making Your Own Folders

If you want to store your files in an independent folder of your choosing, create a new folder:

1. Click **Start, Computer.**

2. Change to the disk or folder in which you want the new folder located.

3. Click **New folder** in the toolbar or right-click a blank area in the folder pane, point to **New,** and click **Folder.**

4. Type a name for the folder (255 characters or fewer). As you start typing, the **New folder** name is deleted and is replaced by what you type. You can use any character or number, but you cannot use any of the following characters: \ / : * ? " < > |.

5. Press **Enter.**

## Deleting and Recovering Files: The Recycle Bin

Windows comes complete with its own trash compactor, called the Recycle Bin, conveniently located in the upper-left corner of your desktop. Whenever a file or folder has outlived its usefulness, either drag it over the **Recycle Bin** and release the mouse button, or select the item(s) and then right-click one of the selected items and click **Delete.** When prompted to confirm, click **Yes.**

To bypass the Recycle Bin and permanently delete an item, hold down the **Shift** key while clicking **Delete** and then click **Yes** to confirm. Be careful with this!

> **WHOA!**
>
> Never delete or move files or folders stored in a program's folder, because doing so may harm your program and render it unusable. If you want to remove a program, use the Windows utility for installing and removing programs, as explained in Chapter 9.

If you accidentally delete an item, you can usually recover it, unless you deleted the item a long time ago or emptied the Recycle Bin. To recover an item, double-click the Recycle Bin, right-click the item, and click **Restore.**

To empty the Recycle Bin, first be sure the Recycle Bin contains only files and folders you will never need. Then right-click the **Recycle Bin** icon and click **Empty Recycle Bin.**

To change the properties of the Recycle Bin, including the maximum amount of disk space it uses, right-click the **Recycle Bin** icon, click **Properties**, enter your preferences, and click **OK**.

## Renaming Folders and Files

To rename a file or folder, right-click the item's name, click **Rename**, type the new name, and press **Enter**.

## Moving and Copying Folders and Files

The most straightforward way to move items is to open two windows: one that shows the item(s) you want to move and another that shows the future destination of the items. Then simply drag any one of the selected items over the destination and release the mouse button to drop the items in place, as shown in Figure 8.9. Hold down the **Ctrl** key while dragging to copy the items instead of moving them. When you hold down the Ctrl key, a plus sign appears next to the mouse pointer, indicating that the items will be copied, not moved.

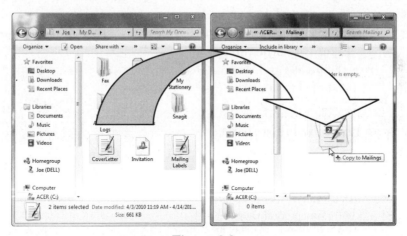

**Figure 8.9**
*Drag and drop items to copy or move them.*

Here's a quicker way to copy or move files:

1. Select the items you want to copy or move in the folder pane.

2. Display the desired destination folder in the navigation pane. You may need to click arrows to the left of items in the navigation pane to display the destination folder.

3. Drag any one of the selected items over the destination folder and drop it in place, keeping the following important information in mind:

   • If you drag an item to a *different disk*, Windows assumes that you want to *copy* the item instead of move it. To move the item, hold down the **Shift** key while dragging.

   • If you drag a folder or file to a different folder on the *same disk*, Windows assumes that you want to *move* the item to the new destination. To copy the item, hold down the **Ctrl** key while dragging.

   • If you're not sure, use the right mouse button instead of the left while dragging. When you release the button, a menu appears asking whether you want to move or copy the items.

Sometimes the easiest way to move a file or folder is to cut and paste it (especially if you don't have the benefit of a two-paned Explorer window). Right-click the icon for the item you want to move and click **Cut** (to move the item) or **Copy** (to copy it). (To copy the objects instead, right-click an object and click **Copy**.) Change to the disk or folder in which you want the cut item placed. Right-click the disk or folder icon (or right-click a blank area in its contents window) and click **Paste**.

## Copying Files to a CD or DVD

Copying files to a CD or DVD requires a slightly different approach than copying files on a hard disk drive, because the blank disc must first be prepared to store files and may then need to be properly "closed" so it can play on other computers and devices. (In this section, you learn how to copy computer files to a disc. To burn an audio CD, see Chapter 30. To burn a video DVD, see Chapter 32.)

Windows can burn files to a disc using either the Windows Live File System format or the Mastered format.

   • **Windows Live File System:** Live File System discs are generally better for storing computer files, because you can add and remove files after burning files to the disc.

   • **Mastered:** Mastered discs are generally better for storing music and pictures, because they're more compatible with regular CD, DVD, and Blu-ray players.

To burn files to a disc using Live File System, follow these steps:

1. Insert a blank disc. The AutoPlay dialog box appears, displaying Blank CD or DVD options.

2. Click **Burn files to disc**. The Burn a Disc dialog box appears.

3. Type a name for this disc in the Disc title box, click **Like a USB flash drive**, and click **Next**. Windows formats the disc (which can take some time) and then displays the AutoPlay window.

4. Click **Open folder to view files**. Windows opens an empty disc folder window for that disc.

5. Copy files or folders to the disc as explained earlier in this chapter, or select a group of items you want to copy, right-click one of the items, point to **Send to**, and click the disc drive that contains the blank disc. As you add files to the disc, Windows automatically burns them to the disc.

6. Eject the disc as explained earlier in this chapter (see "Loading and Unloading CDs and DVDs"). Windows automatically "closes" the session and ejects the disc.

To burn files to a disc using Mastered, follow these steps:

1. Insert a blank disc. The AutoPlay dialog box appears, displaying Blank CD or DVD options.

2. Click **Burn files to disc** and click **OK**. The Burn a Disc dialog box appears.

3. Type a name for this disc in the Disc title box, click **With a CD/DVD player**, and click **Next**. Windows displays an empty disc folder window.

4. Copy files or folders to the disc as explained earlier in this chapter, or select a group of items you want to copy, right-click one of the items, point to **Send to**, and click the disc drive that contains the blank disc. As you copy items to the disc, a notification appears indicating that you have files waiting to be burned to the disc.

5. When you're done copying items, click the notification balloon to display the window that contains the files waiting to be written to the disc.

6. Click **Burn to disc** (in the toolbar near the top of the window), and then follow the wizard's instructions to burn the files to the disc and eject it.

# Sharing Folders and Files with Other Users

Normally, each user's libraries remain off-limits to other users on this computer or on other computers that comprise a network. Windows provides two ways to share folders or files in your library with other users.

- Share among members of the same homegroup, as explained in Chapter 11.

- Copy the files or folders you want to share to the Windows Public folder, as shown in Figure 8.10.

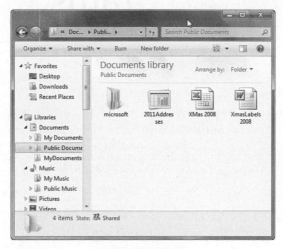

**Figure 8.10**
*Files or folders in the Public folders are shared.*

To make sure Public folder sharing is enabled, click **Start**, **Control Panel**, **Choose homegroup and sharing options** (under Network and Internet), **Change advanced sharing settings**. Scroll down until you see **Public** and click the down arrow to the right. If the following is not enabled, select it: **Turn on sharing so anyone with network access can read and write files in the Public folders**. Click **Save changes**.

## The Least You Need to Know

- To display the disks, folders, and files on your PC, click **Start**, **Computer**.

- To move a file, drag it over the destination disk or folder icon and drop it in place. To copy a file, hold down the **Ctrl** key while dragging.

- To add a folder to a library, right-click the folder, point to **Include in library**, and click the desired library.

- To perform a quick search for anything on your PC, click **Start** and start typing one or more words to describe what you're looking for.

- To burn computer files to a blank CD or DVD, insert the disc, follow the onscreen cues, and remember that Live File System is usually best for burning computer files.

# Running, Installing, and Uninstalling Programs

**In This Chapter**

- Running programs from the Start menu
- Making your favorite programs more accessible
- Picking programs your computer can run
- Installing a program
- Getting rid of the programs you don't use

Without programs, a computer is just a fancy box packed with electronic circuitry. Programs enable you to harness the power of that circuitry and use it to perform specific tasks such as typing a letter, keeping your checkbook balanced, surfing the World Wide Web, playing video games, and so much more.

This chapter shows you how to take control of programs. Here you learn how to run programs already installed on your computer, buy and install programs, and uninstall programs you no longer use.

## Running Your Programs

Whenever you install a program, the installation utility places the program's name on the Start, All Programs menu or one of its submenus. To run the program, you simply click **Start**, **All Programs**, click the desired program group (if necessary), and click the program's name. (See Figure 9.1.) If you don't see the program you want to run, start typing its name in the **Search** box, and Windows will help you find it.

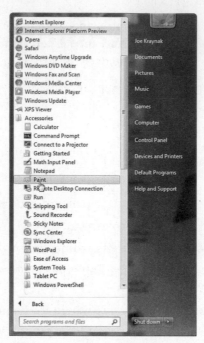

**Figure 9.1**

*Find programs on the Start, All Programs menu.*

As you run programs, Windows automatically adds them to the Start menu's left pane so you can find them more easily next time. Programs you use often stay put, while those you use less often may get bumped off the menu, but you can still always find them on the All Programs menu or one of its submenus. For additional suggestions on how to put programs within easy reach, check out Chapter 6.

> **INSIDE TIP**
>
> You can quickly run a program and open a document simply by double-clicking the document. Windows runs the program associated with that document type, and the program opens the document.

## Using Jump Lists for Quick Access to Programs and Files

As you use various programs to create, save, and edit documents (see Part 3), Windows keeps track of what you're doing and creates a jump list for every program, which contains the names of the files you worked on most recently. To access a program's jump list, do this:

- **From the Start menu:** Jump lists appear only for pinned or recently used programs that appear in the Start menu's left pane. To view a program's jump list, click **Start** and then mouse over the program.

- **From the taskbar:** Jump lists appear only for pinned or currently running programs that appear in the taskbar. To view a program's jump list, right-click a program's icon in the taskbar.

After displaying a program's jump list, you can perform any of the following tasks:

- **Open an item:** Click the item to open it in the program associated with it.

- **Remove an item:** Right-click the item and click **Remove from this list**.

- **Copy an item:** Drag the item off the jump list and drop it wherever you want. For example, you can drag an item from its jump list into an e-mail message to attach the file to your message. (See Chapter 21 for more about e-mail.)

- **Pin an item to the list:** Pinning an item to the jump list moves it to the top portion of the list, where it remains until you remove it. This is useful for documents you frequently open and work on. Right-click the item and click **Pin to this list**.

- **Unpin an item from the list:** To unpin an item, right-click it and click **Unpin from this list**.

You can clear the history of recently opened programs, files, folders, and websites from the Start menu and taskbar. You may want to do this if you share a computer with someone and don't want that person to be able to see what you've been doing. To clear the history, follow these steps:

1. Right-click a blank area of the taskbar and click **Properties**.

2. Click the **Start Menu** tab.

3. Under Privacy, click the check box (to remove the check mark) next to **Store and display recently opened files in the Start menu** and **Store and display recently opened items in the Start menu and the taskbar**.

4. Click **OK**.

# Buying Software Your Hardware Can Run

Before you purchase any program, read the minimum hardware requirements printed on the outside of the package to determine whether your computer has what it takes to run the program. Be sure to note the following information:

- **Operating system:** Your PC can probably run older programs, but you're better off with Windows 7 versions.

- **Free hard disk space:** Be sure your hard disk has enough free disk space. To find out how much free disk space your computer has, Click **Start**, **Computer**. Windows displays the amount of used and free storage space on each disk drive.

- **CPU requirements:** CPU stands for central processing unit, and it's the brain of your computer. If the program requires at least a 1.5GHz 64-bit (x64) processor and you have a 1GHz 32-bit (x32) processor, your computer won't be able to run the application effectively, if at all. Following this list is an explanation of how to check system information on your PC.

- **Type of monitor:** All newer monitors support DVI and/or VGA. Some may support HDMI, too. See Chapter 2 for more about different types of monitors.

- **Graphics card:** Some games and graphics programs require a specific type of graphics card (display adapter).

- **Joystick:** Although most computer games allow you to use your keyboard and mouse, games are usually more fun if you have a joystick or something else that's a little more versatile.

- **CD or DVD drive:** Because of their size, many newer software packages (including Windows Vista) come on DVDs. Check for the required speed of the drive, too.

- **Sound card:** Games and programs for recording and mixing audio may require a special sound card or other recording equipment.

- **Amount of memory:** If your computer does not have the required memory (also known as RAM, short for "random access memory"), it might not be able to run the program, or the program might cause the computer to crash (freeze up).

You can find out most of what you need to know about your computer from the System Information utility. Click **Start**, **All Programs**, **Accessories**, **System Tools**, **System Information**. The System Information window appears (see Figure 9.2), displaying the operating system name and version number, the type and speed of your processor, and the amount of RAM—physical (actual RAM) and virtual (hard drive space used as RAM).

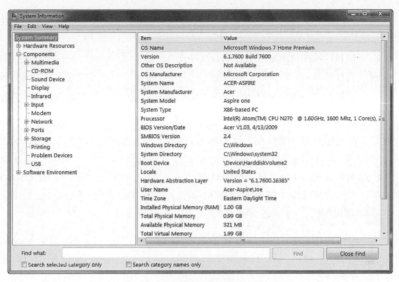

**Figure 9.2**
*The System Information utility.*

Click the plus sign next to Components to explore information about other components of your computer, including the CD-ROM drive, sound device, display, hard drives (under Storage), and so on.

# Where to Find Programs

You can find programs and games online and offline. The following sections point out some of the most common methods of acquiring programs and some of the pros and cons of each.

## The Usual Places You Shop

You can find programs and games online and offline. Following are some of the most common places to go to acquire programs and some of the pros and cons of each:

- **Offline retail stores:** You can find PC-based programs just about anywhere you can buy computers and office supplies, including Walmart, Target, Staples, Office Depot, and Amazon.com.

- **Software developers:** Most software developers, including Microsoft, sell their programs directly to consumers online and usually let you try before you buy. You usually have the option to download the program and start using it right away or order the "media version" (on CD or DVD).

- **Shareware/Freeware sites:** Shareware sites, like download.cnet.com, are the ultimate in try-before-you-buy. You download the program and use it for the specified trial period; if you like it, you buy it. Freeware is like shareware, but you're not expected to pay … ever. (To avoid viruses and other malware, download only from trusted, well-established sites.)

Security settings in your browser may prevent you from downloading or installing a file. If this happens, you usually see a security message at the top of the browser window indicating what's going on and how to proceed.

# Installing Your New Program

Nearly every program on the market comes with an installation file (usually called Setup or Install) that does everything for you. If the program is on CD or DVD, you can usually pop the disc into the appropriate drive, and Windows will automatically initiate the installation routine. You click a few options to tell the installation utility that it can install the program according to the default settings, and then you can kick back and watch the installation routine do its thing.

**WHOA!**

Windows may prompt you for permission before installing a program. If you're not logged onto Windows as an administrator, you may need an administrator to enter a password before you can continue.

If the installation doesn't start automatically when you insert the disc, here's what you do:

1. If you haven't inserted the program disc into the drive, insert it now.

2. Click **Start**, **Computer**.

3. Double-click the icon for the drive that contains the disc. This displays a list of files and folders on the disc.

4. Double-click the file named **Setup**, **Install**, or its equivalent. This starts the installation utility.

5. Follow the onscreen instructions to complete the installation.

If you downloaded a program, it may come as a compressed file (often called a *zip file*), which typically appears as a folder with a zipper on it and .zip in the file name. In most cases, you open the folder as you usually do (see Chapter 8), double-click the **Setup** or **Install** file, and proceed with the installation. If that doesn't work, try extracting the contents of the folder first. Right-click the compressed folder, click **Extract all**, and then click **Extract**. Windows extracts the contents and displays it in a separate window, where you can launch **Setup** or **Install**.

# Removing a Program You Never Use

Your hard disk isn't an ever-expanding universe on which you can install an unlimited number of programs. As you install programs, create documents, send and receive e-mail messages, and view web pages, your disk can quickly become overpopulated. One of the best ways to reclaim a hefty chunk of disk space is to remove (uninstall) programs you don't use.

To remove a program safely and completely, always use the Windows Add/Remove Programs utility:

1. Click **Start**, **Control Panel**.

2. Under **Programs**, click **Uninstall a program**.

3. Click the program you want to uninstall and then, in the toolbar (near the top of the window), click **Uninstall**. (See Figure 9.3.)

4. Click **Yes** to confirm.

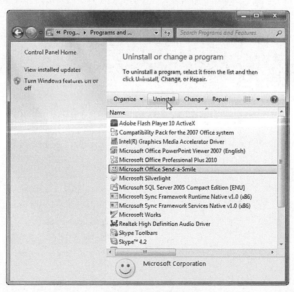

**Figure 9.3**
*Let Windows remove the program for you.*

Some programs enable you to install or uninstall various components of the program. For example, you can install Microsoft Office without installing one of its programs, such as Access. In such cases, when you click a program to uninstall, you may see additional options in the toolbar, including Change and Repair.

## The Least You Need to Know

- To run a program, click **Start**, **All Programs**, click the desired program group, and click the program's icon.
- Not all programs run on all computers. Before buying a program, be sure your PC meets the requirements printed on the program's box.
- To access details about the components that comprise your computer, click **Start**, **All Programs**, **Accessories**, **System Tools**, **System Information**.
- To install a program, insert its installation disc or locate and double-click its **Setup** or **Install** file.
- To remove a program you no longer use, open the Windows **Control Panel**, click **Uninstall a program** under **Programs**, and follow the onscreen prompts.

# Installing and Managing Additional Hardware Devices

**In This Chapter**

- Exploring popular add-ons and upgrades
- Adding external devices to your PC
- Upgrading RAM and installing expansion cards
- Installing another internal hard drive
- Upgrading portable PCs

Even if you purchased a PC with everything you thought you needed, you may discover new gadgets you simply can't live without. In addition, over time, you may want to take advantage of newer technology that your older PC is ill equipped to deal with. Instead of buying an entirely new PC, you may be able to upgrade your PC for a fraction of the cost. This chapter shows you how.

## Upgrade or Buy a New PC?

I generally prefer upgrading my old PC to buying a new one for several reasons, including the fact that transferring programs, documents, e-mail, and everything else from an old PC to a new one is a hassle. I'm also not too fond of our throw-away culture. I'd rather repair than replace, even when repairing costs a little more. However, sometimes it makes sense to replace the entire PC:

- The upgrades cost more than half as much as a brand-new PC.
- You currently have a portable PC with limited upgrade options.
- Your PC is more than three years old (or less for a portable PC, because it's likely to get banged around a bit more). If you upgrade and then a major component of the PC goes belly up, that old PC can turn into a money pit.

In addition, some of the newer software can have trouble with the older hardware.

- Someone you know could really put your old PC to good use.

- Even with all the upgrades you want, your PC still wouldn't be able to do what you want it to do.

Make a list of all the upgrades you plan to make, shop around to determine the cost of each upgrade, total the amount, and compare it with the price of a new PC. The comparison may be enough to convince you to move up to a newer model.

> **INSIDE TIP**
>
> If you're thinking of replacing or upgrading your PC simply because it's slow, consider giving your PC a tune-up first (as explained in Chapter 34) and troubleshooting for performance issues (as explained in Chapter 35).

# Exploring Upgrades and Optional Accessories

When you're ready to soup up or accessorize your PC, you may want to know what your options are. The following list presents the most popular and useful upgrades and accessories:

- **Memory (RAM):** If your system has a meager 1GB RAM, adding another gigabyte or 3 can give it an instant performance boost.

- **External hard drive:** External hard drives are easy to install and are great for backing up files. Also, if you're running out of storage on your internal hard drive, you can move your photos, video, and other large files to the external drive to clear some space.

- **Internal hard drive:** If your PC has a vacant drive bay (a place for mounting another drive), you can significantly boost available storage by installing another internal drive.

- **Optical disc drive:** You may want to install a new disc drive to take advantage of a newer disc format, such as Blu-ray; upgrade from -R to +RW; or have two disc drives to simplify the process of copying discs.

- **Wi-Fi and/or Bluetooth adapter:** If your PC doesn't support wireless connectivity (Wi-Fi for wireless Internet or Bluetooth for wireless devices, such as a wireless keyboard or mouse), you can add this functionality. You can purchase a single adapter that supports both Wi-Fi and Bluetooth.

- **Webcam:** A webcam enables you to videoconference with your PC and take snapshots and record video of yourself while sitting at your PC.

- **Video card:** When you're upgrading to a new monitor (say, from VGA to DVI) or adding a second monitor, you may need to add a video card. Newer video cards typically have several ports for VGA, DVI, and perhaps even HDMI.

- **TV tuner:** Planning to watch TV on your PC? Then you'll need to add a TV tuner card or add a video card that includes a built-in tuner.

- **Memory card reader:** A memory card reader enables you to transfer data from flash memory cards commonly used to store photos in digital cameras and other devices.

- **Network adapter:** Most newer PCs have a local area network (LAN) port, as described in Chapters 1 and 2. If your PC has no LAN port, you can add one.

- **Sound card:** If you've decided to transform your PC into your family entertainment system, you may want to change or add a sound card to produce theater-quality sound.

- **Digital media server:** Media servers store, organize, and distribute digital media, including movies and music, throughout the house. The server is usually part of the home network (cable or wireless) and may be a specialized device or a full-featured computer. It usually has a multiformat disc player for transferring music and video to the server's hard drive, which is usually massive compared to that of a standard PC. The media server also includes a remote control.

- **Media center extender:** A media center extender enables you to place your digital media server in a separate room and stream the audio or video to the home theater or stereo system.

# Installing External Devices

The easiest upgrades are those you can make simply by plugging an external device into one of your PC's existing ports or bringing a wireless device within range of the wireless adapter.

## USB

You can add a webcam, hard drive, optical disc, wireless modem, TV tuner, card reader, Wi-Fi adapter, Bluetooth adapter, printer, keyboard, mouse, game controller (such as a joystick), and other devices. USB enables you to connect up to 127 devices to a host, which is far more than most users ever dream of connecting.

When shopping for USB devices, make sure you purchase devices that your PC supports. Most PCs sold after 2002 support USB 2.0, which is 40 times faster than the old USB 1.0. If you're not sure, click **Start**, right-click **Computer**, and click **Properties**, **Device Manager**. Click the plus sign next to Universal Serial Bus controllers. If you see "Enhanced" anywhere in the list, your PC supports USB 2.0.

Connecting a USB device to your PC is a snap—you just plug it in. You don't have to turn off your PC, because USB devices are *hot swappable*. However, some manufacturers may recommend installing software that came with the device first.

**DEFINITION**

**Hot swappable** means you don't have to turn off the power to your computer to connect or disconnect the device.

Even if a device is hot swappable, just to be safe, perform the following steps when connecting a USB device for the first time:

1. Install any software included with the device.

2. If the device needs to be plugged into a power outlet (as in the case of a USB printer), plug in the device.

3. Turn on the device, if necessary.

4. Connect the device, using a USB cable, to your PC.

To safely disconnect a USB device, first eject it in Windows. Right-click the USB icon in the notification area and then click the **Eject** option for the device you want to disconnect, as shown in Figure 10.1. (You may need to click the up arrow to the left of the notification area to access the USB icon.) Wait for Windows to indicate when you can safely disconnect the device, and then unplug it. Ejecting is especially important when disconnecting an external hard drive or a flash drive, because unplugging it while Windows is using the device could damage or destroy files being stored on the device.

**Figure 10.1**
*Eject a USB device before disconnecting it.*

If you run out of USB ports, connect a USB hub, which enables you to plug numerous devices into a single port. Be aware, however, that hubs come in two types: powered and not powered. (All of the USB ports on your PC are powered.) Some devices, including USB hard drives and optical drives, require a powered USB port. Powered hubs require two connections: one to a power source and the other to an open USB port on your PC.

## Wireless (Bluetooth and Wi-Fi)

Because wireless devices (Bluetooth and Wi-Fi) are cable-free, they're the easiest to connect:

1. Make sure the device has power and is turned on. You may need to plug the device into a power outlet or install batteries.

2. Make sure the device is in range of your PC's wireless adapter (typically 6 to 9 feet for Bluetooth and 100 feet for Wi-Fi).

3. In Windows, click **Start**, **Control Panel**, **Add a device**. The Add a device window appears, and Windows searches for and detects the new device (assuming that all goes as planned).

4. Click the icon for the device, click **Next**, and follow the onscreen instructions to complete the installation.

If Windows doesn't detect the wireless device, check the following:

- The device has power, is turned on, and is not in sleep mode. Try turning the device off and then on to bring it out of sleep mode.

- The device isn't already installed. Click **Start**, **Devices and Printers** to see if the device is already installed. (If Devices and Printers doesn't appear on your Start menu, click **Start**, **Control Panel**, **View devices and printers**.)

- The device is within range of your PC's wireless adapter. Try moving the device closer to your PC.

- No other wireless devices are interfering with this one. Try removing any cordless phones, microwave ovens, or other devices that commonly cause interference out of the vicinity.

- Your wireless adapter is properly connected and turned on, if necessary.

- Your PC's Bluetooth radio transmitter is on. Many portable PCs have an external switch for turning Bluetooth on or off.

- Your wireless device is set up to be discoverable. You may need to press a button on the device, flip a switch, or enter a menu setting to place the device in discoverable mode.

# Installing Internal Devices and Upgrades

Installing devices inside the PC's system unit is a little more involved and riskier than installing external devices. To reduce the risk, take the following precautions:

- Back up the files on your PC. (See Chapter 35.)

- Turn off your PC and unplug it from the power source.

- Wear an antistatic wrist strap to protect sensitive electronic components from getting fried.

- Hold memory modules and expansion cards by their edges, to avoid touching any of the electronic components.

- Don't force anything.

- Make sure everything you plug in is securely plugged in before closing the case and turning on the power.

## RAM Upgrades

To upgrade your PC's memory, you can add one or more memory modules. Depending on how your PC is configured, you may need to remove low-capacity memory modules before you can install higher-capacity modules.

Consult your PC's documentation or manufacturer to determine the type of memory modules your PC can use—modules may look the same and be completely different. If you can't determine the type of memory from your manufacturer or your PC's documentation, an online memory dealer may be able to help. For example, www. crucial.com has a utility that can scan your PC and recommend the type of memory your PC uses, along with other useful information, including the maximum amount of memory your PC can have.

Installing RAM is pretty easy. Following all precautions given earlier, proceed as follows:

1. Open the case (system unit), following your manufacturer's instructions.

2. Locate the memory modules on the motherboard, and note the position of the modules so you can insert the new modules in the same position.

3. If all the slots are occupied, remove one or more modules to make room for the new ones. This typically requires moving the clips on either side of the module away from the module and then pulling the module out of the slot. (The clips hold the module securely in place.)

4. Insert the new memory modules into the slots, press them securely in place, and then hold down the module while pushing the clips back into place. (See Figure 10.2.)

5. Close the case. You may want to hold off on securing the case with screws until you're sure the memory upgrade works.

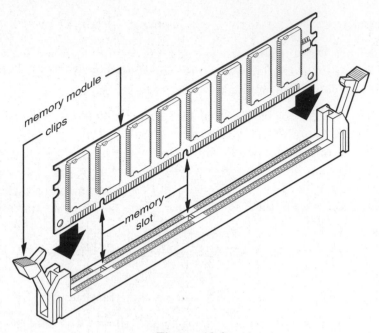

**Figure 10.2**
*Install memory modules in your PC's memory slots.*

To find out how much memory your PC has, run the System Information utility, as explained in Chapter 9.

## Expansion Cards

On desktop PCs, the motherboard has several expansion slots for installing expansion cards (also referred to as adapters). Common cards enable you to add USB and FireWire ports to your PC, upgrade its audio and video capabilities and performance, add a network adapter (wireless or LAN), and add Bluetooth capability. To install an expansion card, follow all the precautions given earlier and then proceed as follows:

1. Install the software included with the device if the device documentation instructs you to do so.

2. Turn off and unplug your PC.

3. Open the case (system unit), following your manufacturer's instructions.

4. Remove the metal cover plate (one screw) near the open expansion slot you want to use.

5. Insert the new card so that the contacts on the card match up with the contacts in the expansion slot, and press down firmly on the card until it is fully seated. (See Figure 10.3.)

6. Replace the screw you removed in Step 4 to anchor the card in place, and then close the case.

7. If you installed the card to connect an external device, connect the device to the card.

8. Turn on your PC and log on to Windows. Windows should identify the card and load any drivers it needs to use the card.

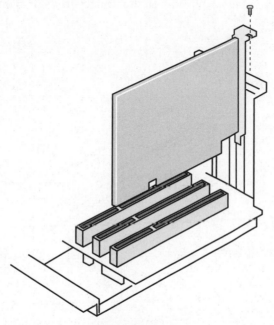

**Figure 10.3**
*Install an expansion card.*

## Installing an Internal Disk Drive

The difficulty level for installing an internal disk drive varies. If you're adding another hard drive or adding or replacing a CD or DVD drive, you follow a basic four-step process. Here's a simplified overview:

1. Run the CD that came with the drive, to install the driver, and then turn off the PC.

2. Mount the drive in an open drive bay.

3. Connect one end of the data cable to the drive and plug the opposite end into one of the drive ports on the motherboard, as shown in Figure 10.4.

4. Connect the power supply to the drive's power outlet.

The process gets more involved depending on what you're doing. For example, you may need to flip some tiny switches on the drive to help your PC identify it. If you're replacing a hard drive, you may need to format the new drive and then transfer files from the old drive to the new one. Fortunately, most new disk drives include detailed instructions, along with software that can make your job much easier. I strongly recommend that you read and follow the manufacturer's instructions.

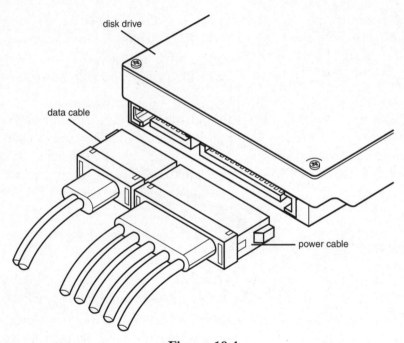

**Figure 10.4**
*Connect a data cable and power cable to the drive.*

The key is to buy the right type of drive (you may need to open the case and peek inside at the cables):

- **SATA:** Newer PCs often come with a SATA hard drive that uses a very narrow cable with a 7-pin connector that plugs into a small port on the motherboard.

- **IDE 80-pin:** PCs equipped with newer IDE hard drives use a wide, typically gray ribbon cable with a 40-pin connector that plugs into a relatively large port on the motherboard. You can count the ridges in the cable to determine whether your computer uses an 80-pin or 40-pin cable.

- **IDE 40-pin:** PCs equipped with older IDE drives use a ribbon cable that looks almost exactly like the IDE 80-pin cable, but with half the number of wires (and fewer and larger ridges). If the drive comes with an 80-pin cable and your PC uses a 40-pin cable, use the 80-pin cable.

# Upgrading Laptops, Notebooks, and Netbooks

Laptop, notebook, and netbook PCs tend to be limited in terms of their ability to upgrade. You may be able to upgrade the PC's memory and add an external monitor, but it's not likely to have an open drive bay and expansion slots. The best option is to look for a USB device that provides your PC with the desired functionality.

If your portable PC has an ExpressCard slot, you may also be able to use ExpressCard devices to improve audio output, add USB and/or FireWire ports, add Wi-Fi capability, install an eSATA port for a high-speed external hard drive, and more. When purchasing ExpressCard devices, make sure you're getting the right card for your PC. Standard ExpressCards are 54mm wide and can accept 34mm cards. The 34mm slots are often used on smaller portable PCs to save space and consume less battery power.

## The Least You Need to Know

- If your PC is only one to three years old, you can probably upgrade it for less than the cost of a new PC and have it do everything you need it to.
- Adding RAM is one of the easiest ways to improve your PC's performance, particularly if your PC slows down when you're running multiple programs.
- The easiest way to upgrade a PC is to add an external device that plugs into one of the PC's USB ports.
- Desktop PCs have expansion slots into which you can plug expansion cards that can add to or improve upon your PC's features.
- Although portable PCs have limited upgrade options, a number of add-ons are available as USB devices.

# Networking Your PC at Home and on the Road

### In This Chapter

- Setting up a wireless network at your home or business
- Sharing network folders and files
- Sharing a high-speed Internet connection
- Sharing a network printer

People generally network their PCs for three reasons:

- To share files and other resources, including a printer, a high-speed Internet connection, and a backup drive among two or more computers, as shown in Figure 11.1.

- To establish a connection with a *Wi-Fi hotspot*. A *hotspot* is a location that offers a wireless network connection for connecting to the Internet. You're likely to find hotspots in coffee shops, hotels and motels, and airports.

- To allow friends, roommates, or family members to play multiuser games.

In this chapter, you discover the four most common ways to network computers, how to use the Windows networking features to set up a network and share files and resources, and how to connect to a Wi-Fi hotspot when you're on the road with your PC.

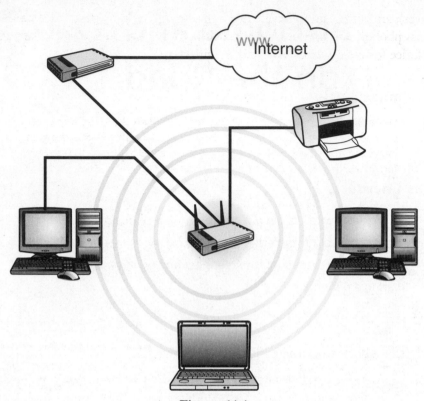

**Figure 11.1**
*Networked computers can share files, folders, Internet access, and printers.*

# Exploring Your Networking Options

When planning your network, the first step is to decide which type of networking hardware you want to use. The following sections discuss your options and some important considerations for making the best choice for your situation and needs. The costs involved are comparable for each option.

## Wireless (Wi-Fi)

Wi-Fi networks enable computers to communicate via radio waves. The biggest advantages of wireless are that you can set up a network without having to run cables, and you can move the computers almost anywhere in your home or office without losing your connection.

The three main drawbacks are that wireless is generally slower than the other three options; Wi-Fi networks are less secure (because data is transmitted through airwaves); and signal interference can be caused by walls, pipes, electrical wiring, cordless phones, and microwave ovens. Still, Wi-Fi is almost always the most attractive choice for most homes and small businesses.

> **WHOA!**
>
> Some Wi-Fi signals can reach pretty far—150 to 350 feet—so be sure to secure your network to keep unauthorized users (such as your neighbors) from accessing your data or using your broadband Internet service (which you're paying for). To learn more about network security, see Chapter 29.

Wi-Fi data transfer rates vary depending on the standard, as you'll see later. A maximum data transfer rate (under ideal conditions) of 54 megabits per second (Mbps) is pretty standard. At that rate, it takes about 1.5 seconds to download a 10MB file. The newest Wi-Fi standard can transfer data at speeds up to 600Mbps under ideal conditions.

## Ethernet

Fast, reliable, secure, and inexpensive, Ethernet networks are an excellent choice if all your computers are in one room or you don't mind running network cables throughout your home or business.

Ethernet networks have data transfer rates of 10, 100, or 1,000Mbps, depending on the type of cables. Transferring a 10MB file over a 100Mbps connection takes about 1 second.

## HomePNA

Secure and potentially inexpensive, Home Phoneline Networking Alliance (HomePNA) enables you to network computers over existing phone lines. HomePNA 2.0 is relatively slow, with a data transfer rate of 10Mbps—about the same speed as a slow wireless network. HomePNA 3.0 features data transfer rates of up to 128Mbps—about double the speed of most wireless networks.

## Powerline

Fast (up to 200Mbps), reliable, secure, and inexpensive, Powerline networking enables you to connect computers using existing electrical wiring in your home or business. The main drawback of powerline networks is that electrical "noise" on the line can interfere with the signal.

## Hybrid

You can combine the networking technologies discussed here to create a hybrid network. For example, you can build an Ethernet network that connects all the computers in your office and then use a wireless or phone line connection for a computer generally used in a more remote room of your house.

# Networking Hardware Checklist

Chances are good that if the computers you plan to network are relatively new, some or all of them have a LAN port (for an Ethernet network) or some sort of Wi-Fi capability. Knowing which hardware you already have on hand may influence your choice of networking configuration.

In the following sections, you take inventory of the hardware you already have and determine which hardware you need for each of your networking options.

## Wireless Networking Hardware

To set up a wireless network, you need two things:

- **Wireless router or access point:** A *wireless router* is best and essential if you plan to share an Internet connection, because it can assign an Internet address to each networked computer and provides a more secure connection between your network and the Internet. An *access point* merely enables two or more computers to connect with one another. (Most wireless routers have several LAN ports on the back as well, for hardwiring computers and other devices to the network.)

- **Wireless adapters:** Every computer must have a wireless networking adapter or built-in Wi-Fi support that's compatible with the router. (Compatibility is a function of the frequency the devices use to communicate: 2.4GHz or 5GHz.) Almost all portable PCs have a built-in wireless adapter.

Range and maximum data transfer rates vary according to the standards the hardware supports, as presented in Table 11.1.

802.11g has been the most popular option for wireless home networking, due to its low cost and backward compatibility with the earlier 802.11b standard. However, many other devices in a home operate on the 2.4GHz frequency, which makes it more susceptible to interference. Consider devices that support the 802.11a and 802.11n standards.

**Table 11.1   Wireless Networking Standards**

| Standard | Max. Speed | Range | Frequency | Interference Susceptibility |
|---|---|---|---|---|
| 802.11n | 600Mbps | 250 feet | 2.4GHz, 5GHz | Moderate |
| 802.11g | 54Mbps | 150 feet | 2.4GHz | High |
| 802.11a | 54Mbps | 100 feet | 5GHz | Low |
| 802.11b | 11Mbps | 150 feet | 2.4GHz | High |

Determining whether a PC already has a wireless networking adapter is pretty easy. Click **Start, Control Panel, Hardware and Sound, Device Manager**. Click the arrow to the left of Network adapters and look for an entry that includes "Wireless Network Adapter." Unfortunately, determining the standard(s) the adapter supports is not so easy. Check your PC's documentation or the box it came in, contact the manufacturer, or search for the make and model online.

**INSIDE TIP**

If you're going to share an Internet connection, don't run out and buy a wireless router just yet. First choose an Internet service provider (ISP), as explained in Chapter 8. You may receive a combination modem/wireless router as part of your subscription.

## Ethernet Networking Hardware

To build an Ethernet network, make sure you have these essentials:

- **Wired router, hub, or switch:** A *router* is best and essential if you plan to share an Internet connection, because it can assign an Internet address to each networked computer and provides a more secure connection between your network and the Internet. A *hub* is just a basic connection box, while a *switch* is sort of like a hub but faster. Make sure the router, hub, or switch has enough LAN ports to accommodate all of your computers.

- **Ethernet adapters:** Each computer must have an Ethernet adapter (often called an *NIC* or *network interface card*). An Ethernet port looks like an oversized telephone jack and is usually labeled "LAN" (for local area network).

- **Ethernet cable:** Make sure you have enough Ethernet cable to connect each computer to the hub or switch.

Some newer, high-tech homes have built-in Ethernet, so be sure to check the wall jacks to determine whether you have any LAN jacks. This can save you from having to run cables.

## HomePNA Networking Hardware

To set up a HomePNA, make sure you have the following:

- **Phone jacks:** To connect via existing phone lines, you must have a phone jack in every room in which you plan to use the networked computers, and they must all be on the same phone line.

- **HomePNA network adapters:** You'll need an adapter for each computer on the network.

- **Telephone cables:** Every computer requires a telephone cable long enough to reach between the adapter and the phone jack.

- **Wired Ethernet router:** If the computers will share an Internet connection, a router is required to more securely connect your network to the Internet.

## Powerline Networking Hardware

Here's what you need to set up a Powerline network:

- **Power outlets:** You need a power outlet in every room in which you plan to use a networked computer, and all the outlets need to be on the same "grid."

- **Powerline network adapters:** You'll need an adapter for each computer on the network.

- **Wired Ethernet router:** If the computers will share an Internet connection, a router is required to more securely connect your network to the Internet.

# Setting Up Your Network

After you've decided on the type of network you want and gathered the requisite hardware, you're ready to set up your network, as explained in the following sections.

## Installing the Hardware

Following the manufacturer's instructions, install or connect a network adapter to every computer that doesn't already have one. See Chapter 10 for more information about installing new hardware devices.

If you're going to use a wireless router, choose a location and position it in a way to reduce potential interference:

- **Choose a central location.** If you're going to be using computers all over your home or office, position the router as close to center as possible. If you're using computers in only a portion of your home or office, choose the center location in that portion.

- **Reduce potential obstructions.** Choose a location off the floor and away from walls, metal filing cabinets, and anything else that might block the signal.

- **Reduce potential interference.** Position your router away from microwave ovens and the most common areas where you use a cordless phone, if possible. Networking equipment that uses a 5GHz frequency can help reduce interference from cordless phones and microwaves. 802.11a and 802.11n devices are less susceptible. If your network primarily uses 802.11g (2.4GHz) networking equipment, shop for phones and other devices that operate at a higher frequency, such as 5.8GHz.

## Setting Up Your Internet Connection (Now or Later)

If you plan to share an Internet connection, now is a good time to set it up. See Chapter 18 for details on how to establish an Internet connection.

Chances are pretty good that if you have high-speed Internet service, your service provider sent a technician to set up the modem on one of your computers and establish the connection for you. All you have to do is disconnect the modem's cable from the PC and plug it into the designated Internet port on the back of the router—the port is typically labeled "Internet," "WAN" (wide area network), or "WLAN" (wireless local area network).

Some services supply a combination modem/router, which makes your job even easier—just plug the device into the designated port on any of your networked computers.

## Connecting the Cables and Cords

The process for connecting the computers and other devices on your network varies, depending on the type of network.

**WHOA!**

Hold off on turning anything on until you've connected all the cables. I'll show you how to turn on everything in the proper sequence and proceed with setting up your network.

Make the following connections based on your network configuration:

- **Wireless:** Plug the wireless router into your surge protector.

- **Ethernet:** Connect the Ethernet cable from each computer's LAN port to the router, hub, or switch, and then plug the router, hub, or switch into your surge protector.

- **HomePNA:** Using standard telephone cables, connect each computer's HomePNA network adapter to a phone jack.

- **Powerline:** Plug each computer's Powerline adapter into an electrical outlet.

## Connecting a Printer (Now or Later)

Now you should have everything connected except, perhaps, the printer. This varies based on the type of printer you have and how you want to connect it:

- **Network printer, wired:** If your printer has a LAN port, you can connect it to the router. All computers on the network can then use the printer independently through the router.

- **Network printer, wireless:** This printer is similar to a wired network printer, but it connects to the network through the wireless router. (Some wireless network printers also include a LAN port.)

- **USB printer:** Connect the printer to a USB port on the computer from which you'll do most of your printing. The other computers can then access the printer through this computer. The only drawback is that the computer attached to the printer must be turned on for the other computers to use it.

- **Bluetooth printer:** If all your networked computers are Bluetooth enabled and within range, they can connect to the printer independently. Otherwise, the computer must connect to the printer through one of the Bluetooth-enabled computers.

For more about setting up your printer, see Chapter 17.

## Turning Everything On

In certain cases, you can turn on all the computers and the modem, printer, router, and other devices in any sequence, and everything works fine. Sometimes, however, something doesn't work—for example, if you turn on the computer and router before turning on the modem, the modem may have trouble establishing an Internet connection.

The proper sequence for powering up your network is to work from the outside (peripherals) back to the computer:

1. Turn on the modem and wait for the lights to indicate that the modem has established a connection.

2. Turn on the router and wait about 30 seconds for it to detect the modem.

3. Turn on the computer you want to use.

If you're setting up a wired network (Ethernet, HomePNA, or Powerline), all computers on the network that are turned on should be connected, but you may still need to set up your router to establish an Internet connection. Check the installation instructions included with your router. Setting up a wireless network is more involved, as explained in the following section.

## Setting Up a Wireless Router

Most routers include a setup disc. After turning on the router and at least one of the computers on the network, insert the disc into one of the computers that's up and running. Windows should automatically launch the router setup routine from the disc. If it doesn't, find the Setup or Install file on the disc and double-click it. (See Chapter 8 for more about finding and executing files.)

The steps for setting up a router for the first time vary depending on the router and the manufacturer's setup routine. However, they all require that you do the following:

1. **Establish an Internet connection.** Because all of your computers will connect to the Internet through the router, you may need to provide the router with the username and password your ISP has assigned to you. (See Chapter 18 for details.)

2. **Give your network a name.** Most routers initially use a default network name, but for security purposes, assigning a unique name is a good idea. Network names are case sensitive, and every computer on the network needs to use the same network name to connect.

3. **Choose an encryption level,** such as WiFi Protected Access (WPA) or WPA-2. This secures the network by blocking unauthorized access and encrypting data as it flows through the network.

4. **Specify a passphrase (password).** A secure passphrase includes a mix of upper- and lowercase letters, numbers, and symbols (-, _, &, $, and so on). Initially, all computers on your network will use the same passphrase.

Write down the network name, encryption level, and passphrase, because you'll need to enter this information on all of the computers you want to include in the network.

## Running the Set Up a Network Wizard

If your router did not include a disc, you can use Windows to set up your network. Windows features a Set Up a Network Wizard that leads you step by step through the process of configuring all computers on your wireless network to establish a connection with the network:

1. Click **Start**, **Control Panel** to display the Control Panel.

2. Click **Network and Internet** and then **Network and Sharing Center**.

3. Below Network and Sharing Center, click **Set up a new connection or network**.

4. Click **Set up a new network**, and then follow the wizard's instructions to set up your network.

The Set Up a Network Wizard can save the network settings to a USB drive to make it easier to add other computers to the network. You can then insert the USB drive into another computer and, in the AutoPlay dialog box, select Wireless Network Setup Wizard to have Windows automatically configure the computer to connect to the network. Otherwise, take the following steps to add another computer to the network:

1. Click **Start**, **Control Panel**, **Network and Internet**.

2. Below Network and Sharing Center, click **Connect to a network**.

3. Click the wireless network from the list that appears and click **Connect**, as shown in Figure 11.2.

4. Follow the onscreen instructions to enter whatever information is required, such as the network name, encryption level, or passphrase/security key.

**Figure 11.2**
*Choose a network.*

## Choosing a Network Location

Networking computers increases their exposure to unauthorized access and to malware (viruses, spyware, and so on), especially if the computers share an Internet connection. The risk level varies depending on the network. A home network is relatively safe, whereas a Wi-Fi hotspot outside your home poses a greater risk.

Whenever you connect to a network for the first time, Windows prompts you to choose a network location, which contains security settings appropriate for the type of network you're connecting to. To choose a network location, click **Start**, **Control Panel**, **Network and Internet**, **Network and Sharing Center**. Below View your active networks, click your current network location (**Home**, **Work**, or **Public**) and then choose the desired location:

- **Home network:** On a home network, you know all the networked computers and users, so Windows can let down its guard. Computers on a home network can join a homegroup, and network discovery is turned on, so networked computers and devices can identify one another and access shared resources.

- **Work network:** Network discovery is enabled, so networked computers can see shared resources on your computer and vice versa, but you can't create or join a homegroup.

- **Public network:** This option attempts to keep your PC and any shared resources invisible and inaccessible when connecting in a public place, such as a coffee shop, or connecting directly to the Internet without the protection of a router.

## Testing Your Network

To test your network, make sure everything is turned on, and then click **Start**, **Computer**, **Network**. You should see an icon for every computer on the network, as shown in Figure 11.3.

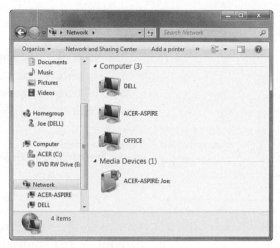

**Figure 11.3**
*Icons for networked computers.*

If you don't see icons for the other networked computers, run the Network troubleshooter:

1. Click **Start**.

2. Type **network trouble** (in the Search box).

3. Click **Identify and repair network problems**. This runs the Network troubleshooter, which tries to diagnose the problem.

4. Follow the onscreen instructions to diagnose and correct the problem. (For more about troubleshooting, see Chapter 35.)

You can also check the status of your network at any time, from any of the computers on the network. Click **Start**, **Control Panel**; then below Network and Internet, click **View network status and tasks**. Near the top of the window, Windows displays a graphic showing your computer connected to the network, which is connected to the Internet (assuming you set up an Internet connection).

# Sharing Files in a Homegroup

The easiest way to share files, folders, and other network resources (including a printer) is through homegroups. A *homegroup* is a collection of computers, all running Windows 7, that share pictures, music, videos, documents, and even a printer.

## Creating a Homegroup

You can set up a homegroup in Windows, and each user can choose which folders and files to share with other users and networked computers that join the homegroup. (Only PCs running Windows 7 Premium or Ultimate can create homegroups, but if a networked PC is running the Basic or Starter edition, it can still join a homegroup.) To create a homegroup, here's what you do:

1. Click **Start, Control Panel, Choose homegroup and sharing options** (below Network and Internet).

2. Click **Create a homegroup**.

3. Choose the items you want to share, as shown in Figure 11.4, and click **Next**. For example, you may want to share music and photos but not documents. Windows displays a password you can use to connect networked PCs to the new homegroup.

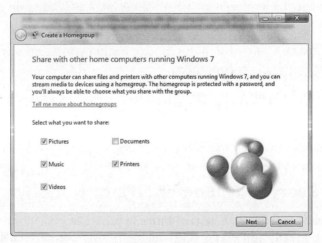

**Figure 11.4**
*Specify the libraries and content types you want to share.*

4. Jot down the password for future reference and click **Finish**. (You can always view the password on this PC later by performing Step 1 and then clicking **View**.) Windows returns you to the Change homegroup settings page, where you can change your preferences.

5. Click **Cancel**. All user accounts on this computer are now members of the homegroup and can share files.

After you create a homegroup on a PC, this PC and all of its users belong to that homegroup. Each user can perform Step 1 above to access a screen that enables them to choose which libraries they want to share. For other PCs on the network to share files, folders, and other resources, they must join the homegroup, as explained in the following section.

> **WHOA!**
>
> If you're networking PCs running earlier versions of Windows, creating home-groups may not enable sharing on all PCs. For instructions on how to proceed, click **Start**, **Help and Support**, and search the Windows 7 help system for "networking different windows versions."

## Joining a Homegroup

After you've created a homegroup, other Windows 7 PCs can join the homegroup by performing the following steps:

1. Click **Start**, **Control Panel**, **Choose homegroup and sharing options** (below Network and Internet).

2. Click the **Join now** button.

3. Follow the onscreen instructions to enter the homegroup password and choose the libraries you want to share.

## Sharing with Everybody, Somebody, or Nobody

These steps work well for sharing the entire contents of your library folders, but say you want to share only certain files or you create a new folder you'd like to share. In such cases, you can choose specifically what you'd like to share (or not share) and how much control over those items other users will have:

1. Click **Start, Computer**.

2. Navigate to the folder that contains the item(s) you want to share or prohibit other users from sharing. (See Chapter 8 for details about navigating disks and folders.)

3. Click the file or folder to select it. (To select additional items, hold down the **Ctrl** key while clicking them.)

4. Click **Share with** (in the toolbar near the top of the window).

5. Click the desired share option: **Nobody** (to block access), **Homegroup (Read)**, **Homegroup (Read/Write)**, or **Specific people**.

6. If you chose Specific people, use the File Sharing dialog box to select the people to share with and specify the level of access for each person; then click **Share** and then **Done**.

> **INSIDE TIP**
>
> To quickly enter share settings for an item, right-click the item, point to **Share with**, and click the desired setting: **Nobody**, **Homegroup (Read)**, **Homegroup (Read/Write)**, or **Specific people**.

## Checking an Item's Share Setting

To determine whether a resource is shared, click it and then check the details pane (shown in Figure 11.5), which shows whether the item is shared and with whom.

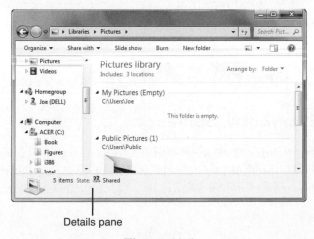

Details pane

**Figure 11.5**
*Check the details pane to determine whether an item is shared.*

## Accessing Shared Disks, Folders, and Files

Your network is up and running and you've chosen to share libraries or folders on the networked computers. Now, how do you get to those shared files and folders? Simply click **Start**, **Computer**. In the navigation pane (left), below Network, click the desired homegroup or computer. The folder pane (right) displays the shared folders or files in the homegroup or on the computer you selected. You can navigate the folders just as if they were stored on this computer, as explained in Chapter 8.

## Mapping a Network Drive to Your Computer

If you frequently access a particular disk or folder on the network, you can map the folder to a drive on your computer. If you share your Music library on the network, for example, you can map it to a drive letter. Whenever you want to access the folder, you simply change to that drive.

To map a shared folder to your computer, take the following steps:

1. On the network computer from which you want to access the shared folder, display the icon for the folder you want to map to a drive.

2. Right-click the folder icon and click **Map network drive**. The Map Network Drive window appears.

3. Open the **Drive** list and click the letter you want to map this folder to.

4. Make sure **Reconnect at logon** is checked so that the mapped network drive will be available whenever you log on.

5. Click **Finish**. Windows creates an icon for the new network drive and opens a window displaying its contents.

# Installing a Printer on Your Network

The steps for installing a printer on your network depend on the printer and how it's connected to the network:

- **Network printer:** If your printer is connected to the router or is a wireless printer, you install it as a *network printer*, meaning all networked computers access the printer independently (not through another computer).

- **Shared printer:** If your printer is connected to one of your networked computers—for example, with a USB cable—you can set it up as a *local printer* and then share it. Other computers on the network can then access the printer through this computer.

## Installing a Network Printer

To install a network printer, follow these steps:

1. Click **Start**, **Devices and Printers**.

2. Click **Add a Printer**. The Add Printer dialog box appears.

3. Click **Add a network, wireless or Bluetooth printer**, click **Next**, and follow the onscreen instructions.

After the network printer is set up, you can use it to print documents just as if the printer were connected to your computer. However, if you did not set up the network printer as your default printer, you must select the printer when you choose to print your document.

## Sharing a Printer

To share a printer, first install it as a local printer on one of your networked computers, as explained in Chapter 17. Assuming that the computer that's connected to the printer has joined the network's homegroup, the printer should be available to all computers in that homegroup. If the printer is not available, make sure it's shared:

1. Click **Start**, **Devices and Printers**.

2. Right-click the printer you want to share and click **Printer properties**.

3. Click the **Sharing** tab, select the **Share this printer** check box, and click **OK**.

Other computers on the network can now choose this shared printer, as explained in Chapter 17.

# Securing Your Network

A broadband Internet connection is typically an *always-on* connection. That is, as long as you leave your modem, router, and computer on, you're connected to the Internet. This makes your network more vulnerable to attacks from snoopy people and perhaps even Internet vandals. With the proper know-how, someone on the Internet can connect to your computer, peek at your documents, and even destroy valuable data.

You can't completely protect your computer or network from such threats, but you can significantly deter potential break-ins by implementing various security measures. For details on how to protect your computer and your network from online threats, visit Chapter 29.

## The Least You Need to Know

- To network your computers, install a single, centralized router and make sure each computer you want on the network has a compatible network adapter or LAN port.

- Learn how to adjust your router settings to enable its firewall, enter encryption settings, and specify a passphrase that all computers need to log on to the network.

- To share files, folders, and other network resources, create a homegroup and have all networked computers join the homegroup.

- To access a shared folder, click **Start**, **Computer**, and then click a homegroup or computer (below Network).

- When using your PC in a public Wi-Fi hotspot, change your network location to Public.

- Always have at least one firewall running: the router's firewall when you're home and the Windows firewall when you're on the road.

# Getting Down to Business

Playing Solitaire and fiddling with the Windows desktop can keep you entertained for hours, but you didn't lay down a few hundred bucks for a PC only to use it as a 99¢ deck of playing cards. You want to type letters, crunch numbers, decorate your documents with dazzling graphics, and take control of your personal finances ... you want to use your PC to get more out of life!

In Part 3, you become productive with your PC as you learn how to type and format letters, add images, create automated accounting worksheets, print documents and mailing labels, pay bills online, and manage your personal finances. Along the way, you even learn how to perform some basic tasks that apply to most applications, including saving, naming, and opening the files you create.

# Typing and Other Word Processing Chores

## In This Chapter

- Starting out right with a template
- Making your text big and pretty
- Saving and opening document files
- Editing your documents and undoing changes
- Checking a document's spelling and grammar

With the popularity of the Internet and other computer technologies, it's easy to forget that many people still use a computer primarily to type and print documents. In this chapter, you learn how to type, format (style), edit (cut and paste), and save a document in a typical word processor.

**Note:** The figures in this chapter show Microsoft Word 10 in action. Word 10 relies more on toolbars (ribbons) and buttons, whereas other versions of Word and other word processors are more menu based, but you'll perform the same tasks regardless of which one you're using. If you don't have Word or another high-end word processor installed on your computer, you can follow along by using Windows WordPad. Click **Start**, **All Programs**, **Accessories**, **WordPad**.

## Starting with a Document Template ... or Not

In most word processors, you don't have to start from scratch. You can begin with a template. Here's the standard routine for creating a new document from a template:

1. Click **File**, **New** to start creating a new document.

2. If the program displays a pane or dialog box with one or more Template options, click the option to browse the templates installed on your computer.

3. Click a category of templates, such as **Brochures** or **Letters**. The word processor displays thumbnail versions of the available templates in this category, as shown in Figure 12.1.

4. Click a template to preview it.

5. When you find a template you like, click the button or link to create a new document using this template.

Preview area

Templates

**Figure 12.1**
*You can start with a predesigned template.*

**INSIDE TIP**

Many templates use text boxes to control the position of blocks of text onscreen, which can be a little confusing when you first encounter them. To edit the text, click in the text box and make your changes. (For more about moving, resizing, and creating your own text boxes, check out Chapter 13.)

Of course, you can start from scratch if you really want to. In most applications, you press **Ctrl+N** or click the **New Blank Document** (usually somewhere near the upper-left corner of the window), and a new blank document pops up on the screen.

# Making the Transition to the Electronic Page

Your word processor displays a vertical line called the *cursor* or *insertion point* to show you where the characters will appear when you start typing. If you change to Draft view, as explained later in this chapter, a horizontal line appears at the end of the document, as shown in Figure 12.2. As you type, this line moves down automatically to make room for your text. (You can't move the cursor or insertion point past this line, no matter how hard you try.)

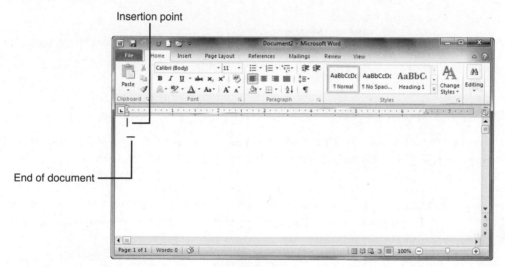

**Figure 12.2**
*Start typing!*

## Keyboarding Tips

The best way to learn how to type in a word processor is to start typing. As you type, keep the following key points in mind:

- Press the **Enter** key only to end a paragraph and start a new paragraph. Within a paragraph, the program automatically *wraps* the text from one line to the next as you type.

- Don't press the **Enter** key to insert a blank line between paragraphs. Later in this chapter, I show you a better way to add space between paragraphs.

- Use the mouse or the arrow keys to move the insertion point in the document. If you're working on a long document, use the scrollbar to move more quickly and then click in the document to move the insertion point where you want it.

- Delete to the right; backspace to the left. To delete a character that's to the right of the insertion point, press the **Delete** key. To delete characters to the left of the insertion point, press the **Backspace** key.

- As you type, you may see squiggly red or green lines below words or phrases. The red lines indicate possible typos or misspellings, while the green lines flag potential grammatical errors. Try right-clicking green or red underlined text to view possible corrections. (For more about correcting spelling and grammatical errors, see "Checking Your Spelling and Grammar," near the end of this chapter.)

- Open the **Insert** menu for options that enable you to insert today's date and time, symbols, pictures, tables, and so on.

## Getting a Better View

Word processors offer various views of a page and enable you to zoom in or out. To change views, you typically open the **View** menu and click one of the view options, as shown in Figure 12.3:

**Print** or **Page Layout** provides a more realistic view of how your pages will appear in print. This uses a lot of memory, however, and might make scrolling a little jerky.

**Full Screen Reading** displays two pages side by side, which is great if you're composing a book, booklet, or pamphlet.

**Web Layout** displays a document as it will appear when displayed online in a web browser.

**Outline** allows you to quickly organize and reorganize your document by dragging headings from one location to another in the document.

**Normal** or **Draft** focuses more on text and less on formatting, page layout, and graphics, so it uses less memory, making scrolling faster and smoother.

Choose a view          Zoom in or out

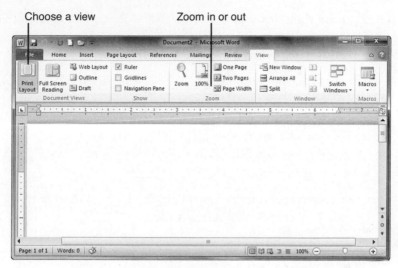

**Figure 12.3**
*Get a better view.*

# Controlling the Look and Layout of the Text

When you first start typing, you might notice that the text looks rather bland. Word processors left align *everything*, single-space lines of text, and choose the dullest type style available. The following sections show you how to give your text a facelift and take control of alignment, line spacing, and spacing between paragraphs.

## Styling Your Text

To change the appearance of existing text, drag over the text to *highlight* it and then select the desired text formatting, including the font and type size, as shown in Figure 12.4. (For more about highlighting text, see "Selecting Text," later in this chapter.)

You can apply formatting before you type text, too. Simply enter your formatting preferences and then start typing.

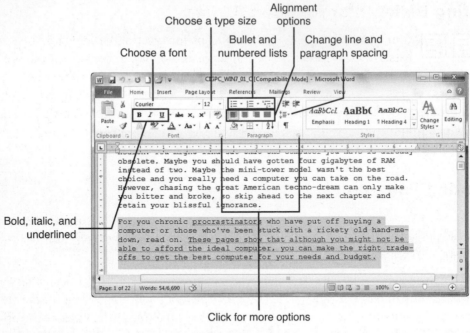

**Figure 12.4**
*Style your text.*

## Aligning Text Left, Right, or Center

As you type a document, you might want to center a heading or push a date or address to the right side of the page to set it apart from surrounding text. To quickly change the text alignment, click anywhere inside the paragraph and then click one of the following buttons in the Formatting toolbar:

 **Align Left** pushes all lines of the paragraph against the left margin.

 **Center** positions each line of the paragraph at an equal distance from both the left and right margins.

 **Align Right** pushes all lines of the paragraph against the right margin. This is a useful option for placing a date in the upper-right corner of a page.

 **Justify** inserts spaces between the words as needed to make every line of the paragraph the same length, as in newspaper columns.

## Creating Bulleted or Numbered Lists

Your word processor also has buttons for creating bulleted and numbered lists. To convert existing paragraphs into a list, drag over the paragraphs you want to transform into a list and click the desired button: **Numbering** or **Bullets**. To create a list from scratch, press **Enter** to create a new paragraph, click the **Numbering** or **Bullets** button, and start typing. When you press **Enter** to create a new paragraph, your word processor automatically creates a new paragraph starting with a bullet or the next number in the list.

## Indenting Paragraphs

To indent the first line of a paragraph, you can press the **Tab** key at the beginning of the paragraph, or choose **Format, Paragraph** and enter a setting for the *first line indent*.

Most word processors display a ruler, as shown in Figure 12.5, which lets you quickly indent paragraphs and set *tab stops*. (Tab stops determine where the insertion point stops when you press the **Tab** key.) To toggle the ruler on or off in Word 2007, click the **View Ruler** button above the vertical scrollbar on the right.

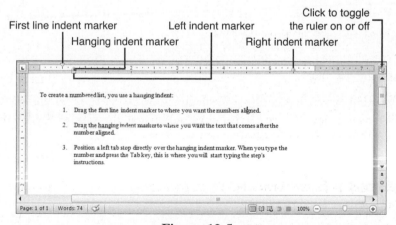

**Figure 12.5**

*Use the ruler to quickly indent paragraphs and set tabs.*

To indent text and change margins and tab stop settings, select the paragraph(s) you want the change to affect (to modify a single paragraph, just be sure the insertion point is somewhere inside the paragraph) and take one of the following steps:

• To place a tab stop, click the button on the far left end of the ruler to select the desired tab stop type (left, right, center, or decimal). Then click in the lower half of the ruler where you want the tab stop positioned.

- To move a tab stop, drag it left or right. To delete it, drag it off the ruler.

- To indent the right side of a paragraph, drag the right indent marker to the left.

- To indent the left side of a paragraph, drag the left indent marker to the right. (The left indent marker is the rectangle below the upward-pointing triangle.)

- To indent only the first line of a paragraph, drag the first line indent marker to the right. (This is the downward-pointing triangle on the left.)

- To create a hanging indent, drag the hanging indent marker to the right. (This is the upward-pointing triangle on the left.)

## Changing the Line Spacing

Here's a section just for students. If you're working on a five-page report and you have only two and a half pages of material, you can stretch it out by double spacing! Press **Ctrl+A** to select all the text and then enter your line spacing preference:

- In many word processors, you change line spacing by clicking **Format**, **Paragraph**, and using the resulting dialog box to choose **Single**, **Double**, or a custom line-spacing option.

- In some programs, you can select the desired line spacing from a list on one of the toolbars.

- A quicker way to change line spacing is to select the text and press one of the following keystrokes: **Ctrl+2** for double-spacing, **Ctrl+5** for 1.5 line spacing, and **Ctrl+1** for single spacing.

## Inserting Space Between Paragraphs

Leaving space between paragraphs helps the reader easily see where one paragraph ends and another begins. Of course, you can insert blank lines between paragraphs by pressing the **Enter** key twice at the end of a paragraph, but that's a sloppy technique that limits your control over paragraph spacing later.

By specifying the exact amount of space you want inserted between paragraphs, you ensure that the amount of space between paragraphs is consistent throughout your document.

To change the space between paragraphs, drag over the paragraphs to highlight at least a portion of each paragraph you want the change to affect. (You don't need to highlight all of the first and last paragraphs.) Now specify the amount of space you'd like before and after each paragraph:

- In many word processors, you change line spacing by clicking **Format**, **Paragraph** and using the resulting dialog box to specify the amount of space you'd like before and after the paragraphs.

- In some programs, you can select the desired space before and after the paragraphs from a list on one of the toolbars.

> **NOTE**
>
> In most cases, 6 points of extra spacing before or after each paragraph does the trick.

# Save It or Lose It

Unless you're the type of person who loves the thrill of risking everything for no potential gain, you should save your document soon after you type a paragraph or two. This prevents you from losing all you've done when you exit the program or in the event of a power outage. Once the document is saved to your PC's hard drive, you can open it at any time to work on it.

## Saving a Document

 Here's the standard operating procedure for saving documents in most Windows programs:

1. Click the **Save** button or press **Ctrl+S**.

2. Click in the **File name** text box and type a name for the file, as shown in Figure 12.6. The name can be up to 255 characters long, and you can use spaces but not any of the following taboo characters: \ / : * ? " < > |.

3. *Optional:* Select the disk drive and folder where you want to save the document.

4. Click the **OK** or **Save** button. The file is saved to the disk.

Select a drive or folder

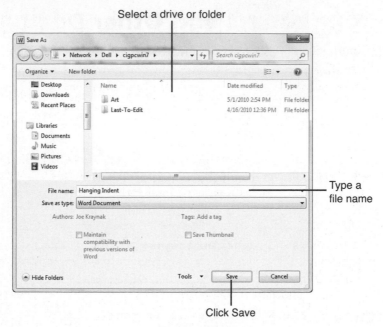

Type a
file name

Click Save

**Figure 12.6**
*Save your document.*

From now on, saving this document is easy; you don't have to name it or tell the program where to store it ever again. The program saves your changes in the document you already created and named. You should save your document every 5 to 10 minutes to avoid losing any work. In most programs, you can quickly save a document by pressing **Ctrl+S** or by clicking the **Save** button on the program's toolbar.

Most new word processors are set up to save files in the Documents library. If you create your own folders for storing documents, you might want to set up one of these folders as the one your word processor looks to first. (See Chapter 8 for instructions on changing the default save folder in Windows 7.)

## Opening a Document

To open a document, click the **Open** button in one of the program's toolbars, navigate to the folder in which the document is stored (usually the Documents library), and double-click the document file.

Another way to quickly access documents you've recently worked on is to use the Windows 7 jump lists, as explained in Chapter 9.

# Editing Your Letters and Other Documents

To fix flaws and purge errors from your documents, you need to master the tools of the editorial trade. The following sections show you how to use your word processor's editing tools to copy, move, and delete text, and how to check for and correct spelling errors and typos.

## Selecting Text

Before you can do anything with the text you just typed, you must select it. You can always just drag over text to select it (as explained earlier in this chapter), but word processors offer several quicker ways to select text. Table 12.1 describes these techniques.

**Table 12.1   Quick Text-Selection Techniques**

| To Select This ... | Do This ... |
| --- | --- |
| Single word | Double-click the word. |
| Sentence | Ctrl-click anywhere in the sentence. |
| Paragraph | Triple-click anywhere in the paragraph. |
| Several paragraphs | Position the pointer to the left of the paragraphs until it changes to a right-pointing arrow, and then double-click and drag up or down. |
| One line of text | Position the pointer to the left of the line until it changes to a right-pointing arrow and then click. (Click and drag to select additional lines.) |
| Large block of text | Click at the beginning of the text, scroll down to the end of the text, and Shift-click. |
| Entire document | Press **Ctrl+A**. |
| Extend the selection | Hold down the **Shift** key while using the arrow keys, Page Up, Page Down, Home, or End. |
| Rectangular block | Hold down the **Alt** key while dragging over the text. |

## Cutting and Pasting Without Scissors

Every word processor features the electronic equivalent of scissors and glue. With the Cut, Copy, and Paste commands, you can cut or copy selected text and then insert it in a different location in your document. You can even copy or cut text from one document and paste it in another document.

To cut or copy text, first select it, and click either the **Cut** or the **Copy** button on the toolbar. Move the insertion point to where you want the text inserted, and click the **Paste** button. Note that cutting a selection deletes it, whereas copying it leaves the selection in place and creates a duplicate.

> **INSIDE TIP**
>
> Master the drag and drop! To quickly move selected text, just drag it to the desired location in the document and release the mouse button. To copy the text instead of moving it, hold down the **Ctrl** key while you drag.

Whenever you cut or copy data in any Windows program, Windows places the data in a temporary storage area called the *Clipboard*. To paste an item from the Clipboard into your document, move the insertion point where you want the item inserted and do one of the following:

- Click the **Paste** button to paste the most recent item you cut or copied.

- To paste something you previously cut or copied, click the little button to the lower right of the Clipboard and select the item you want to paste.

For quicker copy and paste maneuvers, use the keyboard: **Ctrl+C** to copy, **Ctrl+X** to cut, and **Ctrl+V** to paste.

## Oops! Undoing Changes

What if you highlight your entire document, intending to change the font size, and press the **Delete** key by mistake? Is your entire document gone for good? Nope.

As you cut, paste, delete, and perform similar acts of destruction, your word processor keeps track of each command and lets you recover from the occasional blunder. To undo the most recent action, click the **Undo** button.

Click the **Redo** button to undo Undo, or repeat the action you just performed. You can also undo and redo with keystrokes: **Ctrl+Z** undoes an action, and **Ctrl+Y** undoes Undo or repeats the action you just performed.

> **WHOA!**
>
> Be sure you use the Undo feature before closing your document. After you save your document and close it, you cannot reopen it and undo actions you performed during a previous work session.

# Checking Your Spelling and Grammar

Earlier in this chapter, you learned that Word automatically checks for typos and spelling errors as you type. If these autocheck features distract you, you can turn them off. (Check your word processor's Help system for details.)

If you disable the spelling and grammar checks, you can initiate a spelling check manually, typically by pressing **F7** or clicking the **Spelling and Grammar** button on one of the program's toolbars.

Word starts checking your document and stops on the first questionable word (a word not stored in the spelling checker's dictionary or a repeated word, such as *the the*). The Spelling and Grammar dialog box displays the word in red and usually displays a list of suggested corrections, as shown in Figure 12.7. (If the word appears in green, the grammar checker is questioning the word's usage, not its spelling.) You have several options:

- If the word is misspelled and the Suggestions list displays the correct spelling, click the correct spelling and then click **Change** to replace only this occurrence of the word.

- Double-click the word in the Not in Dictionary text box, type the correction, and click **Change**.

- To replace this misspelled word and all other occurrences of the word in this document, click the correct spelling in the Suggestions list and then click **Change All**.

- Click **Ignore** or **Ignore Once** if the word is spelled correctly and you want to skip it just this once. Word will stop on the next occurrence of the word.

- Click **Ignore All** if the word is spelled correctly but is not in the dictionary and you want Word to skip all other occurrences of this word in the document.

- Click **Add** or **Add to Dictionary** to add the word to the dictionary so that the spelling checker never questions it again in any of your Office documents. (All Office applications share the dictionary.)

 **INSIDE TIP**

To check the spelling of a single word, right-click it.

Don't place too much trust in your spell checker. It merely compares the words in your document with the words in its dictionary and highlights any string of text that's not in the dictionary. If you typed "its" when you should have typed "it's," the spelling checker won't flag the error, although the grammar checker might. Likewise, if you type a scientific term correctly that is not in the spelling checker's dictionary, the spelling checker will flag the word, even if it is correct. Proofread your documents carefully before considering them finished.

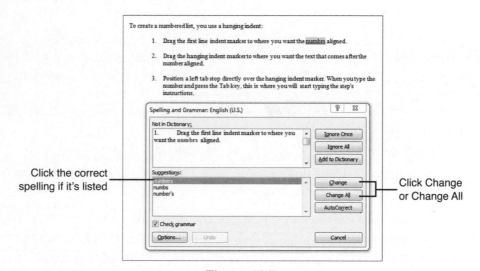

**Figure 12.7**
*If Word finds a misspelling and displays the correct spelling, your options are easy.*

When Word completes the spelling check, it displays a dialog box telling you so. Click **OK**.

## The Least You Need to Know

- Click **File**, **New** to start with a template or a new, blank document.
- Use the **Zoom** option to zoom in if the text is too small.
- Click and drag the mouse pointer over text to highlight it.
- Use the formatting buttons to quickly style and align your text.
- To avoid losing your document, press **Ctrl+S** to save it to your computer's hard disk.
- To undo your most recent action, click the **Undo** button.

# Working with Graphics

## In This Chapter

- Designing greeting cards, newsletters, and more
- Decorating your documents with ready-made clip art
- Scanning drawings, photos, or illustrations
- Getting creative with a paint or draw program
- Adding text with text boxes

In this age of information overload, most of us would rather look at a picture than wade through a sea of words. We don't want to read a newspaper column to find out how many trillions of dollars we owe as a nation. We want a graph that shows how much we owed in 1960 and how much we'll owe in 2020, or maybe a map that shows how much of our nation we could have housed with $200,000 homes given the amount of our debt. We want *USA Today!*

But what about the documents you create? Are you as kind to your audience as you expect the media to be to you? Do you use pictures to present information more clearly and succinctly? Do you *show* as well as *tell?* After reading this chapter, you'll know about several types of programs that can help you answer "yes" to all these questions.

 **NOTE**

This chapter contains general guidance that applies to most graphics applications, but features vary among applications. If something isn't working as expected, check the program's help system, as explained in Chapter 5.

# Laying Out Pages in a Desktop Publishing Program

With a PC and a desktop publishing program, you can create your own greeting cards, invitations, brochures, flyers, business cards, calendars, newsletters, and any other fancy documents you can imagine. The desktop publishing program does most of the heavy lifting. In Microsoft Publisher, for example, a Publishing Wizard leads you step by step through the process of choosing a template, entering your text, and positioning graphics and other objects on the page.

When you're done, you have a page or several pages, each of which is decorated with *text boxes* and clip art, as shown in Figure 13.1. Throughout this chapter, you learn how to manipulate the objects in a publication, including clip art and text boxes.

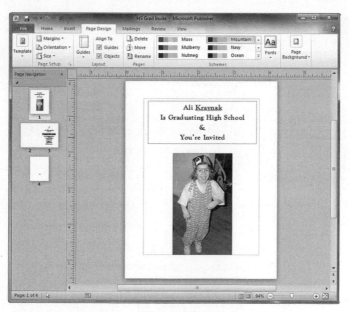

**Figure 13.1**
*Create your own publications.*

Of course, you can combine text and graphics on a page in a word processor, but a desktop publishing program supports more precise positioning of objects. With a desktop publishing program, for example, you can print objects upside down and right side up on the same page so that when you fold the page, you end up with a greeting card. In a word processor, you might be able to pull off that same feat, but it would take the better part of your day. Word processors are better for creating long documents that don't require intricate formatting and layout.

# Inserting Ready-Made Clip Art Images

The easiest way to begin adorning your documents with graphic objects is to insert *clip art images*—small images rendered by professional artists. Suppose you're creating a newsletter and you want to spruce it up with some pictures, perhaps a picture of a fireworks display beside the announcement for the company picnic. All you do is select **Insert**, **Clip Art**; search for and select the image you want to use; and choose the command to insert it, as shown in Figure 13.2.

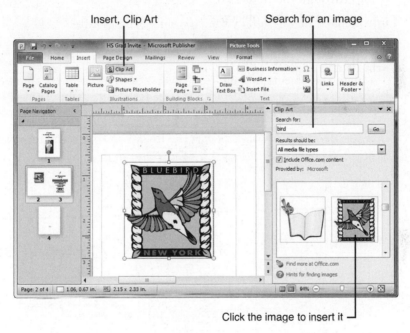

**Figure 13.2**
*You can paste a piece of clip art onto a page.*

Most word processors and desktop publishing programs include their own clip art galleries. You can also purchase clip art libraries on disc and find gobs of clip art on the web. (Check out the Open Clip Art Library at www.openclipart.org.)

# Wrapping Text Around Images

When you lay a picture on top of text, the text typically moves to make room for the picture. In most programs, you can right-click the image, click the option to format the object, and then use the resulting dialog box, as shown in Figure 13.3, to choose the desired text wrap option.

- **In Line with Text:** Not shown in Figure 13.3, this option is typically the default setting and treats the image like text. If the image is at the beginning of the paragraph, for example, text following the image begins near the lower-right corner of the image and wraps below it.

- **Square** places the picture on an imaginary rectangle and wraps the text around the rectangle. For example, if you have a circular picture, you can set text wrapping to **Square** to make the text wrap in a more regular pattern around the image.

- **Tight** makes the text follow the contour of the picture.

- **Top and Bottom** places text above and below the picture but does not wrap it around the sides.

- **Through** (or **Behind text**) allows text to appear in front of the image, which is great for using an image as a background.

- **None** (or **In Front of Text**) places the image on top of the text, which is usually not desirable unless you're using a transparent image.

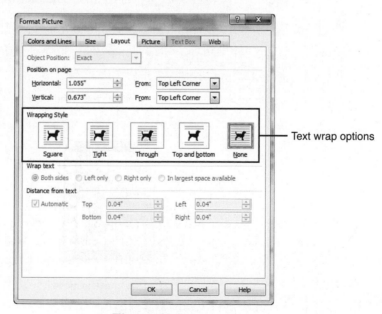

**Figure 13.3**
*Choose a text wrap option.*

> **WHOA!**
>
> Your text wrapping choice seriously affects how the image moves when you drag it. Choosing no text wrapping gives you the most freedom—you can drag the image anywhere, even on top of a chunk of text. If the image refuses to budge when you drag it, the text wrap setting may be restricting its movement.

# Resizing and Reshaping Images

Changing the size of an image is a fairly standard operation. When you click the picture, squares or circles (called *handles*) surround it, as shown in Figure 13.4. To move the image, position the mouse pointer over the image itself (not over a handle) and drag the image to the desired location.

To change the size and dimensions of the image, use the following techniques:

- Drag a top or bottom handle (not in the corner) to make the picture taller or shorter.

- Drag a side handle (not in the corner) to make the picture thinner or wider.

- Drag a corner handle to change both the height and width proportionally.

- If the image has a green circle handle floating above it, drag the green handle to spin the image around its center point.

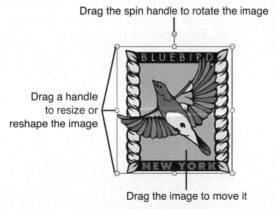

**Figure 13.4**
*You can quickly resize and reshape an image.*

Check the picture toolbar for additional options, including a **Crop** button for trimming the edges of an image. If you don't see a picture toolbar, try right-clicking the image and clicking the option for turning on the toolbar, or right-clicking a blank area of any toolbar and clicking the picture toolbar option.

# Inserting Other Pictures

Clip art galleries are not the only source of graphic images. You can obtain digitized photos using a digital camera (as explained in Chapter 31), scan images (as explained in the next section), draw your own images, obtain images someone else has created and sent to you, or copy images from the web.

Although you can obtain images from numerous sources, the process for inserting an image in most programs is fairly standard:

1. Change to the document you want to add the picture to.

2. Click **Insert**, **Picture**. An Insert Picture dialog box appears.

3. Select the image file you want to insert and click the **Insert** button.

# Scanning Photos, Drawings, and Illustrations

Another way that we, the artistically challenged, overcome our lack of talent is to scan photos and other images into the PC using a gadget cleverly called a *scanner*. A scanner is sort of like a copy machine, but instead of creating a paper copy of the original, it creates a digital copy that can be saved as a file. You can then print the image, fax it, or even insert it in a document.

Most scanners on the market are *flatbed* scanners. You lay the picture face down on the scanner's glass and run the scan program by pressing a button on the scanner, using an application included with your scanner, or scanning from a graphics program.

Whichever way you choose to scan, the scanning program typically displays a dialog box, like the one shown in Figure 13.5, which prompts you to specify the type of document you're scanning and any preferences. After entering your preferences, click the button to commence the scan. The scanner scans the document and saves it as an image to your PC's hard drive.

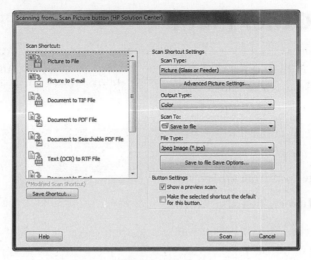

**Figure 13.5**
*Enter your scanning preferences.*

# Drawing and Painting Your Own Illustrations

Clip art, photos, and scanned images are a great source of ready-made art, but when you need a custom illustration, why not draw it yourself? Most word processors and desktop publishing, spreadsheet, and presentation programs include their own drawing tools that enable you to draw lines, arrows, basic shapes, and other objects. Some programs even provide tools for creating organizational charts, flow diagrams, and pyramids.

In addition, Windows includes its own Paint program that transforms your monitor into a virtual canvas on which you can paint using an onscreen brush, pen, and "can" of spray paint.

**NOTE**

Paint programs and drawing tools differ in how they treat objects. In a paint program, objects consist of thousands of tiny colored dots that comprise the image. Drawing tools treat each shape as a continuous line. Drawn objects are easier to resize and move because you manipulate the shape instead of trying to move a bunch of dots.

## Drawing Lines, Squares, Circles, and Other Shapes

Drawing tools consist of onscreen pens, rulers, and templates that enable you to draw lines and basic shapes to create your own custom illustrations. By assembling a collection of these lines and shapes, you can create sophisticated illustrations to adorn your documents.

In recent versions of Microsoft Office, you can access the drawing tools from the Insert ribbon (toolbar). Other programs may include a toolbar with buttons for inserting lines, arrows, and basic shapes. If a program's drawing tools are not visible, check its help system to find out how to access them.

To draw a line or shape, follow these steps:

1.  Click the button for drawing the desired line, arrow, or shape. When you move the mouse pointer over the page, it changes into a crosshair pointer.

2.  Move the crosshair pointer to the position where you want one corner or one end of the object to appear.

3.  Hold down the mouse button and drag the pointer away from the starting point in the desired direction until the object is the size and shape you want, as shown in Figure 13.6.

4.  Release the mouse button.

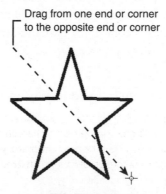

Drag from one end or corner
to the opposite end or corner

**Figure 13.6**
*You can drag a line, arrow, or shape into existence.*

To save some time and reduce frustration when drawing objects, try some of the following tricks of the trade:

- To draw a uniform object (a perfect circle or square), hold down the **Shift** key while dragging.

- To draw the object out from a center point, hold down the **Ctrl** key while dragging. Without the Ctrl key, you drag the object out from its corner or starting point.

- To select an object, click it.

- To delete an object, select it and press the **Del** key.

- To move an object, select it and drag one of its lines.

- To resize or reshape an object, select it and drag one of its handles.

- To copy an object, hold down the **Ctrl** key while dragging it.

- To quickly change the appearance of an object, right-click it and select the desired option from the shortcut menu.

After you have an object on the page, you can use some of the other drawing tools to change qualities of the object, such as its fill color and the color and width of the line that defines it. Select the shape whose qualities you want to change, click the button for the aspect of the object you want to change (line thickness, line color, or fill color), and choose the desired option.

## Painting the Screen with Tiny Colored Dots

Have you ever seen a painting by Georges Seurat, the famous pointillist? His magnificent paintings consist of thousands of tiny dots. Paint programs use the same technique to generate an image. Each image you create in a paint program consists of thousands of tiny, onscreen colored dots called *pixels*.

**DEFINITION**

Your monitor is essentially a canvas made up of hundreds of thousands of tiny lights called **pixels.** Whenever you type a character in a word processing program or draw a line with a paint or draw program, you activate a series of these pixels so they form a recognizable shape onscreen.

Windows comes with a paint program, called Paint, which you can find on the **Start**, **All Programs**, **Accessories** menu. Run Paint to display a screen like the one shown in the Figure 13.7.

When you have the Paint screen up, play around with some of the line, shape, and paint tools. The procedure is pretty basic: click a line, shape, or paint tool (such as the Airbrush tool), choose a line thickness, and click a color. Then drag the mouse pointer over the "canvas." To fill a shape with color, click **Color 2** and the desired color, and then click **Fill** and choose the desired fill style.

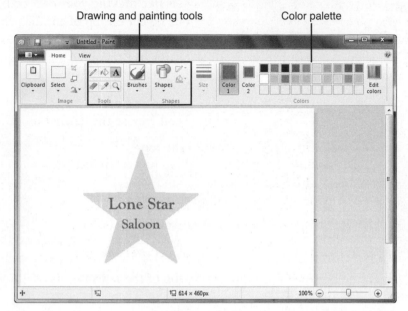

**Figure 13.7**
*Paint is a paint program that comes with Windows.*

# Adding Text in a Box

In a desktop publishing document, all text appears inside one or more text boxes. You can also use text boxes in a word processor document to add margin notes or sidebars.

To create a text box, click **Insert**, **Text Box**. If prompted, select the type of text box you want. Some programs automatically insert a text box. In other programs, you use the mouse to "draw" the text box on the page, just as you draw other graphic objects. After creating the box, type your text inside it and format the text however you wish.

To change the appearance of the box itself (for example, add a border or shading), right-click the text box, select the command for formatting the text box or "shape," and then enter your preferences.

**INSIDE TIP**

Moving a text box is kind of tricky. You can't just drag the center of the box, as you do when you move a picture. First click the outline of the box so handles appear around it. Then drag the border that defines the box, being careful not to drag a handle, which would resize the box instead of move it.

# Manipulating Overlapping Objects

Working with two or more objects on a page is like making your own collage. The trouble with objects is that when you place one object on top of another, the top object blocks the bottom one and prevents you from selecting it. You have to flip through the stack to find the object you want. It's like trying to eat the pancake on the bottom of the stack first.

Most programs that enable you to stack objects offer tools to help you rearrange the objects in a stack. You select the object and then choose the desired action:

- **Bring to front:** Brings an object to the top
- **Send to back:** Sends an object to the bottom
- **Bring forward:** Moves the object one layer up
- **Send backward:** Moves the object one layer down
- **Bring in front of text:** Layers the object over the text
- **Send behind text:** Lays the text on top of the object

If you have a half-dozen objects on a page and you want to nudge them all to the right, you don't have to move each object individually. Shift-click each object that you want to move, or drag a selection box around all the objects. Drag one of the objects, and all the rest follow, like little sheep. To group the objects and make them act as a single object, right-click one of the selected objects and click **Group**. (To ungroup the objects, right-click the grouped object and click **Ungroup**.)

## The Least You Need to Know

- When you need some professionally drawn, ready-made art, check out the clip art collections included with your word processor and other programs and on the Internet.
- To move an image, drag any part of it. To resize an image while retaining its relative dimensions, drag a corner handle.
- In any of the Office applications, you can insert images by using the **Insert**, **Picture** command.
- To draw a line, shape, or text box onscreen, click the button for the object you want to draw, position the mouse pointer where you want one end or corner of the object to appear, and drag away from that point.
- You can create a free-floating text box on a page by clicking **Insert**, **Text box**.

# Crunching Numbers with Spreadsheets

## In This Chapter

- Comparing your checkbook and a spreadsheet
- Typing data into a spreadsheet
- Adding formulas to a spreadsheet
- Charting values in a spreadsheet

There's no mystery to spreadsheets. A checkbook is a spreadsheet. A calendar is a spreadsheet. Your 1040 tax form is a spreadsheet. Any sheet that has boxes you can fill in is a type of spreadsheet.

So what's so special about computerized spreadsheets? For one thing, they do the math for you. For example, a computerized grade book spreadsheet can add each student's grades, determine the average for each student, and even assign the correct letter grade for each average. And that's not all. The spreadsheet can also display the averages as a chart, showing how each student is doing in relation to the other students or highlighting a student's progress or decline in performance. In this chapter, you learn what it takes to create your own spreadsheets and some of the things you can do with them.

## A Computerized Ledger Sheet

A spreadsheet is a grid consisting of a series of *columns* and *rows* that intersect to form thousands of small boxes called *cells*, as shown in Figure 14.1. Most spreadsheet applications display a collection of spreadsheets (also called *worksheets*) in a workbook. You can flip the pages in the workbook by clicking the *worksheet tabs*.

Column

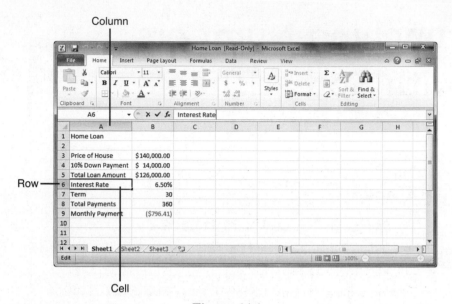

Row —

Cell

**Figure 14.1**
*An Excel worksheet.*

Look across the top of any computer spreadsheet, and you'll see the alphabet (A, B, C, and so on). Each letter stands at the top of a *column*. Along the left side of the spreadsheet, you'll see numbers representing *rows*. The place where a column and row intersect forms a box, called a *cell*. This is the basic unit of any spreadsheet. You type text, values, and formulas in the cells to make your spreadsheet.

To keep track of where each cell is located and what each cell contains, the spreadsheet uses *cell references*.

**DEFINITION**

A **cell reference** is made up of a column letter and row number. For example, the cell that's formed by the intersection of column B and row 3 has the reference B3. Just pretend you're playing bingo.

To select a cell, click it, as shown in Figure 14.2. To select a block of cells, click and drag over the cells to highlight them. To select a row, click the row number that's to the left of the desired row or click and drag over two or more row numbers to select multiple rows. To select a column, click the letter that's above the desired column or click and drag over two or more column letters to select multiple columns.

The selected cell's cell reference appears at the top or bottom of the spreadsheet

Formula bar

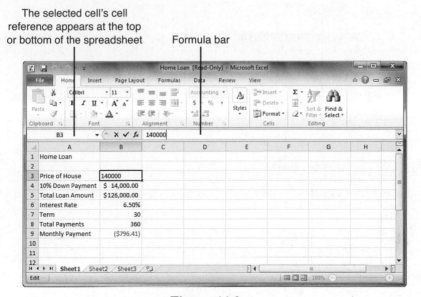

**Figure 14.2**

*The selected cell's contents appear in the formula bar.*

# Building a Spreadsheet from the Ground Up

Creating a spreadsheet involves the following basic steps (don't worry; I go into more detail later in this chapter):

1. Design the spreadsheet.

2. Label the columns and rows.

3. Enter your data.

4. Enter the formulas and functions for calculations.

5. Format the cells (to display dollar signs, for instance).

No law says you have to perform the steps in this order. Some users like to enter their formulas before entering their data so that the formulas calculate results as they work. Regardless of how you proceed, you'll probably have to go back to previous steps to fine-tune your spreadsheet.

**NOTE**

If you need a spreadsheet for a common task, such as determining a loan payment, check to see if your spreadsheet program features a template for the task so that all you have to do is plug in your data. Select **File**, **New**, and choose the option for creating a spreadsheet from a template. Excel comes with dozens of templates, and later versions of Excel enable you to copy additional templates from Microsoft's website.

## Designing the Spreadsheet

If you have a form that you want your spreadsheet to look like, use it as a model. For example, if you're going to use the spreadsheet to balance your checkbook (there are better programs for this, as discussed in Chapter 16), use your most recent bank statement or your checkbook register to model the columns and rows.

If you don't have a form, draw your spreadsheet on a piece of paper to determine the columns and rows you need. It doesn't have to be perfect—just something to get you started.

## Labeling Columns and Rows

When you have some idea of the basic structure of your spreadsheet, you're ready to enter *data labels* (or *labels* for short). Labels are descriptive names for the columns and rows.

To enter a label, click in the cell where you want it to appear, type the label, and press **Enter**. If your label is a number (for example, 2011), you may have to type something in front of it to tell the spreadsheet to treat it as text rather than as a value. In most applications, you type an apostrophe (') or a quotation mark ("). Usually, whatever you type appears only in the input line until you press **Enter**. Then the label is inserted into the current cell. (If you type an apostrophe, it remains invisible in the cell, although you can see it when the entry is displayed on the input line.)

If an entry is too wide for a cell, it overlaps cells to the right of it … unless the cell to the right has its own entry. In such a case, the entry on the left appears chopped off (hidden). If you click the cell, you can view the entire entry on the input line. If you want to see the entire entry in the cell, you can widen the column, usually by dragging the right side of the column header, as shown in Figure 14.3.

Formula bar

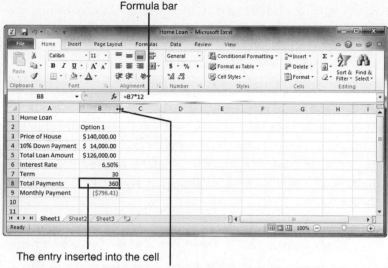

The entry inserted into the cell

If an entry is too wide for a cell, drag the right side
of the column header to increase the column width

**Figure 14.3**
*Select a cell and type your entry.*

## Editing Your Entries

When you make mistakes or change your mind about what you entered, the best way to make corrections usually is to replace the entry. The easiest way to do this is to click the cell that contains the entry, type the replacement, and press **Enter**. That's all there is to it.

To edit an entry in most spreadsheet programs, double-click the cell, use the arrow keys or click to position the insertion point, and type your changes.

## Entering Values and Dates

After you've labeled your rows and columns, you're ready to enter your raw data: the values that make up your spreadsheet.

Also, you don't need to enter dollar or percent signs or commas, although you do need to type any decimal points. You can have the spreadsheet add these symbols for you when you format the cells. For now, just type the number.

Type dates in the proper format for your spreadsheet. In most spreadsheets, you must type the date in the format mm/dd/yyyy (02/25/2011). When you format the cells, you can choose how the spreadsheet displays dates. (Check your spreadsheet application's help system for other acceptable date formats.)

If a value you type is too wide for a cell, the spreadsheet may display a series of number signs (#) or asterisks (*) instead of the value. Don't worry—your entry is still there. You can click the cell to see the entry in the formula bar, and if you make the column wider, the spreadsheet will display the entire value.

To enter values or labels quickly, many spreadsheets let you copy entries into one or more cells or *fill* selected cells with a series of entries. For example, in an Excel spreadsheet, you can type **January** in one cell and use the **Fill** command to have Excel insert the remaining 11 months in 11 cells to the right. Fill also enables you to duplicate entries. For example, you can type **250** in one cell and use the **Fill** command (or drag the Fill handle down, as shown in Figure 14.4) to enter 250 into the next 10 cells down.

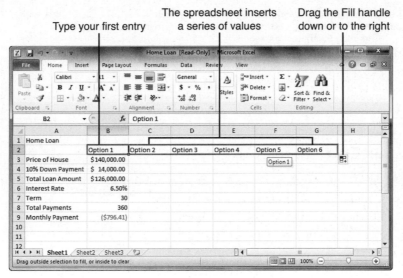

**Figure 14.4**
*Excel's Fill feature in action.*

## Calculating with Formulas and Functions

At this point, you should have rows and columns of values. You need some way to total the values, determine an average, or perform other mathematical operations. That's where formulas and functions come in. Spreadsheets use formulas to perform calculations on the data you enter. With formulas, you can perform addition, subtraction, multiplication, or division using the values contained in various cells.

Formulas typically consist of one or more cell references and/or values and a mathematical operator, such as + (addition), − (subtraction), * (multiplication), or / (division).

For example, if you want to determine the average of the three values contained in cells A1, B1, and C1, you use the following formula:

=(A1+B1+C1)/3

To enter a formula, move to the cell where you want the formula to appear, type = followed by the formula, and press **Enter**. Some spreadsheets assume you want to type a formula if you start your entry with a column letter. Other spreadsheets require you to start the formula with a mathematical operator, such as an equals sign (=) or plus sign (+). Figure 14.5 shows a basic formula in action.

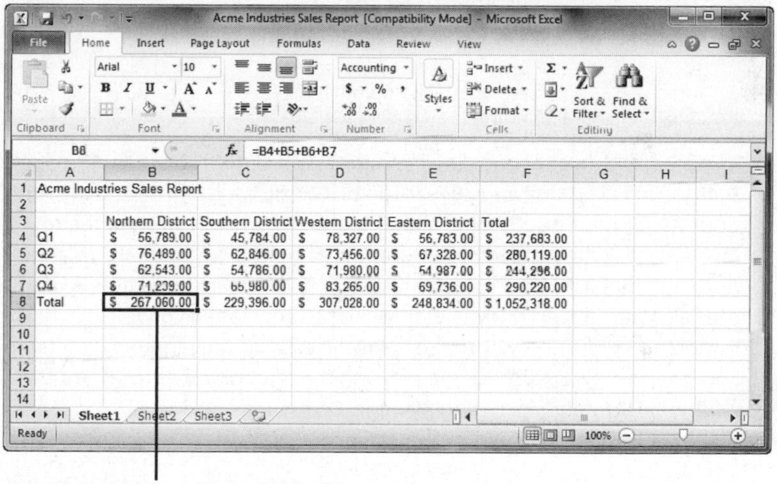

This formula totals the values of cells B4
to B7 and displays the total in cell B8

**Figure 14.5**
*A formula at work.*

Most spreadsheets let you enter formulas in either of two ways. You can type the formula directly in the cell where you want the result inserted, or you can use the mouse to point and click on the cells whose values you want inserted in the formula. To use the second method, called *pointing*, you use the keyboard and mouse together. For example, to determine the total of the values in B4, B5, B6, and B7, you perform the following steps:

1. Click the cell where you want to enter the formula, B8 in this example. The formula's result appears in this cell.

2. Type = to mark this as a formula.

3. Click cell **B4** to add the cell's address to your formula.

4. Type + to add the value from a second cell.

5. Click cell **B5**.

6. Type **+** to add the final value.

7. Click cell **B6**.

8. Type **+** to add the final value.

9. Click cell **B7**.

10. Press **Enter** to accept the formula.

If any of the cells in the formula (B4, B5, B6, or B7) contains a value, the formula's result appears in the cell where you entered the formula.

> **INSIDE TIP**
>
> If your spreadsheet application has a toolbar, it probably has an AutoSum button. (In Excel 2007 and 2010, click the **Formulas** tab to access the AutoSum button.) To quickly determine a total, in the cell where you want the total inserted, click the **AutoSum** button. If neighboring cells contain values, AutoSum highlights the values. If the wrong values are highlighted, drag over the cells that contain the values you want to add. When you release the mouse button and press **Enter**, the spreadsheet performs the required calculations and inserts the result. (Click the arrow to the right of the AutoSum button for additional formulas, including Average, Count, Max, and Min.)

## Using Ready-Made Functions for Fancy Calculations

Creating simple formulas such as one for adding a column of numbers is a piece of cake, but creating the formulas required for a mortgage refinance spreadsheet can pose quite a challenge. To help you in such cases, many spreadsheet applications offer predefined formulas called *functions*.

Functions are complex ready-made formulas that perform a series of operations on a specified *range* of values. For example, to determine the sum of a series of numbers in cells A1 through H1, you can enter the function **=SUM(A1:H1)** instead of entering =A1+B1+C1+ and so on.

Every function consists of three elements:

- The = sign indicates that what follows is a function.

- The function name (for example, SUM) indicates the operation to be performed.

- The argument (for example, A1:H1) gives the cell references of the values that the function will act on. For example, =SUM(A1:H1) determines the total of the values in cells A1 through H1.

**INSIDE TIP**

Use this mnemonic device to remember the order in which a spreadsheet performs mathematical operations: My (multiplication) Dear (division) Aunt (addition) Sally (subtraction). To change the order of operations, use parentheses. Any operation inside parentheses is performed first.

Although functions are fairly complicated and intimidating, many spreadsheets have tools to help. For example, Microsoft Excel offers an Insert Function tool that leads you through the process of inserting functions. It displays a series of dialog boxes asking you to select the function you want to use and pick the values for the argument. Figure 14.6 shows the Insert Function tool in action.

Tell Insert Function where the values the function
needs are stored, and it creates the function for you

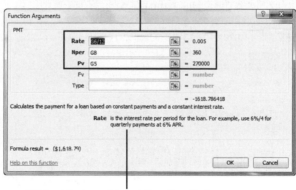

Click a blank, and Insert Function displays
a description of the required entry

**Figure 14.6**

*The Insert Function tool makes it easier to work with functions.*

## Making the Cells Look Pretty

When you have the basic layout of your spreadsheet under control, you can *format* the cells to give the spreadsheet the desired "look." The first thing you might want to do is change the column width and row height to give your entries some breathing room. You may also want to format the values—tell the application to display values as dollar amounts or to use commas to mark the thousands place.

You also can change the type style and type size for your column or row headings, change the text color, and align the text in the cells. For example, you may want to center the headings or align the values in a column so the decimal points line up. To improve the look of the cells themselves, and to distinguish one set of data from another, you can add borders around the cells and add shading and color to the cells.

To format cells, select the cells you want to format and use the controls on the Home tab to apply the desired formatting.

Many newer spreadsheet applications have a Format as Table feature that enables you to select the look you want your spreadsheet to have. The application applies the lines, shading, and fonts to give your spreadsheet a makeover, as shown in Figure 14.7.

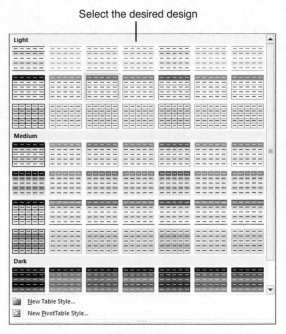

**Figure 14.7**
*Some applications can format your spreadsheet for you.*

After you've formatted your spreadsheet, you can print it. With some spreadsheet applications, such as the latest version of Excel, you can even publish your spreadsheet and charts electronically on the World Wide Web. (See Chapter 17 for more about printing documents.)

# Instant Charts (Just Add Data)

People, especially management types, like to look at charts. They don't want to have to compare a bunch of numbers. They want the bottom line; they want to see immediately how the numbers stack up. Most spreadsheet applications offer a charting feature to transform the values you entered into any type of chart you want: bar, line, pie, area, or high–low (to analyze stock trends). The steps for creating a chart are simple:

1. Drag with the mouse over the labels and values you want to include in the chart. (Labels are used for the axes.)

2. In Excel, display the **Insert** ribbon and click the type of chart you want. (This command varies in different spreadsheet applications. You may need to open the **Insert** menu, choose **Chart**, and then pick a chart type.)

The application transforms your data into a chart and inserts it into the spreadsheet, as shown in Figure 14.8.

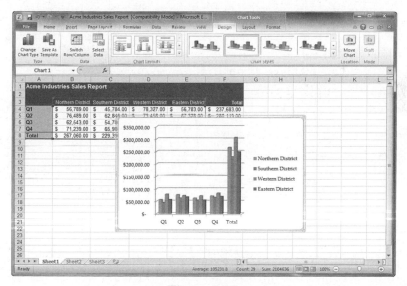

**Figure 14.8**
*Most spreadsheet applications can transform raw data into a chart.*

# Special Spreadsheet Printing Considerations

When you print a letter or other document created in a word processing application, you typically don't need to worry that your paragraphs will be too wide for the pages. The word processor automatically wraps the text to make it fit. Spreadsheets, however, can be much wider than a typical 8½-by-11-inch sheet of paper. To accommodate extra-wide spreadsheets, your spreadsheet application features special print options.

Before you start tweaking the spreadsheet layout and adjusting print settings to make a spreadsheet fit on 8½-by-11-inch pages, check your page setup to determine how your spreadsheet application is prepared to print your spreadsheet(s). Frequently, the application inserts awkward page breaks, omits titles and column headings from some of the pages, and uses additional settings that result in an unacceptable printout.

Recent versions of Excel automatically display a preview of your spreadsheet when you attempt to print it using the File, Print command.

Along the top of the preview area, you're likely to see several buttons that enable you to flip pages, zoom in and zoom out on the page, and change some common print settings. If your spreadsheet application displays a **Margins** button, click it to display margin and column markers; you can drag the markers to adjust column widths and page margins right onscreen. If your application displays a **Page Break Preview** button, click the button to see how the application will divide your spreadsheet into pages; you can drag the page break bars to adjust the page breaks before printing.

If your spreadsheet is close to fitting on a single page, you usually can adjust the left and right margins to pull another column or two (or a couple of rows) onto the page. (Or choose the **Scale to Fit** or **Print to Fit** option when you print the spreadsheet.) If the spreadsheet still doesn't fit, you may need to adjust the page setup. Check the **Page Layout** tab or select **File**, **Page Setup** to access the page setup options.

The page setup options enable you to adjust the print orientation (portrait or landscape), paper size, margins, and print quality. They also enable you to add a header or footer, which comes in handy for automatically numbering your pages.

## The Least You Need to Know

- A cell can contain any of the following entries: a row or column heading, a formula, a function with an argument, or a value.
- Formulas perform calculations on the values in the cells. Each formula consists of one or more cell references or values, along with one or more math operators.
- A function is a ready-made complex formula that performs calculations on a range of values.
- You can format the cells in a spreadsheet to control the text size and style, row height, column width, borders, and shading.

# Creating an Address Book and Printing Mailing Labels

## In This Chapter

- Creating an address list
- Generating mailing labels
- Printing addresses on envelopes

You need to send holiday cards or invitations to 150 family members. The mere thought of addressing the envelopes by hand makes your fingers ache. The solution? Merge your address book with a specially coded document to generate a mailing label for everyone on your list! In this chapter, I show you how to generate and print mailing labels and return address labels, and print an address and return address on individual envelopes.

# Creating a Data Source with Names and Addresses

To perform a mail merge, you need a list of recipient names and mailing addresses. When performing a mail merge, this collection of names and addresses is referred to as the *data source*. You can use any of the following several data sources for the mail merge:

- The Microsoft Works or Word address book (your list of contacts)
- A Microsoft Works or Excel spreadsheet with column headings, as shown in Figure 15.1
- A table created in your word processor
- A Microsoft Works or Access database
- An Outlook address book

Before performing a mail merge using a table or spreadsheet, make sure your table or spreadsheet has a row of bold column headings at the top, like **LastName**, **FirstName**, **Address**, **City**, **State**, and **Zip**. Don't use spaces in the column headings. Your word processor uses the column headings to extract information from the table or spreadsheet. Although the column headings are not essential, you'll find them very helpful in extracting address information and arranging it properly on the labels.

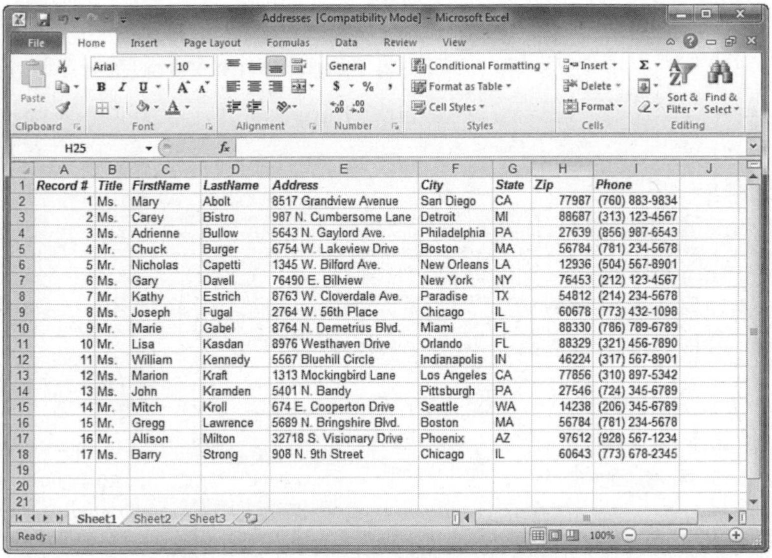

| Record # | Title | FirstName | LastName | Address | City | State | Zip | Phone |
|---|---|---|---|---|---|---|---|---|
| 1 | Ms. | Mary | Abolt | 8517 Grandview Avenue | San Diego | CA | 77987 | (760) 883-9834 |
| 2 | Ms. | Carey | Bistro | 987 N. Cumbersome Lane | Detroit | MI | 88687 | (313) 123-4567 |
| 3 | Ms. | Adrienne | Bullow | 5643 N. Gaylord Ave. | Philadelphia | PA | 27639 | (856) 987-6543 |
| 4 | Mr. | Chuck | Burger | 6754 W. Lakeview Drive | Boston | MA | 56784 | (781) 234-5678 |
| 5 | Mr. | Nicholas | Capetti | 1345 W. Bilford Ave. | New Orleans | LA | 12936 | (504) 567-8901 |
| 6 | Ms. | Gary | Davell | 76490 E. Bilview | New York | NY | 76453 | (212) 123-4567 |
| 7 | Mr. | Kathy | Estrich | 8763 W. Cloverdale Ave. | Paradise | TX | 54812 | (214) 234-5678 |
| 8 | Ms. | Joseph | Fugal | 2764 W. 56th Place | Chicago | IL | 60678 | (773) 432-1098 |
| 9 | Mr. | Marie | Gabel | 8764 N. Demetrius Blvd. | Miami | FL | 88330 | (786) 789-6789 |
| 10 | Mr. | Lisa | Kasdan | 8976 Westhaven Drive | Orlando | FL | 88329 | (321) 456-7890 |
| 11 | Ms. | William | Kennedy | 5567 Bluehill Circle | Indianapolis | IN | 46224 | (317) 567-8901 |
| 12 | Ms. | Marion | Kraft | 1313 Mockingbird Lane | Los Angeles | CA | 77856 | (310) 897-5342 |
| 13 | Ms. | John | Kramden | 5401 N. Bandy | Pittsburgh | PA | 27546 | (724) 345-6789 |
| 14 | Mr. | Mitch | Kroll | 674 E. Cooperton Drive | Seattle | WA | 14238 | (206) 345-6789 |
| 15 | Mr. | Gregg | Lawrence | 5689 N. Bringshire Blvd. | Boston | MA | 56784 | (781) 234-5678 |
| 16 | Mr. | Allison | Milton | 32718 S. Visionary Drive | Phoenix | AZ | 97612 | (928) 567-1234 |
| 17 | Ms. | Barry | Strong | 908 N. 9th Street | Chicago | IL | 60643 | (773) 678-2345 |

**Figure 15.1**

*You can use an Excel spreadsheet as your data source.*

# Using Mail Merge to Generate Mailing Labels

Microsoft Word and the Works word processor both allow you to perform a mail merge to generate mailing labels, and they both work basically the same way. You create a blank document formatted for the type of labels you want to use, such as Avery 8160, and then add field codes to the document, like this:

<<FirstName>> <<LastName>>

<<Address>>

<<City>>, <<State>> <<Zip>>

When you perform the merge, your word processor uses the field codes to retrieve the designated data for each recipient in your address list and create a label for each of them. The process varies depending on whether you're using Microsoft Word or Microsoft Works.

# Running Mail Merge in Microsoft Word

To perform a mail merge in Word, here's what you do:

1. Make sure your data source (address list file) is closed. (These steps assume you have an existing address list, as explained previously in this chapter.)

2. Start with a new, blank document.

3. Initiate mail merge. In Word 2010 and 2007: Click the **Mailings** tab and click **Start Mail Merge**, **Step by Step Mail Merge Wizard**.

4. Under Select document type, click **Labels** and then click **Next: Starting document**.

5. Select the starting document.

6. Click **Label options**.

7. Select the label product and product number to represent the type of labels you'll be printing on, and click **OK**.

8. Click **Next: Select recipients**.

9. Click **Select Recipients**, **Use Existing List**.

10. Click **Use an existing list** and then click **Browse**. The Select Data Source dialog box appears.

11. Navigate to the folder in which your address file is stored, select the document, and click **Open**. If you're prompted to select a table, click one of the tables and click **OK**.

12. Review the list of recipients, as shown in Figure 15.2. (You can remove the check mark next to any recipient's name to exclude someone from the mail merge.) Click **OK**.

13. Click **Next: Arrange your labels**. At this point, Word wants to know where you want the address placed and how you want the name, address, city, state, and zip code arranged.

14. Click **Address Block** and make sure the preview area displays the desired arrangement of address elements. If the arrangement is wrong or something is missing, click the **Match Fields** button to correct it.

15. Click **OK**, click **Update all labels**, and then click **Next: Preview your labels**. Word shows you the first sheet of labels.

16. Print the labels on a plain sheet of paper and then place it on top of a sheet of labels to see whether the text lines up okay with the labels. If the text is printing off the labels or too close to an edge, you can click the **Previous** link and use the rules to adjust the margins for the labels. Be sure to click **Update all labels** after making your adjustments.

17. When everything looks okay, click **Next: Complete the merge**.

18. Load your labels into your printer and click **Print**.

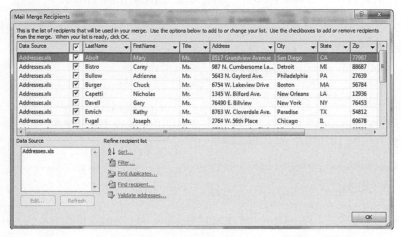

**Figure 15.2**
*The Mail Merge Wizard takes you through the process step by step.*

## Performing a Mail Merge in Microsoft Works

You can create an address list in Microsoft Works using the Microsoft Works spreadsheet or database, or you can create a table in the word processor, as discussed earlier. After creating an address list, close the file and perform a mail merge to generate your mailing labels:

1. In the Microsoft Works word processor, click **Tools**, **Labels** or use the Works Task Launcher to start a labels task.

2. In the Labels dialog box, click **Mailing labels** and then click **OK**.

3. Choose the label product and product number for the labels you're going to print, such as Avery 8160, and then click **New Document**. The word processor creates a new document and displays the Open Data Source dialog box.

4. Click **Merge from the Address Book** or click **Merge information from another type of file** and use the resulting dialog box to choose your data source. The Insert Fields dialog box appears.

5. In the label area of the document (not shaded), click where you want to insert a field.

6. In the Fields list, click the field you want to insert, as shown in Figure 15.3, or click **Address Block** (if you're using the Address Book as your data source) to insert a single field that includes the name and address.

7. Click **Insert**.

8. Repeat Steps 5 to 7 to insert additional fields, if necessary.

9. Add punctuation and spacing between the field codes, as necessary.

10. In the Insert Fields dialog box, click **View Results**. Works displays a sample label. You can click the arrows to scroll through the labels.

11. Load your labels into your printer. Click **Print** to complete the merge and print the labels, or click **Print Preview** to complete the merge and preview the labels. (It's a good idea to print one sheet of labels on a blank sheet of plain paper first to check alignment before you print on more expensive labels. You can then adjust the margins on the label that contains the field codes to change the position of text on the labels.)

12. Click **File**, **Save** and then name and save your document.

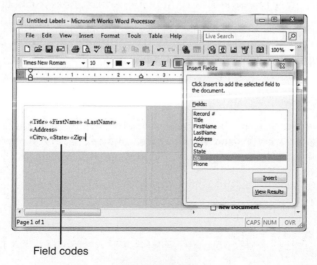

Field codes

**Figure 15.3**
*Insert field codes.*

# Creating Return Address Labels

You can print an entire page of return address labels using Microsoft Word or the Microsoft Works word processor.

## Printing Return Address Labels in Word

To create and print return address labels in Word, here's what you do:

1. Display the Envelopes and Labels dialog box by performing one of the following steps:

   • Word 2010 and 2007: Click the **Mailings** tab and click **Labels**.

   • Earlier versions of Word 2003: Click **Tools, Letters and Mailings, Envelopes and Labels**.

2. Click the **Labels** tab, as shown in Figure 15.4, if not already selected.

3. Click the **Use return address** checkbox or type your return address in the **Address** box. You can drag over your address and right-click it for formatting options.

4. Click the **Options** button, use the resulting dialog box to specify the type of labels you'll be printing on, and click **OK**.

5. Select **Full page of the same label**, if not already selected.

6. Click **Print**. (The first time you print return address labels, print them on a plain sheet of paper to check alignment. If the alignment is off, you can adjust the font and paragraph indents to fix the problem; drag over the address and then right-click it for formatting options.)

**INSIDE TIP**

If you've written a letter that contains your return address, drag over it before clicking **Tools, Letters and Mailings, Envelopes and Labels**. Word will automatically insert that address into the Address box in the Envelopes and Labels dialog box.

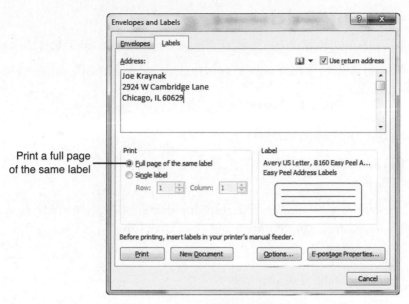

Print a full page of the same label

**Figure 15.4**

*The Envelopes and Labels dialog box.*

## Printing Return Address Labels in Works

To create and print return address labels using the Works word processor, here's what you do:

1. Click **Tools, Labels**.

2. Click **Return address labels** and click **OK**.

3. Choose the label product and product number for the labels you're going to print, and then click **New Document**. The word processor creates a new document for the label product you chose.

4. Type your return address in the upper-left label (the one that's not shaded).

5. Click **Print**.

# Printing on Envelopes

Here's what you do to print a single envelope in Word (the steps are similar with the Works word processor):

1. If you already typed the address in another document, such as a letter, high-light the address so you won't have to retype it.

2. Open the **Envelopes and Labels** dialog box:

    • Word 2010 and 2007: Click the **Mailings** tab and then click **Envelopes**.

    • Earlier versions of Word: Click **Tools**, **Letters and Mailings**, **Envelopes and Labels**.

3. If the **Delivery address:** box is blank, type the recipient's mailing address, as shown in Figure 15.5.

4. If the **Return address:** box is blank, click inside the box and type your return address.

5. Click the **Options** button, use the resulting dialog box to specify the envelope size and printing preferences, and then click **OK**.

6. Load a blank envelope in your printer as indicated on the paper tray, and then click **Print**.

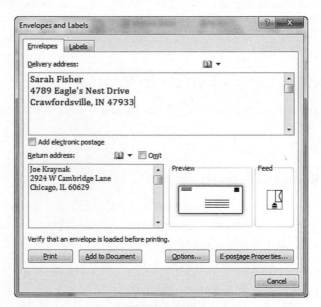

**Figure 15.5**
*Print a single envelope in Word.*

To print multiple envelopes with different addresses and the same return address, perform a mail merge. The steps are similar to those for printing labels, except that you'll have an area on the envelope where you can type your return address.

## The Least You Need to Know

- Before performing a mail merge, make sure you have a data source that contains the names and addresses of all the recipients.

- During a mail merge, a word processor uses field codes to extract names and addresses from a data source to address labels or envelopes to recipients listed in the data source.

- To access the options for printing envelopes and labels in Word 2007 or 2010, click the **Mailings** tab.

- To access the options for printing envelopes and labels in earlier versions of Word, click **Tools**, **Letters and Mailings**, **Envelopes and Labels**.

- In the Works word processor, you'll find the options for printing labels and envelopes on the Tools menu.

# Managing Your Finances

## In This Chapter

- Finances, meet computer
- Draw up a monthly budget
- Manage your money from home
- Pay your bills online
- Using financial calculators

The whole concept of money was supposed to simplify things, to make it easier to exchange goods. Instead of trading a fox pelt for a lobster dinner, you could sell the pelt to someone and then take the money to your local seafood restaurant to pay for your lobster dinner.

Somewhere in history, though, things got all fouled up. We now store our money in banks and use checks and debit cards to get at it, we autopay some of our bills, and we even have chunks of our money removed from our paychecks before we've even touched it to cover taxes and healthcare premiums!

Fortunately, your computer can help you simplify all this. In this chapter, I show you some handy things your computer can do to help you manage your finances.

# Banking Online (Without a Personal Finance Program)

Most of this chapter is about using a personal finance program, such as Quicken or Microsoft Money, to simplify the process of managing all your personal finances—writing checks, paying bills, tracking income and expenses, reconciling your accounts against your monthly bank statements, and more.

But you don't need a personal finance program to tap the power of computerized banking. Many banks, credit card companies, and companies that supply goods and services support online banking and online bill pay so that you can perform your banking and pay bills online.

I can't really step you through the process because most online banking/bill-paying sites behave differently, depending on how they're set up. In most cases, you use your web browser, as discussed in Chapter 19, to pull up the site's opening page. Then you click the option to log in to the system and enter your log-in name and password (you'll have to register first). When you're logged in, the site presents you with a page that allows you to bank online, view your statements, and pay your bills. Figure 16.1 shows a sample online-banking website.

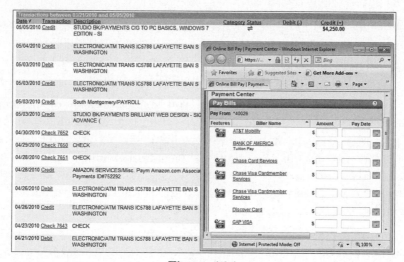

**Figure 16.1**

*With online banking, you can view statements, transfer funds, and pay bills online.*

On a credit card site, you're likely to see your current balance, credit limit, available credit, payment due, payment due date, and a list of transactions on your current statement. (You can view transactions on past statements, too.) Most credit card companies also provide tools that enable you to download data into a personal finance program, if you have one.

> **INSIDE TIP**
>
> If your credit card gives you some sort of perk—frequent flyer miles, free groceries, in-store credit, whatever—pay everything you can with this credit card and then pay the credit card balance in full when you receive your statement. You may even want to set up automatic credit card payments with your utility companies to pay phone, gas, electric, and water bills. Not only does this allow you to earn money with your credit card, but it also simplifies your accounting; you have only one bill to pay each month—your credit card balance.

# Choosing and Setting Up a Personal Finance Program

You can find plenty of personal finance programs, including Quicken, Microsoft Money, and Moneydance. I recommend Quicken because so many financial services support Quicken files. Before choosing a program, ask what your bank recommends. (Quicken is used throughout this chapter to illustrate tasks.)

To start using a personal finance program, you first need to supply the program with information about your accounts. This information typically includes the account name, the type of account (savings, checking, cash, and so on), and the current balance or the balance according to your most recent statement.

To set up an account, you enter the command for creating an account and then follow the onscreen instructions, as shown in Figure 16.2, to supply the requested information.

**Figure 16.2**

*Your personal finance program gathers the information it needs to set up and manage your accounts.*

# Automating the Check-Writing Process

A personal finance program can streamline the check-writing process. You enter the name of the payee and the amount paid. The program inserts the date and spells out the amount for you, as shown in Figure 16.3. The program also copies the required information into the register and calculates your new balance.

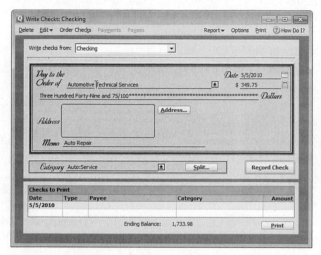

**Figure 16.3**
*Your personal finance program can save you time writing checks.*

Sounds great, and it may be if you write and print a lot of checks. But if you pay most of your bills online, it can be more of a hassle than it's worth. Many users, including me, continue writing checks by hand and use the personal finance program to record the checks, reconcile their balances, and manage their budgets.

# Reconciling an Account with a Statement

Back in the old days, reconciling your checking account with the bank statement was an exercise in frustration. You calculated and recalculated until you started seeing double. With a personal finance program, you simply enter the ending balance (from your most recent statement) and then mark the checks that have cleared, mark the deposits, and record any service charges and interest, as shown in Figure 16.4. The program takes care of the rest, determining whether your register balance matches the balance on your bank statement.

Mark cleared checks          Mark cleared deposits

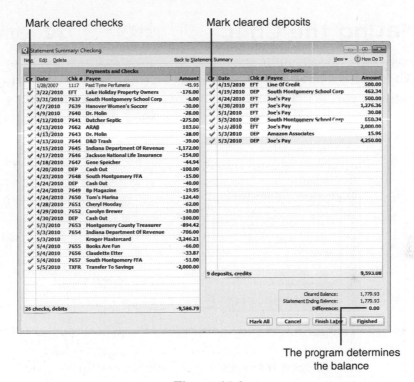

**Figure 16.4**

*Your personal finance program takes the complexity out of reconciling your account.*

If the total on your register doesn't match the total on your bank statement, the program lets you know. If you have to correct an entry in the register, the program automatically recalculates the total, saving you the time of starting over from scratch.

# Banking Online (with a Personal Finance Program)

If your computer connects to the Internet, you may be able to pay your bills using your personal finance program. You can often use online bill paying to pay your utility bills and make credit card and loan payments. If you owe money to a person or business not connected to the system, the online bill-paying service can print and mail an old-fashioned paper check for you!

**WHOA!**

Make sure you aren't paying for a service you already have for free. Check with your bank or credit card company to find out what online bill-paying service they offer for free.

Most banks and credit unions that offer online banking don't require you to use a personal finance program to access it. But if you use a personal finance program to manage your finances, it makes sense to do your online banking through the program. The program can automatically retrieve information from your bank, mortgage company, or credit card company and record it so you don't have to manually enter the information. This keeps your account information current and relatively error-free.

Before you attempt to set up your account online, check with your bank or credit union to determine whether it supports online banking. Tell the bank what program you plan to use, so it can supply you with specific instructions on how to proceed. When you're setting up new accounts, you may be able to automate the account setup by having your personal finance program obtain information directly from the bank. Not only does this save you some time, but it can also prevent costly errors.

# Setting Up Recurring Entries

If you get paid the same amount every two weeks or you have a bill that's the same amount each month (such as a mortgage payment, rent, or budgeted utility payment), you can set up a recurring entry that automatically records the transaction at the scheduled time or reminds you to enter it. If you're set up to pay bills online, you can even automate the payment.

When you enter the command to create a new recurring entry, the program displays a dialog box, requesting details about the transaction. Enter the requested information.

# Tracking Your Budget

To take control of your financial destiny, you have to figure out where all your money is going. For instance, you can't decide whether you're spending too much on car repairs unless you know exactly how much you're spending. Would you save money by buying a new car instead? Is there any way you can set aside some money for investments? With accurate budget information, you can make financially sound decisions.

With most personal finance programs, you can establish a budget and have the program keep track of each expense for you. Many programs come with a set of home or business expense categories you can use when recording your transactions. If an expense is not listed, you can create a new category. Whenever you record a transaction (check, cash, credit card, debit), you specify the category. At the end of the month, you tell the program to generate a budget report, as shown in Figure 16.5. The report displays the total for each category and helps you spot the pork in your budget.

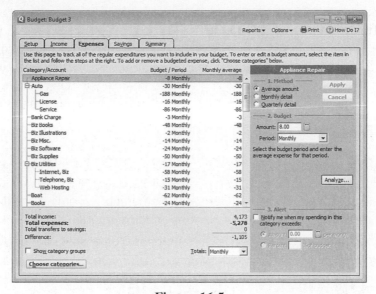

**Figure 16.5**

*A personal finance program can generate a budget report that helps you track your income and expenses.*

# Tapping the Power of Financial Calculators

Personal finance programs typically include several financial calculators that can help you determine the monthly payment on a loan, how much you need to invest to retire comfortably at 65, how much you can save by refinancing your mortgage for a shorter term or a lower interest rate, and so on. You simply plug in the numbers you know, and the calculator supplies you with the missing figures.

If you purchase the basic version of a personal finance program, it may not be equipped with calculators. When you're shopping for a program, be sure you get the version that includes the calculators. They're indispensable ... I guess that's why the software developers charge extra for them.

# Preparing Your Annual Tax Return

About the only thing a personal finance program can't do for you (financially speaking) is your taxes. However, assuming you did a good job of recording all your transactions, accounted for every penny of income and expenses, and assigned a category to each transaction, the program can package up your financial data and ship it off to a tax-preparation program, such as TurboTax.

TurboTax and similar tax-preparation programs lead you through the process of preparing your taxes by asking you a series of questions. You simply answer the questions and supply the requested data, and the program fills out the tax forms for you. The program can even submit your tax returns online so you get your refund sooner.

## The Least You Need to Know

- A personal finance program can help you track your income and expenses and manage your bank accounts.
- Check with your bank to determine whether it offers online banking and how to access its features with your personal finance program.
- By assigning a category to each transaction, you enable your personal finance program to account for every penny of income and expenses and to generate a monthly budget report.
- You can set up recurring entries to have your personal finance program automatically enter transactions on schedule.
- A personal finance program can help you gather all your financial data for the year, simplifying the task of preparing your taxes.

# Printing Documents and Other Creations

## In This Chapter

- Installing a printer
- Previewing your document before printing it
- Tweaking the page margins
- Printing your masterpiece
- Troubleshooting common printer problems

When printing goes as planned, it's a snap. You click the **Print** button and then kick back and play Solitaire while the printer spits out your document. However, not all print jobs proceed without a hitch. You finish your game of Solitaire only to find a stack of papers covered with foreign symbols. Or you get an error message saying that the printer's not ready. After hours of fiddling and fumbling, you find and correct the problem only to face a new problem: getting your printer back online.

In this chapter, you learn all you need to know about glitch-free printing and how to recover from the occasional print failure.

## Connecting Your Printer to Your PC

Before connecting a printer to your PC, read the manufacturer's instructions and install the printer's software, if instructed to do so. Otherwise, when you connect the printer, Windows is likely to recognize it and install a standard printer driver rather than the software designed for the printer.

Now you're ready to connect the printer. In the old days, life was simple. Every PC and just about every printer had a parallel printer port (now obsolete). Now, printers connect to PCs in a variety of ways.

- **USB:** Plug one end of the USB cable into the printer's USB port, and plug the other end into any one of your PC's USB ports. Turn on the printer and PC, unless they're already on. Windows automatically detects the printer.

- **Wi-Fi or Bluetooth wireless:** Turn on the printer, router (if the PC will be connecting to the printer through a router), and PC, in that order. Assuming that the printer and PC both are equipped with a compatible wireless adapter and the devices are within range of one another or the router, Windows automatically detects the printer.

- **Ethernet:** With everything turned off, connect the printer to the router that the PC is connected to, as explained in Chapter 11. Turn on the printer, router, and PC, in that order. Windows automatically detects the printer.

After detecting the printer, Windows leads you through the process of installing the printer driver, if you didn't already install it.

To determine whether your printer is available in Windows, click **Start**, **Devices and Printers**, and look for an icon for your printer. (If your Start menu does not contain the Devices and Printers option, click **Start**, **Control Panel**, **View devices and printers**.) If you see the icon and it has a check mark on it, you're all set—Windows will use this as the default printer. If you see the icon but no check mark, right-click the icon and click **Set as default printer**. If you don't see an icon, proceed to the following section to install the printer in Windows.

**NOTE**

Keeping your printer driver up to date ensures smoother operation and optimum use of your printer's features. Many printers automatically check for and install driver updates via the Internet, but check your printer's documentation or help system for details.

# Setting Up Your Printer in Windows

If your printer came with its own installation disc, use the disc to install the printer. Follow the manufacturer's instructions on whether to run the installation before or after connecting the printer. Insert the disc, and if Windows doesn't launch the installation routine, display the contents of the disc (as discussed in Chapter 8), double-click the **Install** or **Setup** file, and follow the onscreen instructions to complete the installation.

If your printer did not come with a disc, here's what you do:

1. Click **Start, Devices and Printers**.

2. In the toolbar near the top of the window, click **Add a printer**. The Add Printer Wizard appears.

3. Click one of the following options:

   - **Add a local printer:** Choose this option if you're installing a printer connected directly to the computer.

   - **Add a network, wireless or Bluetooth printer:** Choose this option if you're installing a wireless printer or connecting to the printer through a router or another PC on your network.

4. Follow the wizard's instructions to choose a printer, as shown in Figure 17.1, and complete the installation.

**Figure 17.1**
*Windows displays a list of installed printers.*

When you install your printer, click the option to set it up as the default printer. Otherwise, when you print documents, Windows may assume that you want to use a different printer (if other printers have been installed), even if your computer is currently not connected to one of these other installed printers.

# Preprint Checklist

Most programs display a print button in one of their toolbars that enables you to quickly send your document to the printer. It's tempting to click the button and see what happens. Resist the temptation. You can avoid 9 out of 10 printing problems by checking your document in Print Preview first.

To view a document in Print Preview in most applications, open the **File** menu and click **Print Preview** (or its equivalent command), or click the **Print Preview** button in one of the program's toolbars. Flip through the pages to see how they'll appear in print.

If your document looks fine, skip ahead to the "Sending Documents to the Printer" section to start printing your document. If you noticed some problems, proceed to the following section.

# Setting Your Margins and Page Layout

You can correct many undesirable page layout issues by checking and adjusting the page margins and layout settings in your program.

In recent versions of Microsoft Office applications, you click the **Page Layout** tab and use the options in the Page Setup group to enter your preferences, as shown in Figure 17.2.

Click the Page Layout tab

Use these buttons to          Click here for
control your page setup      more options

**Figure 17.2**
*The Page Layout tab.*

**INSIDE TIP**

If you don't see an option you need to access on the Page Layout tab, click the icon in the lower-right corner of the Page Setup group. This displays the Page Setup dialog box, which includes the tabs Margins, Paper (where you can choose a paper source), and Layout (which includes settings for positioning the header and footer). The Layout tab also contains a handy Vertical Alignment option; if you have a short letter or a title page for a report, for example, you can choose to center it vertically on the page so you don't end up with too much white space at the bottom.

To display the page setup options in most other applications, you open the **File** menu and select **Page Setup**. The Page Setup dialog box appears, presenting numerous options for changing the page layout and print settings.

In either case, here are some common settings you might want to adjust:

- **Page margins:** You can set the margins for the top, bottom, left, and right sides of the page. The Gutter setting lets you add margin space to the inside margin of the pages, in case you plan to insert the pages into a book or binder.

- **Orientation:** You can choose to print in portrait mode (right side up) or landscape mode (sideways) on a page. In most cases, you'll be printing in portrait mode. Landscape mode is useful for printing wide spreadsheets and other items that are wider than they are tall.

- **Paper size:** Most documents are printed on standard 8½-by-11-inch paper, but you may need to print a document on legal-size paper or on envelopes. (If your printer has two paper trays, you may also need to specify the paper source—which tray is loaded with the selected-size paper.)

## Adding a Header or Footer

Most applications that allow you to create and print documents include a feature for printing a header (at the top) or a footer (at the bottom) on each page. A typical header or footer contains the title of the document, the date on which it was printed, and the page number (the application can automatically insert the correct page number on each page).

The command for creating a header or footer varies from program to program. In most applications, you click **View**, **Header and Footer**. In recent versions of Microsoft Office, you'll find the header and footer options on the **Insert** tab.

This takes you to an area where you can type your header or footer and use various buttons to switch between the header and footer; insert the date, page numbers, number of pages, and so on; and use a different header or footer for even- and odd-numbered pages (see Figure 17.3).

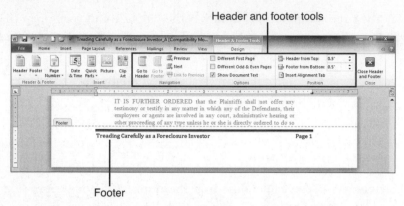

Header and footer tools

Footer

**Figure 17.3**

*You can add a header or footer at the top or bottom of every page.*

# Sending Documents to the Printer

When your printer is installed and online, printing is a snap. Although the procedure for printing might vary, the following steps work in most Windows programs. If you just want to print one copy of your document, using the default settings, click the **Print** button on the toolbar (if available). If you need to customize a bit, follow these steps:

1.  Open the document you want to print.

2.  Click **File**, **Print**. (In Office 2010 and 2007 applications, click the **Office** button, point to **Print**, and click **Print**.) The Print screen appears, prompting you to enter instructions. Figure 17.4 shows the print screen from Microsoft Word 2010.

3.  Enter your preferences and click the **Print** button.

To enter default settings for your printer (including the quality settings), click **Start**, **Devices and Printers**. Right-click your printer's icon and select **Properties**. Enter your preferences and click **OK**. The default settings control the operation of the printer for all applications. You can override the defaults any time you print a document. Overriding the defaults does not change the default settings.

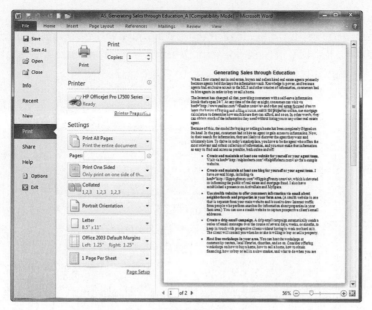

**Figure 17.4**
*The Print screen lets you change the settings.*

# Managing Background Printing

If you ever need to stop, cancel, or pause and resume printing, you must access the print queue (a line for documents waiting to be printed). Whenever you print a document in Windows, a picture of a printer appears in the notification area (lower-right corner of the Windows desktop). Double-click the printer icon to access the Print Manager and view the print queue, as shown in Figure 17.5. You then can perform the following steps to stop or resume printing:

- To pause all printing, open the **Printer** menu and select **Pause Printing**.

- To pause the printing of one or more documents, Ctrl+click each document in the queue, open the **Document** menu, and select **Pause Printing**.

- To resume printing, open the **Printer** or **Document** menu and click **Pause Printing**.

- To cancel all print jobs, open the **Printer** menu and select **Cancel All Print Jobs**.

- To cancel individual print jobs, Ctrl+click each print job you want to cancel, open the **Document** menu, and select **Cancel**.

- To move a document within the print queue, drag it up or down.

If you choose to cancel printing, don't expect the printer to immediately cease and desist. Fancy printers have loads of memory and can store enough information to print several pages. If you're serious about canceling all printing, press the **Cancel** button on your printer, too.

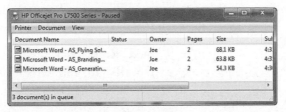

**Figure 17.5**
*You can supervise and control printing using Print Manager.*

**WHOA!**

If you choose to print only one copy of a document but your printer spits out several copies, you most likely printed the document more than once. When the printer doesn't start printing right away, many people lose patience and keep clicking the **Print** button. Each time you click the **Print** button, another copy of the document is sent to the queue, and your printer dutifully prints it.

# Hey, It's Not Printing!

If your printer refuses to print your document, you must do a little detective work. The following questions can help you track down the cause:

- Is your printer plugged in and turned on?

- Does the display on the printer indicate a problem, such as a paper jam or out of ink? Refer to your printer's manual for information on clearing paper jams and solving other common printer-related problems.

- Does your printer have paper? Is the paper tray inserted properly?

- Is the printer's online light on (not blinking)? If the online light is off or blinking, press the power button to turn on the light and make the printer print.

- Is **Print to file** or **Print to Adobe PDF** selected in the Print dialog box? It shouldn't be. This option sends the document to a file on your disk instead of to the printer.

- Is your printer marked as the default printer? Follow the instructions earlier in this chapter to determine whether the printer that's connected to your computer or network is the default printer in Windows.

- Is the printer paused? Double-click the printer icon on the right end of the taskbar, open the **Printer** menu, and be sure **Pause Printing** is not checked. If there is a check mark, click **Pause Printing** to turn off this option.

- Is the correct printer port selected? Right-click the icon for your printer and choose **Properties**. Click the **Details** tab, and be sure the correct printer port is selected.

A network printer that's connected to a central router is usually assigned an Internet Protocol (IP) address that looks something like 192.168.0.3. Check your printer setup using the controls on your printer—it may have an option that allows you to print a Printer Configuration page that includes the printer's IP address. Open your web browser (as explained in Chapter 19), type your printer's IP address in the address bar near the top of the window, and press **Enter**. This may open a page that enables you to check ink levels and enter default settings for your printer.

## The Least You Need to Know

- Before you print a document, click the **Print Preview** or **Print Layout** button to see how the finished product will look.

- To check the page layout settings, click the **Page Layout** tab (in Office 2007 or 2010 applications) or open the **File** menu and click **Page Setup** (in most other applications).

- To quickly print a document, no questions asked, click the **Print** button, if available. For more control over printing, click **File**, **Print**.

- To pause or cancel printing, double-click the printer icon in the notification area to display the Print Manager's print queue. Choose the desired option from the **File** menu.

- If your document doesn't start printing, double-click the printer icon in the notification area to determine what's wrong.

# Tapping the Power of the Internet

Faster than the U.S. Postal Service. More powerful than the Home Shopping Network. Able to leap wide continents in a single click. Look, up on your desktop. It's a phone! It's a network! Yes, it's all those and more. It's the Internet!

With your PC, a modem, and a standard phone line (or, better yet, a broadband connection), you have access to the single most powerful communications and information network in the world: the Internet. The chapters in Part 4 show you how to get wired to the Internet and use its features to exchange electronic mail; find information on just about any topic imaginable; chat with family, friends, and acquaintances; shop for deals; manage your investments; plan your next vacation; and even publish your own creations via the web!

If you're wondering what Google, Facebook, Twitter, and YouTube are all about, this part's for you.

# Getting Wired to the Internet

**In This Chapter**

- Understanding Internet basics
- Deciding on the right connection for you
- Choosing an Internet service provider (ISP)
- Getting on the information superhighway
- Checking out your connection speed

How would you like to access the latest news, weather, and sports without stepping away from your computer? Order items from a computerized catalog? Send a postage-free letter and have it arrive at its destination in a matter of seconds? Mingle with friends, family, and strangers?

With your computer, a modem, and an Internet service provider, you can do all this and more. This chapter introduces you to the wonderful world of the Internet and shows you how to connect your computer to the outside world.

## Understanding How This Internet Thing Works

The Internet is a worldwide network of computers that can communicate with one another and share resources. The computers are all interconnected by a massive collection of fiber-optic cables, phone lines, and wireless signals that facilitate data transfer at lightning-fast speeds.

For your computer to plug into this network and tap its resources, it needs a modem and an Internet service provider (ISP). The modem is the hardware your computer uses to send and receive data on the Internet—it's sort of like a telephone for your computer. The ISP functions as a communications hub between your computer and the Internet. Using the modem, your computer connects to the ISP, and the ISP connects to the Internet, as shown in Figure 18.1.

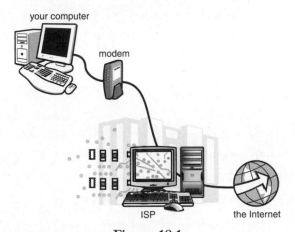

**Figure 18.1**

*Your computer uses a modem to connect to your ISP, which connects your computer to the Internet.*

# Picking a Connection Type

Although myriad options are available for connecting to the Internet, they boil down to two choices: dial-up or broadband.

Dial-up is a slow connection, but it's available wherever you have access to a phone line, which is pretty much everywhere. Your options may be limited because of your location.

Broadband is a fast connection, which you can get through some cable companies, digital satellite services, phone companies, and wireless ISPs, but keep in mind that *fast* is a relative term. A dedicated (leased) line is typically the fastest, followed by fixed wireless (as opposed to mobile wireless), cable, Digital Subscriber Line (DSL), and satellite, but several factors can affect the actual speed at which your computer connects. One user's DSL connection may be faster than another user's cable connection.

If you live in a major metropolitan area, you have plenty of Internet connection types from which to choose: dial-up using a standard modem over your existing phone line, DSL modem, cable modem, satellite, and perhaps even some type of wireless connection (fixed or mobile). Your choice hinges on the following three factors:

- **Availability:** You might not have cable or DSL service in your area, so that can significantly limit your choices. Dial-up service over an existing phone line and satellite service are almost universally available.

- **Speed:** Choose the fastest connection you can afford. You may think you won't use the Internet that much, but when Windows or your other programs need to download huge software updates, you'll be wishing you had a faster connection.

- **Price:** Monthly service charges range from about $15 per month for dial-up service (plus the cost of local phone service) to more than $60 a month for cable or satellite service. (Satellite also costs about $600 up front for the installation, although satellite Internet companies often offer special deals if you make a long-term commitment.)

The following sections provide a brief overview of your choices, but you need to shop around to find out what's available in your area and compare prices.

> **INSIDE TIP**
>
> Connection speeds are measured in kilobits per second (Kbps), which is equivalent to 1,000 bits per second; and megabits per second (Mbps), which is roughly equivalent to 1 million bits per second.

## Turbo-Charging Your Connection with a Cable Modem

Like cable television connections, a cable Internet connection supports high-speed data transfers to your PC, enabling you to cruise the Internet at the same speed you can flip TV channels:

- **Speed:** Rates range from 4Mbps to 20Mbps, although you're likely to experience download rates of 3Mbps to 6Mbps.

- **Cost:** Service costs about $40 or $50 per month, depending on speed, plus $100 for the modem, which you may get for free or be able to rent from the cable company for a few dollars a month.

- **Drawbacks:** You share bandwidth with other users in your area, so the speed of your connection can fluctuate depending on how many users are currently using the service and how much data they're transferring.

## Another Speedy Option: DSL

DSL may be a little more available than cable and cost a little less, but it's also slower:

- **Speed:** Rates range from 768Kbps to 7.1Mbps.

- **Cost:** Service costs about $20 to $40 per month, depending on the speed, plus $100 for the modem, which you may get for free or be able to rent from the phone company for a few dollars a month.

- **Drawbacks:** Your PC must be within about 3 miles of the phone company's switching station.

## Connecting from the Boonies via Satellite

If you can't get cable or DSL, you may need to settle for satellite broadband. Here's how it stacks up:

- **Speed:** Rates range from 500Kbps to 6Mbps but are typically much slower, especially when you're sending data (uploading) from your computer to the Internet.

- **Cost:** Service costs about $60 to $120 per month, depending on speed and bandwidth limit, plus $600 for the hardware and installation (although the satellite company may waive the installation fee if you make a long-term commitment).

- **Drawbacks:** Satellite service is slower, pricier, and less reliable than cable or DSL service, but it's still way better than dial-up. Also ask whether you have to stick one of those ugly satellite dishes on the side of your house or in your yard.

**INSIDE TIP**

If you choose satellite, consider using a dial-up account as a backup for when you can't connect in storms or dense cloud cover.

## On the Go with Wireless Internet

Wireless Internet comes in two basic forms: fixed and mobile. With *fixed wireless*, you install an antenna on your home or workplace and connect to a specific signal tower. Fixed wireless is beginning to compete with cable, DSL, and satellite, especially in rural areas. *Mobile wireless* is more like the wireless Internet you might have for an iPhone or similar device. You can connect to the Internet wherever your service provides coverage. Here's how wireless stacks up:

- **Speed:** Speeds vary greatly, typically from 256Kbps to 1Mbps for residential use. With the latest wireless technologies, speeds top out at about 100Mbps for mobile users and 1Gbps for fixed wireless (wireless service for users at stationary locations), but residential users will see speeds more in the range of 1Mbps to 10Mbps.

- **Cost:** Costs vary about as much as speeds and are almost always linked to speed. For example, you may pay $29.95 per month for a 256Kbps connection and $60 for a 1Mbps connection. I've seen ISPs that charge hundreds of dollars per month for 1Mbps service in areas where the only other broadband option is satellite.

- **Drawbacks:** Distance from the communications tower, any obstacles between the tower and your PC, and other factors can negatively affect the reliability and speed of the connection. Most services limit you to a certain number of megabytes or gigabytes per month and charge you for any number of megabytes over that amount.

When shopping for a WISP (wireless Internet service provider) and a wireless modem (adapter), keep the following standards and terminology in mind:

- **Wi-Fi:** For connecting to a wireless network at home or an Internet hotspot, look for modems that support the 802.11g (up to 54Mbps) or 802.11n (theoretically, up to 600Mbps) standard, as explained in Chapter 11.

- **WiMAX:** This is like Wi-Fi, but potentially faster and with a much greater range. Through a wireless ISP that supports WiMAX (802.16), you can connect to the Internet whenever you're in the ISP's coverage area.

- **LTE:** Long Term Evolution (LTE) is similar to and in competition with WiMAX.

- **3G:** 3G is short for 3rd Generation wireless communications technology. WiMAX and LTE both support 3G standards.

- **4G:** This high-performance wireless technology supports downloads of up to 1 gigabyte per second (1GBps) for fixed wireless and 100Mbps for mobile users. This is about 10 times faster than with 3G. As of the writing of this book, WiMAX and LTE were evolving toward the 4G standard, and many communications companies in the United States were offering the LTE version of 4G even though it didn't fully support the standard yet.

When you're in the market for a WISP, check out the major providers first, including AT&T, Verizon, and Sprint. Visit their websites and enter your phone number or location to determine whether the WISP provides coverage for your location and whatever areas you travel to most. (See Figure 18.2.)

**Figure 18.2**
*Check each provider's coverage map.*

## Chugging Along with Dial-Up

Because dial-up is the least expensive and most universally available of the lot, the dial-up modem has managed to hang on, but dial-up really can't compete when it comes to speed:

- **Speed:** You'll get 56Kbps tops, but you're likely to see speeds in the range of 28Kbps to 44Kbps for downloads and slower for uploads.

- **Cost:** Expect to pay $10 to $15 per month.

- **Drawbacks:** S-L-O-W.

Dial-up modems are fairly standard, so any new 56Kbps V.92/V.44 modem from any of the major manufacturers (3Com, Zoom, or U.S. Robotics) can handle the job. If you have an open expansion slot in your PC, consider buying an internal modem. If you'd rather use your PC's expansion slots for something else, purchase a USB model.

Most dial-up modems support voice applications, fax, and videophone, but check the product description if you plan to use those features.

# Shopping for an Internet Service Provider

The best way to shop for an ISP is to ask your neighbors and/or local business associates which ISP they use and how they like it. This way, you know the service is available in your area and you can find out about any customer service issues the company may have.

The second-best way to shop for an ISP is to connect to the Internet and search the web for services in your area. You can use a friend or relative's computer, or head down to the public library and use one of its computers.

If you have no way to shop for an ISP online, employ one of the following old-fashioned techniques:

- **Call your phone company.** Most phone companies offer DSL and wireless Internet service—and if they don't, they'll be able to refer you to a company that does. Also, ask about package deals.

- **Call your cable or satellite company.** If you have cable or satellite TV service, your cable or satellite company probably offers Internet service, too. Ask about package deals, especially if you're already a customer.

- **Look in your Yellow Pages under "Internet."** Most phone books list the ISPs in the area.

# Establishing a Connection

If you're getting a broadband connection through your ISP (such as cable, satellite, or DSL), your ISP is going to schedule a date and time for installation, and the installer will set up your connection for you. You'll have an "always on" connection, in which you remain connected as long as your PC, broadband modem, and router (if you use a router) are turned on.

If you choose dial-up service, the ISP provides you with Internet connection settings you must enter to establish a connection, including a phone number, login name, and password. You must then enter the connection settings in Windows:

1. Click **Start, Control Panel, Network and Internet, Network and Sharing Center.**

2. Below Change your network settings, click **Set up a new connection or network.**

3. Click **Set up a dial-up connection** and click **Next**.

4. Follow the Create a Dial-up Connection wizard's instructions to enter the settings required to establish a connection with your ISP, as shown in Figure 18.3.

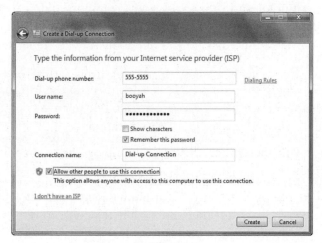

**Figure 18.3**
*Use the Create a Dial-up Connection wizard to enter the dial-up settings.*

With a dial-up connection, your modem must dial in to the ISP and log on to connect before you can access the Internet. When you install software for most ISPs, the installation places an icon on the desktop that you can click or double-click whenever you want to connect. If you don't see an icon for connecting to the service, here's what you do:

1. Click **Start**, **Control Panel**, **Network and Internet**, **Network and Sharing Center**.

2. Double-click the icon for your dial-up ISP. Windows dials in and automatically enters your username and password to log you in.

After you've established a connection, a Dial-Up icon typically appears in the system tray (in the lower-right corner of the Windows desktop). It looks like two overlapping computers. Rest the mouse pointer on the icon to check out your connection speed, or click the icon for additional details. You can right-click the icon and click **Disconnect** to hang up.

# Testing Your Connection Speed

No matter how your computer connects to the Internet, connection speeds can vary depending on the speed of your modem, the condition of the phone and fiber-optic cables, the amount of traffic on the network, and various other factors outside your control. If your Internet connection seems more sluggish than usual, you can check your connection speed at any of several websites:

1. Click the **Internet Explorer** button in the taskbar. The Internet Explorer window appears and then downloads and displays the page it's set up to load upon startup.

2. Click in the address bar near the top of the window, type **http://us.mcafee.com/root/speedometer/default.asp**, and press **Enter**. This connects you to McAfee's Internet Connection Speedometer.

3. Click the **Click here to Test Now** link. The Internet Speedometer sends data to your computer to test your connection speed and then displays the results, as shown in Figure 18.4.

**Figure 18.4**

*You can test your actual connection speed on the web.*

## The Least You Need to Know

- A modem enables your PC to connect to the Internet through an Internet service provider (ISP).

- Cable and DSL Internet services are fast and affordable, satellite is good if you can't get cable or DSL, and wireless Internet is essential if you need to stay connected on the road.

- When you're in the market for an ISP, ask your neighbors or nearby businesses what they use, and contact your cable or satellite TV provider and your phone company to see what they offer.

- Before signing up with a wireless ISP, check its coverage map to ensure that you'll have Internet connectivity where you need it.

- To check the speed of your Internet connection, go to **http://us.mcafee.com/root/speedometer/default.asp** and then click the **Click here to Test Now** link.

# Poking Around on the World Wide Web

## In This Chapter

- Launching your web browser
- Opening specific web pages
- Skipping from one web page to another with links
- Finding stuff on the web
- Bookmarking pages for quick return trips

The single most exciting part of the Internet is the World Wide Web (or web, for short), a loose collection of interconnected documents stored on computers all over the world. What makes these documents unique is that each page contains a link to one or more other documents stored on the same computer or on a different computer down the block, across the country, or overseas. You can hop around from document to document, from continent to continent, simply by clicking these links.

When I say *documents*, I'm not talking about dusty old scrolls or text-heavy pages torn from books. Web documents contain pictures, sounds, video clips, animations, and even interactive programs.

As you'll see in this chapter, the web has plenty to offer, whatever your interests—music, movies, sports, finance, science, literature, travel, astrology, body piercing, shopping, you name it.

## Browsing for a Web Browser

To navigate the web, you need a special program called a *web browser*, which works through your Internet service provider (ISP) to pull up documents on your screen. Windows 7 includes a web browser called Internet Explorer, but plenty of other (free) browsers are available, including Mozilla Firefox (www.mozilla.com), Google Chrome (www.google.com/chrome), Apple Safari (www.apple.com/safari), and Opera (www.opera.com).

To keep things simple, I use Internet Explorer in the examples throughout this chapter. However, if you're using a different browser, don't fret. Most browsers offer the same basic features and similar navigation tools. Be flexible, and you'll be surfing the web in no time.

# Steering Your Browser in the Right Direction

To run Internet Explorer, click its icon (in the taskbar). When your browser starts, it immediately opens a page that's set up as its starting page. (You'll learn how to change your browser's starting page later in this chapter.) You can begin to wander the web simply by clicking links. You can tell when the mouse pointer is over a link because the pointer changes from an arrow into a pointing hand. Click the **Back** button to flip to a previous page, or click the **Forward** button to skip ahead to a page you've visited but backed up from (see Figure 19.1).

Click on link to flip to a page

**Figure 19.1**
*A web browser displays and helps you navigate web pages.*

If you click a link and your browser displays a message that it can't find the page or that access has been denied, don't freak out. Just click the **Back** button and try the link again. If that doesn't open the page, try again later. In some cases, the link may have a typo, the page was moved or deleted, or the service hosting the page is temporarily down. On the ever-changing web, this happens quite often. Be patient, be flexible, and don't be alarmed.

> **WHOA!**
>
> If you're not connected to the Internet when you start your browser, it might display a message indicating that it cannot find or load the page. If you have a standard modem connection, reestablish your connection as discussed in Chapter 18.

# A Word About Web Page Addresses

Every website has an address that defines its location, such as www.si.edu for the Smithsonian Institution or www.walmart.com for Walmart. The next time you watch TV or flip through a magazine, listen and keep your eyes peeled for web addresses. Not only do these addresses look funny in print, but they sound funny, too; for instance, www.walmart.com is pronounced "dubbayou-dubbayou-dubbayou-dot-walmart-dot-kahm."

Web addresses are formally called *URLs* (uniform resource locators). URLs allow you to open specific pages. You enter the address in your web browser, usually in a text box near the top of the window, and your web browser loads the page.

Every web page URL starts with http://. Newsgroup sites start with news://. FTP sites (where you can get or upload files) start with ftp://. You get the idea. HTTP (short for Hypertext Transfer Protocol) is the coding system used to format web pages. The rest of the address identifies a specific site or page. You can omit the http:// at the beginning, and in almost all cases, you can omit the www. as well.

The domain name (site address) is not case sensitive, so joekraynak.com and JoeKraynak.com will both take you to my site, but everything after that might be case sensitive; joekraynak.com/about opens my About page, but joekraynak.com/About results in an error.

# Finding Stuff with Google and Other Search Tools

The web has loads of information and billions of pages, and this vast amount of information can make it difficult to track down anything specific. The web often seems like a big library that gave up on the Dewey Decimal System and piled all its books and magazines in the center of the library. How do you sift through this massive mess of information to find what you need?

The answer: use an Internet search tool. You simply connect to a site that has a search tool, type a couple of words that specify what you're looking for, and click the **Search** button (or its equivalent). The following are the addresses of some popular search sites on the web:

www.google.com          www.yahoo.com

www.ask.com             www.bing.com

Most web browsers have a Search option that connects you to various Internet search tools. Internet Explorer, for example, displays a Search box near the upper-right corner of the window. Simply click in the Search box, type a couple of key words that describe what you're looking for, and click the **Search** button, as shown in Figure 19.2. For more about searching the web Google style, see Chapter 20.

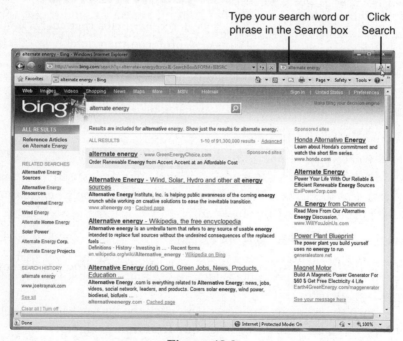

**Figure 19.2**
*Use the Search box to find the desired web content.*

# Locating People Online

You can also use special search tools to find long-lost relatives and friends on the Internet. These search tools are electronic telephone directories that can help you find mailing addresses, phone numbers, and even e-mail addresses. To search for people, check out the following sites:

www.whitepages.com    www.pipl.com

www.spokeo.com       www.anywho.com

www.peekyou.com

The best way to find long-lost friends and relatives, however, is through Facebook, covered in Chapter 22.

# Navigating Multiple Pages with Tabs

Most web browsers, including Internet Explorer, have tabs that enable you to keep multiple web pages open in a single window. You can then quickly switch to a page by clicking its tab.

To open a new tab, click the **New Tab** button, as shown in Figure 19.3, or press **Ctrl+T**. By default, Internet Explorer opens a blank tab. You can then click in the address box and enter a website address to open the desired page.

If you'd rather have Internet Explorer display the page it opens upon startup rather than displaying a blank tab, take the following steps:

1. Click **Tools, Internet Options**. If you don't see "Tools," click **>>** on the right end of the toolbar.

2. Under Tabs, click the **Settings** button.

3. Click the check box next to **Open only the first home page when Internet Explorer starts** to place a check in the box.

4. To open the home page on new tabs, click the button below "When a new tab is opened, open" and then click **Your first home page**.

5. Click **OK**.

Click a tab to display its contents

Enter the address of the page you want to open

Click the tab's Close button to remove it

Click New Tab to add a tab

**Figure 19.3**

*Tabs enable you to open several web pages in a single window.*

**INSIDE TIP**

When clicking links, you can choose to have a link's contents open in a new tab or window. Right-click the link and click **Open in New Tab** or **Open in New Window**.

To have Internet Explorer display a different page upon startup, refer to "Changing the Starting Web Page," later in this chapter.

# Going Back in Time with the History List

Although the Back and Forward buttons eventually take you back to where you were, they don't get you there in a hurry or keep track of pages you visited yesterday or last week. For faster return trips and a more comprehensive log of your web journeys, check out the history list.

Click the **Favorites** button (to the left of the tabs) and click **History**. Click the day or week when you visited the website, and click the website's name to see a list of pages you viewed at that site. To open a page, click its name, as shown in Figure 19.4.

Click Favorites

Click History

Click the website's name

**Figure 19.4**

*Use the history list to retrace your steps.*

If you share your computer with someone, you might not want that person to know where you've been on the web. To cover your tracks, do one of the following:

- Click **Favorites**, **History**; right-click the page, site, day, or week you want to remove; and click **Delete**.

- Click **Tools**, **Internet Options**, **Delete**. Click to place a check box next to each group of items you want to remove and click **Delete**.

# Marking Your Favorite Web Pages

You can add your favorite sites and pages to the Favorites menu for quick return trips. To mark a page, right-click a blank area of the page and select **Add to Favorites**. You can then add and edit the name of the page as it appears in your favorites list, create a new folder (submenu) to store related favorites, and choose the folder where you want to insert your new favorite. When you're done entering your preferences, click the **Add** button. (Other browsers have similar features but may refer to favorites as *bookmarks*.)

**INSIDE TIP**

Right-click a blank area of the page and click **Create Shortcut**. This places a shortcut icon for the page on your desktop.

To quickly open a favorite page, click **Favorites**, click the folder in which you saved the favorite, and then click the page's name.

You can rearrange items on your Favorites menu by dragging and dropping them. If you drag an item over a folder and wait a moment, Internet Explorer opens the folder. You can then drag and drop the item in place.

# Changing the Starting Web Page

Whenever you fire up your browser, it opens with the same page every time. If you have a page you'd like your browser to load upon startup, just let your browser know. To change your starting page in Internet Explorer, take the following steps:

1. Open the page you want to view upon startup.

2. Click **Tools, Internet Options**.

3. On the **General** tab, under **Home page**, click **Use Current**. To open two or more pages upon startup, type the addresses in the Home page text box, one address per line. (Press **Enter** to create a new line.)

4. Click **OK**.

## The Least You Need to Know

- To start Internet Explorer, click its icon in the Windows taskbar.

- Links typically appear as buttons, icons, or specially highlighted text.

- Click a link to load its contents.

- To open a specific page, type its address in the text box near the top of the window and press **Enter**.

- To search for a topic or site on the web, use a search engine, such as www.google.com, and enter a few words to describe what you're looking for.

- To bookmark a page in Internet Explorer, right-click a blank area of the page and select **Add to Favorites**.

# Searching the Web Google Style

## In This Chapter

- Searching for anything and everything on Google
- Browsing the web by category
- Searching for images, video clips, and people
- Using Google in unconventional ways
- Checking out other notable search tools

Google is a search engine—sort of like a web librarian. It finds stuff on the web, indexes it, and then enables people like you and me to search its index to find what we're looking for, including web pages, photos, video clips, maps, and documents.

Performing a basic search on Google is easy and straightforward, but there's much more to it than most people realize.

## Performing a Basic Search

To "google" a topic, go to www.google.com, type a brief description of what you're looking for, and click the **Search** button. Google displays links to web pages it deems are most relevant to what you searched for, as shown in Figure 20.1.

Each item in the search results includes a title, description, address, link to a cached page, and link to similar pages. You can click the title to access the site or page. (A cached page is a backup of a page.)

If nothing on the first page of search results looks promising, you can revise your search or scroll to the bottom of the page, where you'll find links to related searches or the next page of search results.

Web page title

Type a description of what you want    Click Search

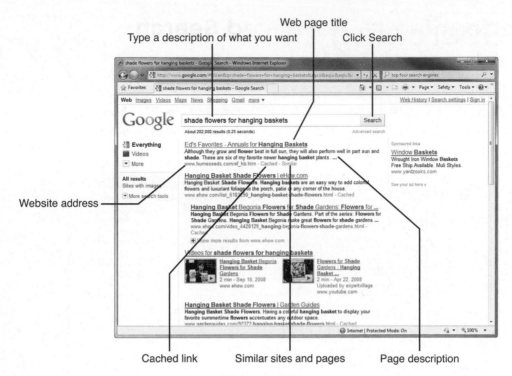

Website address

Cached link            Similar sites and pages        Page description

**Figure 20.1**
*Google a topic of interest.*

**INSIDE TIP**

If your search phrase contains a typo, Google displays search results for pages that include the typo, along with a link (above the search results) that you can click to perform the search again with the correct spelling. Click the link for more accurate results.

# Focusing on Specific Content

You can narrow your search by focusing it on specific content, including images, video clips, blog posts, books, scholarly articles, definitions, and even patents. Before or after performing a search, click one of the content links near the top of the page: **Images**, **Videos**, **Maps**, **News**, or **Shopping**. You can click **More** (to the left of the search results) for additional filter options.

# Performing an Advanced Search

Unless you specify otherwise, Google uses all the words in your search phrase to present you with what it deems most relevant. You can take more control over the results by performing an advanced search. Go to www.google.com and then click **Advanced Search** (to the right of the Search box). Google's advanced search options appear, as shown in Figure 20.2. Enter your search instructions and then click the **Advanced Search** button.

**Figure 20.2**
*Perform an advanced search.*

# Browsing the Website Directory

Most people search Google for specific information and aren't even aware that they can browse Google by category. If you're not sure what you're looking for, this is a great way to find it. Simply head to directory.google.com and then follow the trail of links to the website or page that interests you. (See Figure 20.3.)

**Figure 20.3**
*Browse Google's directory.*

# Adjusting Your Search Settings

Several default settings control the way Google functions and the search results it presents. To check these settings and adjust them, click the **Settings** link in the upper-right corner of any Google page and then click **Search settings**. The Google Preferences page appears, allowing you to enter your preferences for the following options:

- **Interface Language:** Choose the language you want Google to use when displaying text, tips, and messages.

- **Search Language:** Choose the language of the pages you want to see in the results.

- **Safe Search Filtering:** Specify how strict you want Google to be in blocking links to sexually explicit content, including photos and video.

- **Number of Results:** Specify the number of search results you want Google to display per page.

- **Results Window:** You can click the check box to have Google display the search results in a new browser window.

- **Query Suggestions:** You may notice that as you type a search phrase, Google displays a list of search phrases you can choose from so you don't have to keep typing. You can enable or disable this feature.

• **Subscribed Links:** You can subscribe to certain sites to give their content priority in the search results when your search phrase contains specific words. For example, if you subscribe to CalorieLab.com, whenever you include a food item in your search, CalorieLab.com content related to that food item appears at the top of the search results.

When you're done entering your preferences, click the **Save Preferences** button.

# Cool Google Search Tips and Tricks

Google's Search box can perform all sorts of tricks, including presenting the weather for a specific city, displaying conversion rates for different currencies, converting inches into centimeters, and much more, as shown in Table 20.1.

**Table 20.1   Special Google Search Operators**

| To Look Up ... | Type (For Example) ... |
| --- | --- |
| Weather for specific city | weather Chicago, IL |
| Stock quote | ticker BBY |
| Time in city/country | time France |
| News for sports team | New York Yankees |
| Calculation result | (34+27+75)/3 |
| Book author or title | Ralph Waldo Emerson |
| Earthquake activity | earthquake |
| Temperature conversion | 65 Fahrenheit in Celsius |
| Public data | population WY |
| People profile | Sally Strapinski |
| Definition | define: quadruped |
| Local business/restaurant | pizza 60629 |
| Movie showtimes | movies 47933 |
| Health issue | allergy |
| Poison Control Center | poison control |
| Airline departure/arrival | U.S. Airways 504 |
| Currency conversion rate | 300 USD in EUR |
| Map | Boston map |
| Tracking number for package | 1X8888Z99999999 |
| Patent number | patent 4345679 |
| Location based on area code | 812 |

**INSIDE TIP**

To find a business over the phone, try calling 1-800-GOOG-411 (1-800-466-4411)—it's free. When asked, state the business, product, or service, followed by the city and state or zip code, and Google will provide you with the top search results in the area.

# Creating a Google Account

Google has numerous features that require you to have a free Google account, including Gmail (web-based e-mail), iGoogle (personal home page), Picasa Web Albums (for photo sharing), Talk (online chat), and Calendar. To tap Google's full potential, I encourage you to create your own Google account:

1. Head to www.google.com.

2. Click **Sign in** (upper-right corner).

3. Below Don't have a Google Account?, click **Create an account now**.

4. Enter the requested information and word verification, review the Terms of Service, and (if you agree to the Terms of Service), click **I accept. Create my account**.

You can now sign in to Google whenever you like, to take advantage of features and tools too numerous to cover completely in this chapter. Table 20.2 lists website addresses to the most popular features, where you can learn more about them:

**Table 20.2   Popular Google Features and Where to Find Them**

| Feature | Website Address |
| --- | --- |
| Alerts | www.google.com/alerts |
| Free blog | www.blogger.com |
| Bookmarks | www.google.com/bookmarks |
| Calendar | www.google.com/calendar |
| Docs | docs.google.com |
| Gmail | mail.google.com |
| Groups | groups.google.com |
| Customizable home page | www.google.com/ig |
| Maps | maps.google.com |
| Notes | www.google.com/notebook |
| Social network | www.orkut.com |

| Feature | Website Address |
| --- | --- |
| Photo sharing | picasaweb.google.com |
| Web aggregator | www.google.com/reader |
| Subscribed links | google.com/coop/subscribedlinks |
| Chat | www.google.com/talk |
| Videos | video.google.com |

# Checking Out Other Search Sites and Tools

Google is the most popular search engine, but it's not the only one. Some of the other search engines are comparable, while others perform specialized searches. Following are some notable search engines you may want to check out:

- **WhitePages.com** (www.whitepages.com) is excellent for tracking down phone numbers and addresses of individuals and businesses.

- **Yahoo!** (www.yahoo.com) is comparable to Google in connecting you with Yahoo! resources, news, trends, and search.

- **Bing** (www.bing.com) is Microsoft's search engine.

- **Open Directory** (www.dmoz.com) is a hand-crafted, no-frills search directory.

### The Least You Need to Know

- To find anything on the web, go to www.google.com, type one or more words that describe what you're looking for, and click **Google Search**.

- Use the links at the top of any Google page to focus your search on specific content, such as photos or video.

- You can browse Google's directory of websites and pages by going to directory.google.com.

- To look up the definition of a term, type **define:** followed by the term, and press **Enter**.

# Sending and Receiving E-Mail

## In This Chapter

- Addressing and sending e-mail messages
- Checking your electronic mailbox
- Attaching files to outgoing messages
- Following proper e-mail etiquette

How would you like to send a message to a friend and have it arrive in a matter of seconds? Send dozens of messages every day without paying a single cent in postage? Never again stare out your window waiting for the mail carrier?

Well, your dreams are about to come true. When you have a connection to the Internet and an e-mail program, all these benefits are yours. In this chapter, you learn how to start taking advantage of them.

Before you set sail on your maiden voyage, you have a choice to make: do you want to use an e-mail client installed on your computer, access your e-mail via the web, or both? Using an e-mail program installed on your computer allows you to download all incoming messages to your computer and read them at your leisure—regardless of whether you're connected to the Internet. E-mail programs also provide enhanced tools for managing messages. (See the upcoming section "Using an E-Mail Program.") Web-based e-mail offers the advantage of being able to access your e-mail from any computer. You simply use a web browser installed on any computer to connect to the site, log in, and send and receive your messages. (See the "What About Free, Web-Based E-Mail?" section later in this chapter.)

# Using an E-Mail Program

An e-mail program runs on your computer and connects to your Internet mail server to send messages from and receive messages to your PC. You can use any of several programs to access e-mail, including Outlook, Windows Live Mail (download.live.com/wlmail), Eudora (www.eudora.com), and Thunderbird (www.mozilla.com/thunderbird), to name a few.

Versions of Windows prior to Windows 7 include an e-mail program—Outlook Express, Windows Messenger, or Windows Mail. Microsoft Office also includes an e-mail program called Outlook. If you're running Windows 7 and don't have Office, go to one of the websites mentioned in the previous paragraph to download and install the e-mail client of your choice.

In the following sections, I show you how to set up your e-mail account in your e-mail program and use the program to send, receive, and read messages.

## Setting Up Your Account

The hardest part about using an e-mail program is setting it up to connect to your mail server—an electronic post office that routes your incoming and outgoing messages to their proper destinations. To set up your e-mail program, you need the following information from your ISP:

- **E-mail address:** Your e-mail address contains some version of your name or nickname followed by the @ sign and your e-mail server's domain name—for example, jsmith@iway.com.

- **Password:** You pick the password or have one assigned to you.

- **Outgoing mail (SMTP):** The Simple Mail Transfer Protocol (SMTP) server is the mailbox where you drop your outgoing messages. It's actually your Internet service provider's computer. The address usually starts with "mail" or "smtp," as in mail.iway.com or smtp.iway.com.

- **Incoming mail (POP3):** The Post Office Protocol (POP) server is like your neighborhood post office. It receives incoming messages and places them in your personal mailbox. POP server addresses commonly start with pop or mail, as in mail.google.com, but check to make sure.

When you have the preceding information, you must enter it into your e-mail program. To enter e-mail settings in Outlook 2010, click **File**, **Add Account**, and then follow the onscreen instructions to enter your name, e-mail address, password, and any other information required to establish a connection with your e-mail provider.

Figure 21.1 shows the first dialog box in the Add New Account wizard in Outlook 2010. Using your e-mail address and password, Outlook can usually obtain the other settings it requires to access your e-mail server. If it can't connect, you may need to start over and click the option to manually configure your server settings (lower-left corner of the dialog box shown in Figure 21.1).

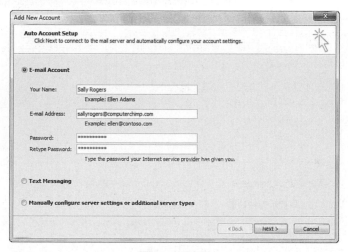

**Figure 21.1**

*Before you can use your e-mail program, you must set up an account.*

## Addressing an Outgoing Message

The procedure for sending messages over the Internet varies, depending on which e-mail program or online service you're using. In most cases, you first click the button for composing a new message. For example, in Outlook 2010, you click the **Home** tab and then the **New E-mail** button and use the resulting dialog box, as shown in Figure 21.2, to address, compose, and send your message.

**NOTE**

Most e-mail programs, including Outlook, feature an e-mail address book or list of contacts. If a contact is in the address book, you simply start typing the person's name or e-mail address in the To box, and the program completes the entry for you. Or, you can click **To** and select the address from the list.

Click to send the message

Type the person's e-mail address

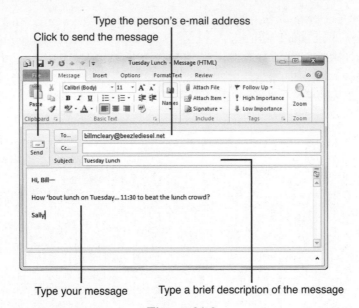

Type your message          Type a brief description of the message

**Figure 21.2**

*Here's how to send mail with a typical Internet e-mail program (Outlook).*

## Checking Your E-Mail

Most e-mail programs check for messages automatically on startup or display a button you can click to fetch your mail (the Send/Receive button in Outlook or the Sync button in Windows Live Mail). The program retrieves your mail and then displays a list of message descriptions. To preview a message, click it, as shown in Figure 21.3. To view the message in its own window, double-click it.

Most e-mail programs use several folders to help you keep your messages organized. For example, Outlook features folders named Inbox, Outbox, Sent Items, and Deleted Items.

To switch from one folder to another, click the desired folder.

Click the message to
preview its contents

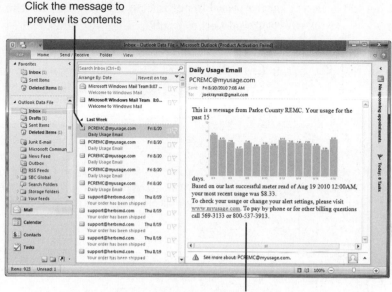

The contents of the message appear in the preview pane

**Figure 21.3**
*You can quickly display the contents of messages you receive.*

## Sending Replies

To reply to a message you received, double-click the message, click the **Reply** button, type your reply, and click **Send**. If you received a message that you want to pass
along to other recipients, you can *forward* the message. Double-click the message you
want to forward, and click the **Forward** button. In the To text box, enter the e-mail
addresses of the people to whom you want to forward the message. If you want to add
an introduction to or comment about the original message, type this text in the message area. When you're ready to forward the message, click the **Send** button.

## Adding Photos and Other Cool Stuff

Almost all e-mail programs, including Outlook, offer a toolbar with buttons for the
most common enhancements. You can use the toolbar to make text bold or italic; add
bulleted and numbered lists; and insert pictures, horizontal lines, links, and other
objects. (If the toolbar does not appear, check the **Format** menu and click the **HTML**
or **Rich Text** option. HTML stands for Hypertext Markup Language, the coding
system used to format web pages. Rich Text is another specification that allows for
fancy formatting in e-mail messages.)

The buttons for inserting pictures and hyperlinks and formatting text work the same way as in your word processing and desktop publishing programs.

To share a link, type the e-mail address or address of the web page you want it to point to and press the **spacebar** or **Enter** key. Most e-mail programs automatically convert web page and e-mail addresses typed in the message area into links. You can also drag links from a web page into the message area and drop them in the message area.

> **WHOA!**
>
> You have no guarantee that the images and formatting you apply will appear in your message when the recipient views it. Many users enable an option in their e-mail programs to view text only. The e-mail program strips out everything but the text.

## Attaching Documents to Your Messages

You can send files along with your messages by creating *attachments*. For instance, if you have a resumé you created in Word, you can e-mail it as an attachment to a friend to review. That person could then open the resumé in Word and view or print it. Without attachments, you would need to copy the text of the resumé and paste it into your e-mail message, losing any formatting you applied to the text and any graphics you inserted.

> **DEFINITION**
>
> An **attachment** is a file in its original condition and format that you clip to an e-mail message. It can be a document, photo, spreadsheet, or any other electronic file.

To send an attachment, compose your e-mail message as you normally do; click the **Attach** or **Insert File** button; and use the resulting dialog box to choose the file you want to send. When you're ready to send the message, along with the attachment, click the **Send** button.

Many word processing and spreadsheet programs have built-in support for e-mail, allowing you to send a document right from the program. In Word 2010, for instance, you can open the document you want to send, open the **File** menu, click **Share**, click **Send Using E-mail**, and click **Send as Attachment**.

If you receive a message that contains an attached file, your e-mail program usually displays some indication that a file is attached. For example, Outlook displays a paperclip icon. If you double-click the message (to display it in its own window), an icon appears at the bottom of the window or in an attachments text box. You can double-click the icon to open the file, or right-click and choose **Save** to save the file to a separate folder on your hard drive.

> **WHOA!**
>
> When you receive an attachment, use an antivirus program to scan the file before opening it (if it's a document) or running it (if it's a program). Programs are especially notorious for carrying viruses, but documents may contain macro viruses, which can cause as much havoc. (Most antivirus programs are set up to run in the background and automatically scan attachments when you choose to open them or save them to disk.)

# What About Free, Web-Based E-Mail?

You've probably heard of "free e-mail" services, such as Gmail (Google Mail), Yahoo!, and Hotmail, and wondered why anyone would need free e-mail. Isn't all e-mail free? Does your ISP charge extra for it? Of course, your e-mail account is included with the service that your ISP provides; your ISP does not charge extra for it. But there are several good reasons to explore these free e-mail services:

- Free e-mail is typically web-based, allowing you to send messages and check your mail from anywhere in the world using any computer that's connected to the Internet.

- Free e-mail lets everyone in your home or business have his or her own e-mail account.

- Free e-mail is good to use when you register "anonymously" for free stuff, keeping your real e-mail address private.

- Free e-mail also provides you with a stable e-mail address so that when you change ISPs, you don't have to change your e-mail address.

To get a free e-mail account, connect to any of the following sites, click the link for free e-mail, register, and follow the instructions at the site to start using your free e-mail account:

| | |
|---|---|
| Gmail | mail.google.com |
| Yahoo! | mail.yahoo.com |
| Windows Live | signup.live.com |
| AOL Mail | mail.AOL.com |

# Emoticons and E-Mail Shorthand

If you want to look like an e-mail veteran, you can pepper your messages with emoticons (pronounced *ee-mow-tick-ons*). These icons look like facial expressions or act as abbreviations for specific emotions. (You might need to turn your head sideways to see the tiny faces.) You can use these symbols to show your pleasure or displeasure with a particular comment, to take the edge off a comment you think might be misinterpreted, and to express your moods.

| Emoticon | Meaning |
|---|---|
| :) or :-) | I'm happy, or it's good to see you, or I'm smiling as I'm saying this. (You can often use this to show you're joking.) |
| :D or :-D | I'm really happy or laughing. |
| ;) or ;-) | Winking. |
| :( or :-( | Unhappy. You hurt me, you big brute. |
| ;( or ;-( | Crying. |
| :\| or :-\| | I don't really care. Straight face. Neutral. |
| :/ or :-/ | Skeptical. Annoyed. |
| :# or :-# | My lips are sealed. I can keep a secret. |
| :> or :-> | Devilish grin. |
| :p or :-p | Sticking my tongue out. |
| <g> | Grinning. (Usually takes the edge off whatever you just said.) |
| <lol> | Laughing out loud. |
| <jk> | Just kidding. |

In addition to the language of emoticons, Internet chat and e-mail messages are commonly seasoned with a fair share of abbreviations. The following table offers samples of the abbreviations you'll encounter and be expected to know.

| Abbreviation | Meaning |
|---|---|
| AFAIK | As far as I know. |
| AFK | Away from keyboard. |
| BRB | Be right back. |
| BTW | By the way. |
| CUL8R | See you later. |
| F2F | Face to face (usually in reference to meeting somebody in person). |

| Abbreviation | Meaning |
|---|---|
| FAQ | Frequently asked questions. (Many sites post a list of often asked questions, along with the answers. They call this list a FAQ.) |
| FTF | Another version of "face to face." |
| FYI | For your information. |
| IDK | I don't know. |
| IMHO | In my humble opinion. |
| IMO | In my opinion. |
| IOW | In other words. |
| KISS | Keep it simple, stupid. |
| LOL | Laughing out loud. |
| NM, NVM | Never mind. |
| OIC | Oh, I see. |
| ROTFL | Rolling on the floor laughing. |
| TTFN | Ta ta for now. |
| TTYL | Talk to you later. |

# E-Mail No-No's

To avoid getting yourself into trouble by unintentionally sending an insulting e-mail message, be sure you use the proper protocol for composing e-mail messages.

The most important rule is to NEVER, EVER TYPE IN ALL UPPERCASE CHARACTERS. This is the equivalent of shouting, and people become edgy when they see this text on their screen. Likewise, take it easy on the exclamation points!!!

Avoid sending bitter, sarcastic messages (flames) via e-mail. When you disagree with somebody, a personal visit or a phone call is usually more tactful than a long e-mail message that painfully describes how stupid and inconsiderate the other person is. Besides, you never know who might see your message; the recipient could decide to forward your message to a few choice recipients as retribution.

Also in a business or educational e-mail, use correct spelling and grammar. Abbreviations for words or sentences, such as CUL8er (for "see you later"), and emoticons may be acceptable in text messaging and e-mailing friends, but they're taboo in formal circles.

If you're in marketing or sales, avoid sending unsolicited ads and other missives. Few people appreciate such advertising. In fact, few people appreciate receiving anything that's unsolicited, cute, "funny," or otherwise inapplicable to their business or personal life. In short, don't forward every little cute or funny e-mail message, "true" story, chain letter, joke, phony virus warning, or free offer you receive.

Finally, avoid forwarding warnings about the latest viruses and other threats to human happiness. Most of these warnings are hoaxes, and when you forward a hoax, you're just playing into the hands of the hoaxers. If you think the warning is serious, check the source to verify the information before you forward the warning to everyone in your address book. Virus hoaxes are posted at www.symantec.com/avcenter/hoax.html and vil.nai.com/vil/hoaxes.aspx.

## The Least You Need to Know

- To set up a new e-mail account in Outlook, click **File**, **Add Account**, and follow the onscreen instructions.

- To create a new e-mail message, click the **Compose Mail** or **New Message** button or its equivalent in your e-mail program.

- Incoming e-mail messages are often stored in the Inbox. Simply click the **Inbox** folder and click the desired message to display its contents.

- To reply to a message, select the message and click the **Reply** button.

- To attach a document to an outgoing message, click the button for attaching a file and select the desired document file.

- DON'T TYPE IN ALL UPPERCASE … and follow all the other rules of proper e-mail etiquette.

# Connecting with Friends and Family on Facebook

**Chapter**

# 22

## In This Chapter

- Grasping the essence of Facebook
- Getting on Facebook and finding your friends
- Navigating Facebook
- Sharing posts, photos, videos, and more
- Adjusting your privacy settings

Everyone these days seems to be on Facebook … everyone except you. Well, that's about to change. It's high time you join your friends and family in the twenty-first century. This chapter introduces you to Facebook, shows you how to register and log in, and then takes you on a nickel tour to get you up to speed on the basics.

## What Is Facebook, Anyway?

Facebook is a free online, social networking venue where friends, family, colleagues, and acquaintances can mingle, get to know one another better, and expand their social circles.

After you register and log in to Facebook, as explained in the following section, you can invite people you know to join you on Facebook and become your friends. Any friends already on Facebook can invite you to become their Facebook friends, too. (The whole making friends thing is covered later in this chapter.)

Once you have a Facebook friend or two, you can begin exchanging notes by posting status updates to your News Feed, as shown in Figure 22.1. A status update essentially tells your Facebook friends what you're doing, thinking, or feeling. Your News Feed is a running record of status updates and more posted by you and your friends. The "and more" can include photos and video clips that you and your friends post, links to interesting stuff on the web, notes you create, results of quizzes and polls you participate in, and more.

News Feed

**Figure 22.1**
*Your News Feed keeps you in the loop.*

That's Facebook in a nutshell, but you can do much more than swap text messages with your buddies. Following are some of the more popular activities you may want to engage in:

- Dig up old friends and classmates and family members who've wandered from the fold

- Expand your social and professional circles by connecting with friends of friends and current and former co-workers

- Share photos, videos, and links to interesting web pages

- Recommend books, movies, and music

- Exchange birthday wishes and gifts

- Play games

- Spread the word about political causes and charities

- Invite guests to parties and other get-togethers, and keep track of who's planning to attend

- Chat with your friends online

- Buy and sell stuff, find a job, and market yourself or your company

# Putting Your Face on Facebook

Before you can join in the revelry, you have to put your face (and name) on Facebook by registering—entering your e-mail address, choosing a password, and providing some basic information about yourself:

1. Fire up your web browser and head to www.facebook.com.

2. Complete the Sign Up form.

3. Click **Sign Up**. Facebook may display a security check screen prompting you to type a string of characters shown on the screen.

4. If a security check appears, type the text that appears as directed, click **Sign Up**, and follow the onscreen instructions to complete the registration process.

After you register, Facebook steps you through the process of finding friends, entering basic information like schools you've attended and places you've worked, and uploading a digital photo of yourself. This serves two purposes: it fleshes out your profile so you're more three-dimensional on Facebook, and it helps your friends, relatives, and acquaintances track you down.

If you're not comfortable making this information public, you can change the settings to prevent others from seeing the information. See "Adjusting Privacy Settings" later in this chapter for details.

# Touring Facebook

After registering, you can log in to Facebook at any time by heading to www.facebook.com and entering your e-mail address and password. When you log in, Facebook gets in your face with all the buttons, bars, links, icons, and menus you need to access everything, as shown in Figure 22.2. This opening screen can seem a little overwhelming at first. This section highlights the main areas you need to focus on and then describes them in more detail.

You can log out of Facebook at any time by clicking **Account** (upper right) and then **Logout**.

Left menu    Core features

Notifications    Top menu

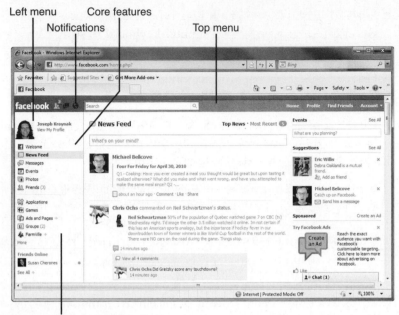

**Figure 22.2**
*Facebook's interface.*

## Scooting Up to the Top Menu

The top menu is Old Reliable. It appears at the top of the screen no matter where you are or what you're doing on Facebook, providing quick access to the following features (from left to right on the bar):

- **facebook:** Clicking the **facebook** icon takes you home—to the screen that greets you when you sign on.

- **Friend Requests:** Click **Friend Requests**, and a menu drops down displaying any Facebook members who are asking to be your friend. The menu also contains a Find Your Friends link to search for your friends on Facebook.

- **Messages:** Click **Messages**, and Facebook displays a list of messages you received from other Facebook members. The menu also contains the Send a New Message link to compose and send a message to someone on Facebook.

- **Notifications:** Click this to see a list of friends who do something notable on Facebook that pertains to you.

Games and bookmarked applications

- **Search:** Click in the **Search** box, type a search word or phrase, and press **Enter** or **Return** on your computer keyboard to search Facebook for people, places, things, or help with a particular feature.

- **Home:** This takes you to your Home page, where you can view your News Feed.

- **Profile:** Clicking this displays your Profile page, where you can access your Wall, information about yourself, your photo albums, and other items of interest. More about the Wall later in this chapter.

- **Account:** The Account menu enables you to configure Facebook by adjusting account settings, privacy settings, application settings, and more. Here you'll also find options for getting help and logging out.

## Catching Up on Your News Feed

The News Feed is the core component of Facebook, providing you with a running account of just about everything you and your Facebook friends are up to and have agreed to share with one another.

You can switch your News Feed to display Top News or Most Recent by clicking the desired option just above the News Feed. Top News displays a list of what Facebook deems are the most interesting posts from your Facebook friends. Most Recent displays all your friends' posts, starting with the most recent.

## Checking Out the Publisher

At the top of your News Feed is your own personal Publisher. Whenever you want to post something to your News Feed, click in the Publisher's text box (the box containing "What's on your mind?"), type your message, and click **Share**. In addition to text messages, you can post photos, videos, links, event announcements, notes, and other stuff you want to share.

## Exploring the Left Menu

The left menu contains links for the most popular features on Facebook, besides the News Feed, including the following:

- **You:** At the top of the left menu is your mug shot (assuming you added one), your name, and a link called Edit My Profile. Click any one of these, and Facebook displays your Profile page or takes you to the profile editor.

- **Core features:** The next section down provides links to gain quick access to the four core Facebook features: News Feed, Messages, Events, and Friends.

- **Applications and Games:** This section contains links to Facebook's collections of applications and games, along with links to popular Facebook applications (apps for short), including ads, pages, and groups (discussion areas).

- **Friends Online:** If friends are currently logged in to Facebook, their names appear here. Click a friend's name to start chatting with that person. Chat is a form of instant messaging in which you carry on a conversation by "texting" one another.

If you don't want to chat, you can go offline, making yourself invisible to your friends—click **Chat** (lower-right corner of the screen), **Options**, **Go Offline**.

# Adjusting Your Privacy Settings

Before you post much information about yourself on Facebook, you should know what sorts of information Facebook shares with others and adjust your privacy settings to your comfort level. To access your privacy settings, click **Account**, **Privacy Settings**. Use the options on the resulting screen, as shown in Figure 22.3, to set your privacy preferences.

Customize your settings

**Figure 22.3**
*Review your privacy settings.*

# Being Friends on Facebook

On Facebook, Friends have benefits. They can communicate with one another via the News Feed and Wall, share photos and videos, invite one another to events, chat, play games together, and much more. To take full advantage of Facebook, you first need to become friends with at least one other Facebook member.

## Befriending and Defriending

Whenever you want to be someone's Facebook friend, you must send the person a friend request. That person can then choose to confirm your request (accept your invitation) or ignore it. When someone sends a friend request to you, you have the same options. Facebook and your existing Facebook friends can also recommend Facebook members you may know.

To find prospective friends on Facebook, click **Friends** (left menu). This displays your Friends page, complete with any friend requests you received but haven't responded to, people you may know (and may want to friend), and a Search for People text box (near the bottom) that you can use to track down people you know by name or e-mail address.

When you find someone you want to friend, sending a friend request is a snap. Click the person's name or photo, click **Add as Friend**, and then click **Send Request**. Assuming the person confirms your request, you become Facebook friends.

## Visiting Walls

Facebook Walls enable friends to communicate more directly with one another, but still in a public setting. Instead of posting a message to your News Feed where a specific friend is less likely to notice it, you can post your message on the friend's Wall, where your friend is very unlikely to miss it.

To access a friend's Wall, simply click the person's name or photo wherever you happen to see it. You can then post something to your friend's Wall just as you post content to your News Feed. This generates a "story" in your News Feed and your friend's News Feed so that any of your mutual friends can check it out.

To access your own Wall, click **Profile** (top menu).

## Checking Out Profiles

Unless you indicate otherwise, most of your profile information is readily accessible to all your Facebook friends. This includes Basic Information, Personal Information, Contact Information (address and phone number, but not your e-mail address, unless you choose to share it), Education and Work experience, and a list of any groups you've joined. (A group is a discussion forum exclusively for members of the group.)

To check out your profile, click **Profile** (top menu). To change information in your profile, click **Edit My Profile**. The resulting screen provides options for changing your basic information, profile picture, relationship status, likes and interests, education and work information, and contact information.

## Defriending Someone

If someone you friended is particularly annoying or you no longer consider the person a friend, you can remove the individual from your inner circle. Click the person's name or photo to pull up his or her profile, scroll to the bottom of the left column, click **Remove from Friends**, and then click **Remove from Friends** again to confirm. Facebook does not notify members removed from friends, but a member is likely to notice at some point.

# E-Mailing Your Facebook Friends

When you have something to say specifically and exclusively to one of your Facebook friends, the last place you want to post it is in your News Feed or on your Wall where everyone can see it. To communicate privately, use Facebook's Messages.

You can send a message to just about anyone on Facebook. Just click the member's name or photo wherever you happen to see it to pull up the member's profile. Below the member's profile picture, click **Send So-and-So a Message**. Add a subject, type your message, and click the **Send** button.

When you receive messages, the **Messages** icon (top toolbar) displays the number of unread messages you've received. Click the icon to view a list of recently received messages; then, click the message you want to read. (You can view all messages by clicking the **Messages** icon and then clicking **See All Messages**, at the bottom of the menu.)

# Help! Navigating Facebook's Help System

Although we cover the most important stuff you need to know to use Facebook, we can't cover everything in such a limited space. If you need help with something that's not covered in this book, head to Facebook's Help system. Click **Account**, **Help Center**. Click an icon for the feature you need help with, shown in Figure 22.4.

Search for answers

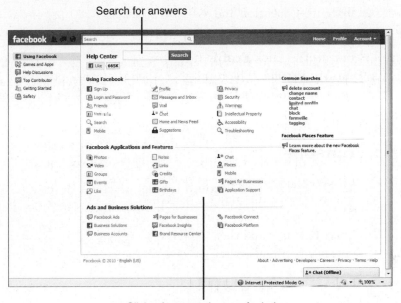

Click a feature to browse for help

**Figure 22.4**

*Facebook's Help Center has an icon for each of the most common features.*

The Help System includes a tab for Getting Started (in the left menu)—a great place for newbies to learn how to find friends, set up a profile, and navigate Facebook. The Safety tab offers guidance for protecting yourself and any teenagers you're responsible for on Facebook.

# Quitting Facebook

For whatever reason, should you decide that you want out of Facebook, you have two exits: you can deactivate your account or delete it.

## Deactivating Your Account

Deactivating your account leaves all your stuff intact. If you quit and get homesick for Facebook, you can always pick up where you left off. To deactivate your account, here's what you do:

1. Click **Account, Account Settings**.

2. In the lower-right corner of the Settings box, click **Deactivate**. Facebook displays the guilt screen, complete with photos of all the friends who will miss you very, very much. Don't look.

3. Scroll down the page to the deactivation options.

4. Click the reason that best describes why you're leaving Facebook.

5. (Optional) Click in the **Please explain further** box and type any additional explanation you'd like to pass along to the folks at Facebook. (Be nice, or at least respectful.)

6. (Optional) If you want to stop receiving e-mail notifications from Facebook whenever your friends invite you to do something or send you a message, click **Opt out of receiving future e-mails from Facebook**.

7. Click the **Deactivate My Account** button. Facebook deactivates your account and displays a message informing you how to return later if you change your mind.

# Deleting Your Account

Deleting an account is a more serious and long-term decision. Everything in your account is erased, including your photos, notes, list of friends, and so on. It's like getting rid of all your stuff and entering a witness-protection program.

If you're sure you want to delete your account, it's pretty simple. Head to https://ssl.facebook.com/help/contact.php?show_form=delete_account, click the **Submit** button, and respond to any confirmation warnings as desired. You're outta there.

## The Least You Need to Know

- To join Facebook, head to www.facebook.com, enter some basic information about yourself, click the **Sign Up** button, and follow the onscreen instructions.

- Post to your News Feed when you want to keep all your friends in the loop. Post to your friend's Wall to communicate more directly to an individual. Send a message to communicate with a friend privately.

- Click **Home** or the **facebook** logo (in the top menu) to return to the place you started when you logged on to Facebook.

- Deactivating a Facebook account does not remove your information. You must delete your account to be completely free of Facebook.

# Sharing Video on YouTube

## In This Chapter

- Finding and watching videos on YouTube
- Getting a few perks with a free YouTube account
- Customizing your home page and channel
- Sharing your own videos
- Getting help

Forget about ABC, CBS, and NBC. YouTube is way more popular, providing you with free access on demand to an unlimited selection of video clips 24/7. Simply head to www.youtube.com, click a link for a video that looks interesting, and then kick back and watch. Of course, you can do a lot more on YouTube, which is what this chapter is all about.

# Searching and Browsing on YouTube

When you go to www.youtube.com, the opening screen displays a sample collection of video clips that members recently added, none of which you may find particularly interesting. If nothing catches your eye, or if you're looking for a specific type of video, you can search for items or browse YouTube's video collection.

## Searching for Specific Video Footage

When you know what you're looking for, or at least have a vague notion, click inside the **Search** box (near the top of the page), type one or more words describing what you're looking for, and then click the **Search** button. YouTube displays a collection of video clips that match your description, as shown in Figure 23.1. Click a clip to play it.

Type one or more descriptive words     Click Search

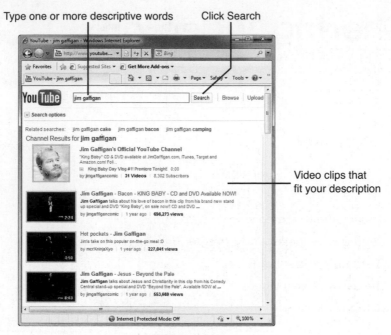

Video clips that
fit your description

**Figure 23.1**

*Search for specific video clips.*

## Browsing YouTube's Video Collection

To browse YouTube's video collection by category, click the **Browse** button near the top of any YouTube page and then click the double down arrow button to the right of Videos/All categories. Click the category of your choice and then use the resulting screen to browse the videos in the selected category. (See Figure 23.2.)

If you click any of the major categories near the bottom of the Categories list, such as Shows or Movies, the Search button changes, so you can limit your search to the selected category. For example, if you click **Movies**, the Search button changes to Search Movies. Click in the Search box, type one or more words describing the movie, and click **Search Movies**.

**INSIDE TIP**

To return to YouTube's opening page, click the YouTube logo in the upper-left corner of any YouTube page.

Categories list          Click Browse     Click to see
                                          most viewed

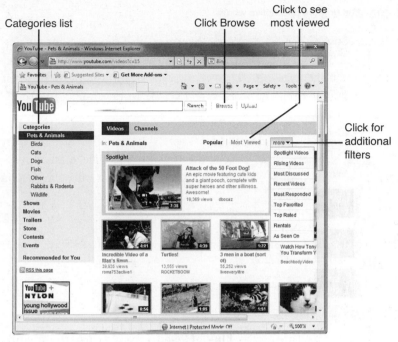

Click for
additional
filters

**Figure 23.2**
*Browse videos by category.*

# Doing More Through a YouTube Account

You can watch most videos without joining YouTube, but if you want to do more than that, create an account, which allows you to do the following:

- Enable YouTube to keep track of the videos you watched so it can recommend other videos you might enjoy.

- Flag videos as your favorites, so you can quickly return to them later.

- Rate (thumbs up or down) and comment on videos.

- Subscribe to channels. (A channel is a collection of videos uploaded by a specific individual on YouTube.)

- Customize your YouTube home page.

- Upload and share your own videos with millions of other YouTube users.

## Creating an Account

To create an account, click the **Create Account** link (upper-right corner), complete the form, and click **I accept**. When YouTube prompts you for your e-mail address, complete the form by entering your e-mail address and the password you want to use (and confirming it), typing the word verification, and then clicking the **Create New Account and Finish**.

YouTube e-mails you a confirmation message. When you receive it, open the message and click the link to activate your account and verify your e-mail address. This opens YouTube in your web browser and automatically logs you into your account.

**NOTE**

You can sign in to YouTube with your Google account and password. For more about Google, see Chapter 20.

## Signing In and Signing Out

You can sign in to YouTube at any time. Head to www.youtube.com and click the **Sign In** link (upper right). Type your username and password in the corresponding boxes. To remain signed in after you exit YouTube, make sure the **Stay signed in** box is checked, or remove the check mark if you want YouTube to sign you out automatically when you leave. Click the **Sign in** button.

If you share your computer with other users, you may want to sign out when you're done watching videos. To sign out, click the **Sign Out** link (upper right).

## Saving Your Favorites

When you come across an amazing video that you're probably going to want to watch again or share with others, add it to your list of favorites. Click the **Save to** button (below the video) and click **Favorites**, as shown in Figure 23.3.

To view a video on your Favorites list, click your username (upper right) and click **Favorites**. This displays a list of your favorites. Click the **Play** button for the favorite you want to watch. (You can remove a video from your list of favorites by clicking the **Remove** button, to the lower right of the favorite.)

Click Save to    Click Favorites

**Figure 23.3**

*Add a video to your list of favorites.*

## Creating Additional Playlists

Your list of favorites is your default *playlist*. You can create additional playlists to more effectively organize your favorite videos. To create a playlist, pull up a video you want to add to the playlist, click the **Save to** button (below the video), and click **Create a new playlist**, as shown in Figure 23.3. Type a name for the new playlist and press **Enter**.

To add a video to your new playlist, pull up the video, click the **Save to** button, and then click the name of the playlist you want the video added to.

## Subscribing to a Channel

If you really like a video, chances are good that you'll enjoy other videos the person has uploaded. Just above the video, click the member's username to access his or her channel. Here you'll find links to any other videos the member has uploaded, along with the member's favorites and playlists (assuming that the person is not preventing them from being shared). To subscribe to the member's channel, click the **Subscribe** button at the top of the page or above any video the member has uploaded.

To manage your subscriptions, click the YouTube logo (upper left), click your user-name (upper right), and click **Subscriptions**.

## Sharing a Video with Others

When you see an incredible (or incredibly funny) video, your first impulse may be to share it with others you think will like it. YouTube provides options that make it easy to share videos via e-mail and on numerous social networking sites, including Facebook and Twitter. To share a video, click the **Share** button, click the desired share option, and follow the onscreen cues to complete the process.

## Rating and Commenting on Videos

Below every video are a thumbs up (Like) button, thumbs down button, and Respond to this video box. Click the thumbs up or thumbs down button to cast your vote for or against the video. To comment on the video, click in the **Respond to this video** box, type your comment, and press **Enter**.

If you feel the video is inappropriate, click the **Flag** button (off to the right), select the reason you think the video is inappropriate, and then click the **Flag this video** button.

# Sharing Your Videos

You may not be Cecil B. Demille or James Cameron, but you can play a more active role on YouTube by contributing (uploading) your own video footage taken using a camcorder, digital camera, or even cellphone. You shoot the video, copy it to your computer, edit it, save it as a file, and then upload the file to YouTube. The following sections show you how to deal with the uploading step. For more about transferring video to your computer, editing it, and saving it as a file, see Chapter 32.

If you have a functional webcam attached to your computer, YouTube also enables you to record video on the fly directly into YouTube.

**WHOA!**

YouTube has a detailed list of rules and regulations governing the content users can post. Don't post sexually explicit video or video that shows bad stuff, including child or animal abuse, drug abuse, underage drinking or smoking, bomb making, gratuitous violence, racist comments, and so on. I encourage you to read YouTube's Community Guidelines at www.youtube.com/t/community_guidelines before uploading any videos.

## Prepping a Video for Uploading

Before uploading a video, edit and save your video to a file that adheres to YouTube's video specifications:

- No longer than 10 minutes

- No larger than 2 gigabytes

- Saved in one of the following file formats:
  .WMV (Windows Media Video)    .3GP (cellphones)
  .AVI (Windows)                .MOV (Mac)
  .MP4 (iPod/PSP)               .MPEG
  .FLV (Adobe Flash)            .MKV (h.264)

Your video editing program, such as Windows MovieMaker or Apple iMovie, enables you to edit and compress video, and should allow you to save the video in one of the acceptable formats. (Keep in mind that compression negatively affects the quality of the video.)

## Uploading Your Video to YouTube

After you've prepped your video and have a suitable file to upload, the actual process of uploading it is a snap:

1. Click the **Upload** link (near the top of the page). If the Upload link isn't there, click the YouTube logo in the upper-left corner of any YouTube page to go to your home page, and then click the **Upload** link.

2. Click the **Upload video** button.

3. Choose the video file you want to upload, and click **Open**.

4. Complete the Video information and privacy settings section, as shown in Figure 23.4, and click **Save changes**.

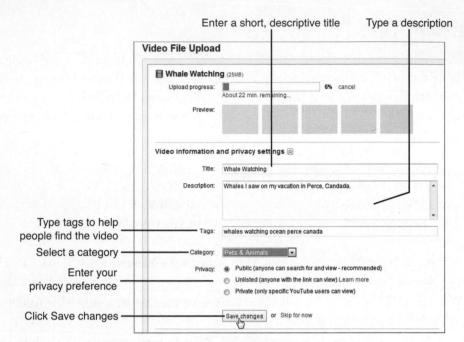

**Figure 23.4**
*Upload a video.*

## Recording a Video with a Webcam

If you have a functioning webcam connected to your PC, you can use it to record live video and instantly upload it to YouTube. Here's how:

1. Click the **Upload** link near the top of the page.

2. Click **Record from webcam.**

3. If an Adobe Flash Player Settings box appears, click **Allow** to give it access to your webcam, click **Remember,** so you won't be asked again, and then click **Close.** Whatever's in front of the camera should now appear in the record area on the screen.

4. Position yourself or whatever you want to "film" in front of your webcam, click the **Record** button, and do your thing.

5. If something bad happens while you're recording, click **Stop** and then **Restart.**

6. When you're done recording, click the **Stop** button.

# Getting Help

You can do more on YouTube than this chapter covers. To learn about additional features or to obtain assistance using a feature, check out YouTube's help system. Scroll to the bottom of almost any YouTube page and click the **Help** link. You can then search the help system for a specific topic or browse to learn more about YouTube.

## The Least You Need to Know

- To search for videos on YouTube, click in the **Search** box (top of the page), type one or more words to describe what you want, and then click the **Search** button.

- To browse YouTube's video collection, click the **Browse** link (to the right of the Search button).

- Register for a free account so you can save your favorite videos for future viewing and personalize YouTube.

- To save a video as a favorite, click the **Save to** button (below the video) and click **Favorites**.

- To upload a video of your own, click the **Upload** link (at the top of almost every YouTube page) and follow the onscreen cues to complete the process.

- To get help, scroll to the bottom of almost any YouTube page and click the **Help** link.

# Passing Notes on Twitter

## In This Chapter

- Creating and logging in to your Twitter account
- Reading and replying to someone else's tweet
- Posting tweets with or without links
- Following others on Twitter and checking out who's following you
- Personalizing Twitter's appearance

In the twenty-first century, hearing it through the grapevine usually means reading it on Twitter. Twitter is a social networking tool that enables users to share very brief text messages (140 characters or less), commonly referred to as *tweets*. At any time of the day or night, hundreds of millions of Twitter users are in the process of sharing tweets with one another, creating a global buzz. This chapter shows you how to join in the chorus of tweeters 'round the world.

# Creating a Twitter Account and Signing In

Before you can do anything on Twitter, you must create an account and sign in. The following sections show you how.

## Creating a Twitter Account

To create a Twitter account, head to twitter.com and click the **Sign Up** button. Complete the Join the Conversation form, shown in Figure 24.1. If you don't want to receive e-mail updates from Twitter, click the check box next to **I want the inside scoop** to remove the check mark. Click the **Create my account** button.

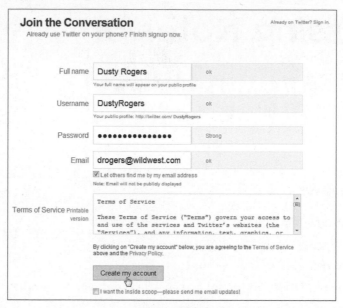

**Figure 24.1**
*Create your account.*

When Twitter asks "Are you human?" click in the **Type the words above** box, type the validation text displayed on the page, and click **Finish**. Twitter creates your account, signs you in, and displays a list of topics you can explore. Before you do that, however, confirm your account. Check your e-mail for a confirmation message from Twitter. When you receive the message, open it and then click the link for confirming your account. Twitter grants you full access to the service and displays its home page.

## Signing In and Signing Out

To sign in to Twitter, go to twitter.com, click the **Sign in** button (upper right), enter your username or e-mail address and password in the designated text boxes, and click the **Sign in** button.

When you're done on Twitter, consider signing out, especially if you're sharing the PC—you don't want just anyone tweeting using your username and identity. To sign out, click the **Sign out** link (upper-right corner).

## Fleshing Out Your Profile

Unless you add more information about yourself, the only thing identifying you on Twitter is your Twitter name. To give yourself more of a presence and improve your chances of connecting with more people, consider fleshing out your profile with a picture, location, website address, and bio. Click **Settings** (upper right), **Profile**, and use the Profile Settings screen, as shown in Figure 24.2, to upload a profile picture and add details about yourself. When you're done, click the **Save** button.

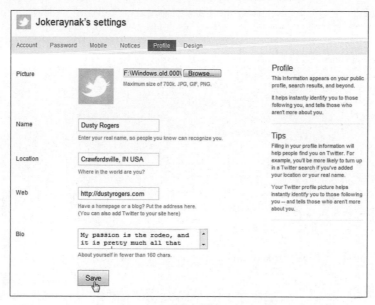

**Figure 24.2**
*Add a picture and details to your profile.*

### Tweaking Your Account Settings

Before you post any of your own tweets, you may want to check out your account settings and perhaps make some adjustments. Click **Settings** (upper right) and then **Account**. You can use the Account Settings screen to change your username, e-mail address, language preference, time zone, location, and tweet privacy preference. You can also choose to let others find you by searching for your e-mail address. Enter your preferences and click the **Save** button.

# Reading and Replying to Tweets

To get a feel for the Twitter community and tweeting, read some tweets and perhaps reply to a tweet or two before posting your own tweets. The following sections show you how.

## Reading a Tweet

When you're interested in learning what others think about a particular topic, you can read all about it on Twitter. On twitter.com, click in the search box, type one or more words describing the topic, and then click the search button, as shown in Figure 24.3.

Twitter displays a list of recent tweets (most recent first) that match the topic description you searched. To see more tweets on this topic, scroll to the bottom of the list and click **more**.

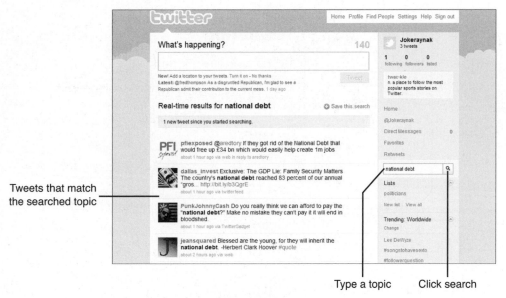

Tweets that match the searched topic

Type a topic    Click search

**Figure 24.3**
*Search for tweets.*

Every tweet contains the name of the person who posted it, followed by a brief message. You can click the member's name to view more tweets by that individual. Below each message is an indication of the time that has passed since the message was posted. A tweet may also contain any of the following:

- A link (or abbreviated link) to a web page or blog post the person wants you to check out.

- An "at" sign (@) followed by a link, indicating that the tweet you're reading is actually a reply to someone else's tweet. To read the original tweet, click **in reply to [person's Twitter ID]**, or if this isn't available, click the link to the right of the @ sign.

- A link preceded by a hashtag (#), indicating a group or extra information. Click the link to view other tweets tagged for inclusion in this group.

- A retweet icon at the beginning of the tweet (just to the right of the person's profile picture with two arrows making a square).

> **INSIDE TIP**
>
> If you're probably going to search for this same topic in the future, click **Save this search** (above the list of tweets that match your search phrase). Saved searches appear in the navigation bar on the right—simply click the link for the saved search whenever you want to repeat it.

## Replying to a Tweet and Retweeting

Twitter is all about interacting with others—engaging in conversations. If a tweet inspires you to respond in some way, mouse over the tweet and click **Reply**, as shown in Figure 24.4. The What's happening? box becomes the Reply to so-and-so box, and Twitter starts you off by adding the @ sign followed by the member's username. Type your reply and then click the **Tweet** button.

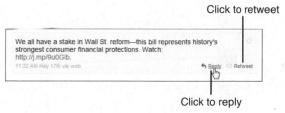

**Figure 24.4**
*Reply or retweet.*

Another way to respond to a message is to retweet it—spread the word by passing the tweet along to all of your followers. Of course, when you're just starting out, you probably have few (if any) followers, so retweeting may not make much sense right now. When you do have some followers, here's how you retweet: mouse over the tweet you want to retweet, click **Retweet**, and then click **Yes** to confirm.

You can always delete a reply or undo a retweet. To delete a reply you posted, mouse over the reply and click **Delete**. To undo a retweet, mouse over the tweet you retweeted and click **Undo**.

## Flagging a Tweet as a Favorite

When you come across a tweet you'll probably want to return to later, mark it as a favorite. Simply mouse over the tweet and click the hollow star that appears to the upper right of it. The star turns solid gold, and Twitter adds the tweet to your list of favorites. To view your favorites, click **Favorites** (in the navigation bar on the right).

# Posting Tweets

Posting a tweet is a snap. Click in the **What's happening?** box and type a message (140 characters or less). As you type, Twitter displays the number of characters remaining, as shown in Figure 24.5—a negative number means you're over the limit. When you're done typing, click the **Tweet** button. Twitter posts your tweet and displays it on your home page.

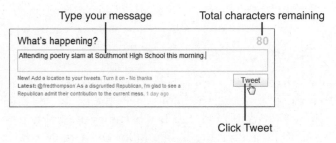

Type your message          Total characters remaining

What's happening?                                    80

Attending poetry slam at Southmont High School this morning.

New! Add a location to your tweets. Turn it on - No thanks
Latest: @fredthompson As a disgruntled Republican, I'm glad to see a        Tweet
Republican admit their contribution to the current mess. 1 day ago

Click Tweet

**Figure 24.5**
*Twitter's home page.*

## Adding a Link

Many tweets consist of a brief message that introduces a web page or blog entry followed by a link to that page or entry. (For more about blogging, see Chapter 28.) To insert a link into your tweet, type the web page address or copy the address from your browser's address box and paste it in your message. (You do not need to include the http:// at the beginning of the address.)

When you click the **Tweet** button, Twitter automatically converts the address into a link prior to posting your tweet, so anyone reading it can simply click the link.

**NOTE**

A long URL can consume a huge portion of your allotted 140 characters. Consider using a free URL abbreviation service, such as bit.ly, to truncate the URL for you. Visit bit.ly for details.

## Deleting a Tweet

You can't edit a tweet, so if you make a mistake or want to remove your tweet for any reason later, delete it. Sign in to Twitter and rest the mouse pointer on the tweet you want to delete. In the lower-right corner of the tweet, a trash can icon appears with the Delete link next to it. Click **Delete** and then click **OK** to confirm.

# Following Users on Twitter

Twitter users who share common interests can choose to follow one another. Friends often use Twitter sort of like Facebook to keep in touch with one another. You and your friends can choose to follow one another—whenever you post a tweet, all your friends are notified. You can also follow complete strangers or politicians, celebrities, athletes, and anyone else who chooses to tweet in public.

To follow someone on Twitter, mouse over his or her username and click the **Follow** button, as shown in Figure 24.6. Whenever you want to check the person's tweets, click **following** (near the top of the navigation bar).

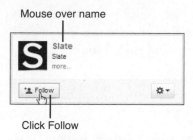

**Figure 24.6**
*Follow someone on Twitter.*

## Searching for People on Twitter

Twitter can help you track down people, businesses, or organizations you may want to follow, assuming they're on Twitter. Click **Find People** (near the top of any Twitter page). In the **Who are you looking for?** box, type the person's or organization's name or e-mail address, and then click **Search**. Scroll down the list, if necessary, to find the individual or organization you're looking for. You can then click the user's name to read tweets or click the **Follow** button to follow that person.

## Seeing Who's Following You

If you have friends on Twitter or post such interesting tweets that complete strangers take an interest, you may begin to gather a following. To see who's following you, click **followers** (near the top of the navigation bar). For each follower, Twitter displays the following three buttons:

- The Follow button enables you to follow the person who's following you.

- The list button enables you to add users to lists to make them more manageable. See the next section for more about lists, including how to create them.

- The third button opens a menu with options for mentioning so-and-so in a tweet, sending the person a direct message (sort of like e-mail), following the person, blocking the person, or reporting the person for spamming you.

## Exchanging Direct Messages in Private

You can send a direct message privately to anyone who's following you. Direct messages are sort of like a cross between an e-mail and a tweet. They're private like e-mail, but brief like tweets. To send a direct message, take one of the following actions:

- From your home page, click **Direct Messages** (right navigation bar), open the **Send _____ a direct message** list, select the desired recipient, type a message in the box, and click **Send**.

- Click **followers** (right navigation bar), click the button to the far right of the desired recipient's name, and click **Direct message so-and-so**. Type your message and click **Send**.

- Click in the **What's happening?** box and type **d+username+message**, dropping the @ symbol; for example, **d JoeKraynak What are you working on?** Click the **Tweet** button. As soon as you type **d** followed by a space, the "What's happening?" changes to "Direct message."

> **INSIDE TIP**
>
> To reply to a follower's tweet with a private message instead of a public response, click **Reply** (below the tweet you want to respond to), replace the @ sign with a *d* followed by a space, type your message after the person's username, and click **Tweet**.

# Learning More About Twitter

This chapter provides you with all you need to know to start using Twitter, but the more you know, the more you'll get out of it. I encourage you to check out Twitter's help system. Just click **Help** near the top of any page to access Twitter's Help Center.

## The Least You Need to Know

- To search for tweets about a specific topic, click in the search box (right navigation bar), type a topic description, and click the search button.

- To post a tweet, click in the **What's happening?** box, type your message (140 characters or less), and click **Tweet**.

- To reply to a tweet, mouse over it, click the **Reply** button, type your reply, and click **Tweet**.

- To follow someone on Twitter, mouse over the person's username and then click the **Follow** button.

- To personalize Twitter, edit your profile, change your account settings, and more, click **Settings** at the top of most Twitter pages and use the resulting options to enter your preferences.

# Communicating One-on-One in Real Time

## In This Chapter

- Instant-messaging friends and relatives with AIM
- Videoconferencing for free with AIM and similar free services
- Making free (or cheap) phone calls with Skype
- Checking out other ways to communicate online

Your PC is no replacement for an iPhone or Android, but when you're sitting in front of a PC equipped with a webcam and microphone, you can do everything you can do with a cellphone and then some … and for a lot less money. Using programs like AOL Instant Messenger (AIM), Google Talk, and Skype, you can communicate in real time with anyone, anywhere in the world via texting, Internet phone, and even video calling, all for free. This chapter shows you how.

## Instant Messaging with AIM

America Online's Instant Messaging program, AIM, is the most popular program of its kind. Millions of people, probably including some of your friends and relatives, use it daily to keep in touch with one another. In the following sections, you learn how to download a free copy of AIM to your PC, install it, and start using it to communicate with your other computer-savvy pals.

### Getting Started with AIM

Most IM programs, including AIM, are free for the taking. You don't even need an AIM account. You can use an existing e-mail address, including the address you use to sign in to Facebook. To download and install a copy of AIM and (optionally) create a username that identifies you on the AIM network, take the following steps.

1.  Connect to the Internet and start your web browser.

2.  Click in the Address bar, type **www.aim.com**, and press **Enter**. AIM's home page appears.

3.  Click **Download AIM**.

4.  When asked whether to run or save the installation file, click the **Run** button.

5.  Follow the onscreen instructions to download and install AIM and set a username and password. (I recommend doing a custom installation so you can see a list of optional components and choose whether to install them.)

AIM starts automatically after you install it and whenever Windows starts. If you exit the program and decide to restart it later, click **Start**, **All Programs**, **AIM**, and click the icon for running AIM. When AIM starts, it prompts you to enter your username and password.

Type your username and password in the appropriate boxes. To have AIM remember your password so you don't have to enter it next time, click **Remember me** and **Remember my password** to place a check in each box. You can also click **Automatically sign me in** and/or **Sign in as invisible** (so your buddies won't know you're online until you want them to). Click the **Sign In** button to go online. At this point, anyone who knows your username can contact you by sending you a message, assuming that you're not invisible.

You can make yourself visible or invisible after signing on. Click the button to the left of your username and choose the desired online status:

*   **Available** lets your buddies know that you're online and taking calls.

*   **Away** lets your buddies know that you're online but away from your PC right now.

*   **Mobile** enables you to set up and turn on IM forwarding so that any instant messages your buddies send you are forwarded to your cellphone.

*   **Invisible** keeps you hidden so your buddies don't know you're online.

## Building a Buddy List

AIM provides a feature called the *buddy list* that enables you to keep track of the people with whom you most commonly interact. To add a buddy to your list, click the **Buddy List** tab, and then click the **+Add** button (just below the tabs) and click

**Add Buddy.** The New Buddy window appears, as shown in Figure 25.1. Enter the necessary contact information and your buddy's AIM username and click **Save**. (If you're wondering what an ICQ number is, ICQ is another instant messaging program AIM supports.)

Click the **Buddy List** tab, and then click the **+Add** button (just below the tabs) and click **Add Buddy**. The New Buddy window appears, as shown in Figure 25.1.

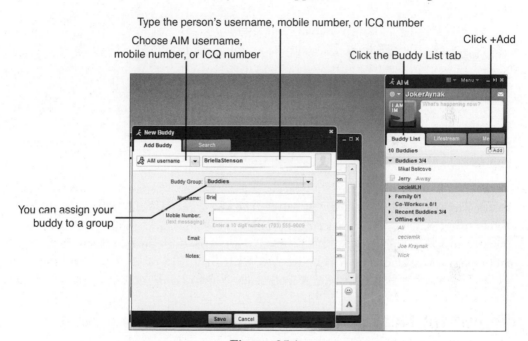

**Figure 25.1**
*Add a buddy to your buddy list.*

**INSIDE TIP**

If you have loads of buddies, create your own buddy groups to make your buddy list less crowded and overwhelming. To create a new group, click the **+Add** button, click **Add Group**, type a descriptive name for the group, and click **Save**.

## Instant Messaging

Whenever you sign on to AIM, AIM checks to see which of the people on your buddy list are currently online and willing to accept messages. When a buddy is online, you simply double-click that person's username in your buddy list and start chatting, as shown in Figure 25.2.

Type your message here and press Enter

Conversation appears here

**Figure 25.2**
*Start sending instant messages!*

In addition to typing text, you can format the text to use a different type style, shrink or enlarge the text, add enhancements such as bold and italics, apply highlighting, insert a link to a web page, or even insert small icons that represent your current emotional state. Click the smiley face icon to display a list of available icons for expressing your mood. Click the **A** icon to view formatting tools.

## Audio Instant Messaging

To engage in audio instant messaging with a buddy who has the proper equipment (speakers and a microphone), double-click your buddy's name; then click the camcorder icon and click **Start an Audio IM**. Your buddy then needs to click **Accept** to answer the "phone."

## Video Instant Messaging

By equipping your computer with an affordable webcam, you can engage in video calls with colleagues and loved ones. To initiate a video call with AIM, click the camcorder icon and then click **Start a Video IM**. A message pops up on your buddy's screen inviting him or her to a video chat. Assuming that your buddy accepts the invitation, his or her image appears on your screen, as shown in Figure 25.3, and your image appears on your buddy's screen.

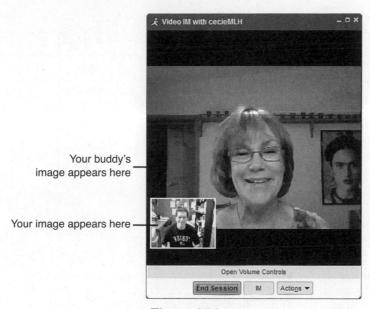

Your buddy's image appears here

Your image appears here

**Figure 25.3**
*With video chat, you and your buddy can see and hear one another chat.*

## Texting a Buddy's Mobile Phone

If your AIM buddies have mobile devices with Internet access, you can text them right from AIM, and they can text you back. First, you must enter your buddy's mobile phone number. Right-click your buddy's name and click **Edit Buddy**. Click in the **Mobile Number** box, type the person's 10-digit U.S. phone number, and click **Save**.

To text the person, right-click his or her name and click **Text Message (SMS)** or press **Alt+Shift+T**, type your message, and press **Enter**. AIM sends the text message to your buddy's mobile device, and the person can then reply to you.

## Getting AIM for Your Cellphone

You can stay in touch with your buddies when you're away from your PC by opening the availability list (to the left of your username) and clicking **Mobile**. When a buddy sends an instant message to your username, the message is automatically forwarded to your cellphone; you can text back a reply, but you can't initiate a discussion.

For additional features, consider logging in to AIM TXT. To log in, text "login" to 246246 and then reply with your username and password. You can then text any of the commands (or their corresponding numbers) listed in Table 25.1 to 246246.

**Table 25.1  AIM TXT Commands**

| Command | To | Example |
| --- | --- | --- |
| login | log in to AIM | login |
| 1 or logout | log out | logout |
| 2 or status | update your status | status home team just took the lead |
| 3 or send | send IM to buddy | send at the mall where are you? |
| 4 or avail | appear as available | avail or what's happening? |
| 5 or away | appear as online but away | away or stepping out for 30 mins |
| 6 or invis | appear offline | invis or at lunch |
| 7 or bl or buddy list | display list of buddies in your Mobile Device group | bl |
| 8 or switchsn | log in with different username | switchsn |
| 9 or help | view examples of AIM TXT commands | help |
| add | add a buddy to your Mobile Device group | add chuck4032 |
| del | delete a buddy from your Mobile Device group | del chuck 4032 |

If you're in the market for a better way to connect your mobile device to AIM, consider purchasing an AIM app. AIM is available for the iPhone, Android, iPad, Blackberry, and other mobile devices. Head to products.aim.com and scroll to the bottom of the page to access links for AIM apps.

# Sampling Other Chat/Instant Messaging Clients

Although AIM may still be the most popular instant messaging client and chat network around, it's certainly not the only option—and it's not necessarily the best. Following are some other online chat/instant messaging clients you may want to check out, along with website addresses where you can go to learn more about them:

- Yahoo! Messenger, at messenger.yahoo.com

- Google Video Chat and Google Talk, at www.google.com/talk

- Windows Live Messenger, at download.live.com/messenger

- Facebook Chat (see Chapter 22)

If you have a diverse group of friends all using different instant messaging clients, conversing with all of them may mean installing and juggling several different clients.

Fortunately, apps that let you access and use multiple services within a single app are available, enabling you to manage and communicate with all your buddies and friends from one account. Following are a few multiprotocol clients you may want to check out:

- Digsby (www.digsby.com)
- KoolIM (www.koolim.com)
- Meebo (www.meebo.com)
- Miranda (www.miranda-im.org)
- Pidgin (www.pidgin.im)
- Trillian Astra (www.trillian.im)

# Placing Really Cheap (or Free) Phone Calls with Skype

If you're traveling to foreign lands or have friends on the opposite side of the globe, the best way to talk to them is to use Skype or an instant messaging program that supports PC-to-PC and PC-to-phone calling.

For quite a while, the only game in town was Skype, and I think it's still the best, but other players are now competing in this space, including Windows Live Messenger and Yahoo! Messenger. The following sections introduce you to the basics of Skype. Competing services function pretty much the same way.

**WHOA!**

If you're wondering what's free and what's not, Skype offers free PC-to-PC calls (audio and video) and instant messaging for Skype users. Skype charges for PC-to-phone calls, and calling a mobile phone costs significantly more. Check www.skype.com for more pricing details and special deals.

## Getting Skype

To get Skype on your PC, head to www.skype.com, click **Get Skype**, click **Get Skype for Windows**, and follow the onscreen cues to download and install Skype. (When you click the button to download Skype, a security bar may appear near the top of your browser window. If it does, click the bar to proceed with the download.) When asked whether to run or save the downloaded file, click the **Run** button.

When the installation is complete, Skype leads you through the process of creating a new Skype account, creating a Skype username, and entering the e-mail and password you want to use to sign in.

To sign in to Skype, click **Start**, **All Programs**, **Skype**, **Skype**, type your login name and password in the appropriate boxes, and then click **Sign in**. The first time you sign in, a welcome screen appears with buttons you can click to learn the basics, test and set up your equipment (speakers, microphone, and webcam), and find Skype members you may know. If the people you want to call don't have Skype accounts, encourage them to sign up.

## Adding Contacts

Skype features several ways to add contacts using a person's Skype username, e-mail address, or phone number:

- **Find people using a list of contacts:** Click **Directory** and then click the **See friends who are already on Skype** link. Use the resulting dialog box to find friends on Facebook, AOL, or Gmail, or in your Microsoft Outlook address book, and then add them as contacts.

- **Find someone you know:** Click **Directory**, click in the **Type Skype name** box, type the person's full name or e-mail address, and click **Search**. If the name of the person you're looking for appears in the list near the bottom of the window, double-click it to add it as a contact.

- **Add a phone number:** Click **New**, **New Contact**. Click the **Save a phone number in your contact list** link (near the bottom). Type the contact's name in the **Name** box, as shown in Figure 25.4. Open the drop-down list and choose Mobile, Home, Office, or Other. Click the flag and select the country you'll be calling. Click in the phone number box and type the person's phone number. Click **Save phone number**.

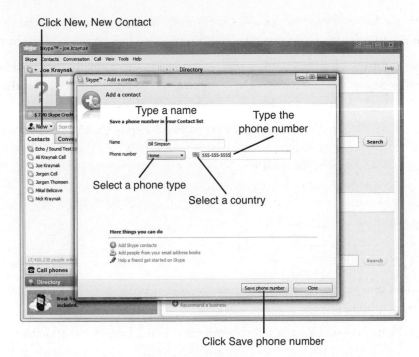

**Figure 25.4**
*Add a contact's phone number.*

## Making Free Skype-to-Skype Calls

You can call, video-call, or instant-message any of your contacts who also use Skype for free, assuming that the person is online, signed on to Skype, and sitting at his or her computer. To place a Skype-to-Skype (PC-to-PC) call, click the person's name in your Contacts list, click the **Skype** tab (if it's not already selected), and then click the **Call** or **Video call** button, as shown in Figure 25.5.

Click the contact's name    Click Call or Video call

**Figure 25.5**
*Place a Skype-to-Skype call for free.*

Skype places the call, and a notification appears on the screen of the person you called. He or she can then answer with or without video or deny the call. Use the buttons near the top or bottom of the call pane to mute your microphone, adjust the volume, turn video on or off, adjust other settings, or hang up, as shown in Figure 25.6.

Mute/unmute    Adjust    Turn video
microphone    volume    on or off

Modify other call settings

**Figure 25.6**
*Manage your call session.*

## Cheap Long Distance with PC-to-Phone Calls

Prior to placing PC-to-phone calls, you need to place some money in your account. Click the **View account** button (upper left) or open the **Skype** menu and click **Account**; then use the resulting screen to buy credits or a subscription:

- **Buy more credit:** For the pay-as-you-go plan, click **Buy more credit** and use the resulting screen and your credit card to add money to your account. As you make calls, money is deducted from your balance.

- **Buy a subscription:** Click the link to find out more about subscriptions and use the resulting web page to purchase a monthly subscription. This enables you to make unlimited calls for a month for a flat monthly fee at a considerably lower per-minute rate.

To place a PC-to-phone call, click the name of the person you want to call in your Contacts list, click the tab for the phone you want to dial, and click the **Call** button, which may appear as Call Phone, Call Home, Call Mobile, or Video Call. When the person answers (or you get the message machine), start talking. When you're done, click the **End call** button (the red button with the phone on it).

## The Least You Need to Know

- Most instant messaging programs allow you to send instant messages to others who use the service and talk with them for free via voice and video.

- To get started with AIM, download the instant messaging client from www.aim. com.

- To add a contact in AIM, click the **+Add** button and then **Add Buddy**, use the resulting dialog box to enter contact information, and click **Save**.

- To contact a buddy who's online, double-click your buddy's name and use the resulting window to exchange text messages or initiate a voice or voice+video call.

- To make free PC-to-PC calls and cheap long-distance calls worldwide, try Skype, at www.skype.com.

# Buying and Selling Stuff Online

## In This Chapter

- Gauging the safety of shopping online
- Finding great deals on comparison-shopping sites
- Becoming a savvy Internet shopper
- Booking travel reservations online
- Buying and selling stuff on eBay and Craigslist

The World Wide Web is home to one of the largest free-market economies in the world. At any time of the day or night, 7 days a week, 365 (and sometimes 366) days per year, you can find millions of people buying, selling, and giving stuff away online. And because the competition is so stiff among sellers, you can often find better deals online than what local brick-and-mortar discount stores offer.

In this chapter, I introduce you to the wonderful world of online shopping and reveal some of the best places to go and strategies to use to find great deals online.

**WHOA!**

Don't automatically assume that just because you're buying something online, you're getting a better deal than what local stores are offering. You must still perform your due diligence and compare prices. In addition, buying online usually means you pay shipping fees, which can boost the price of goods higher than what you'd pay locally.

## Is It Safe?

Generally speaking, shopping online is about as safe as shopping offline. If you head out to your local shopping mall, for example, you take the risk that someone will break into your car, steal your purse or wallet, or even sneak a peak at the name and number on your credit card.

You face similar risks online, but you face these risks whether you shop online or not. As you'll discover in Chapter 29, con artists often phish for information by sending e-mails prompting you to log on to phony sites and supply sensitive information about your accounts.

You can reduce the risks by taking the following precautions:

- Shop only on sites you trust. Buying merchandise from a reputable online retailer like Amazon.com is generally much safer than placing an order on an individual seller's website.

- If you're buying from a little-known company, search the web to find out anything you can about the company. If other shoppers have been burned by that company, they usually post something on the web warning others.

- Enter your name, credit card number, and other sensitive information only on secure websites. You can tell whether a site is secure by looking at the address bar in your browser. The address of a secure site begins with "https" rather than "http." Your web browser may also display a lock icon near the top or bottom of the browser window to indicate that a site is secure.

- If you receive an e-mail message asking for account information, be highly skeptical. Legitimate companies rarely request account information via e-mail or ask that you log in to a website to verify account information.

- Don't place orders on a shared computer. Any information you enter on the shared computer could be stored for future use. If it is, someone else can log into the site where you placed the order and access your account information.

- Pay for orders with a credit card or an escrow service such as PayPal, rather than using a debit card, so you have the opportunity to cancel the order or at least file a dispute if you don't receive your order or are dissatisfied with it. Credit card companies are usually pretty cooperative and successful in ensuring customer satisfaction.

- Overall, trust your instincts. If a deal sounds too good to be true, it probably is. If a website asks for your Social Security number, birthday, driver's license number, or other information that's rarely needed to process a transaction, it's probably up to no good.

# Comparison-Shopping for the Real Deals

Savvy shoppers always compare prices, and you can compare prices online, too. However, several comparison-shopping sites can do all the legwork for you and display a list of merchants who offer the same or similar products.

Check out the following popular comparison-shopping sites; many also offer product reviews to help you make your decision:

- Shopzilla (www.shopzilla.com; see Figure 26.1)

- Google Product Search (www.google.com/products)

- PriceGrabber (www.pricegrabber.com)

- NexTag (www.nextag.com)

- BizRate (www.bizrate.com)

- MonsterMarketplace (www.monstermarketplace.com)

- mySimon (www.mysimon.com)

- CNET Shopper.com (shopper.cnet.com; check it out for computers, cameras, and electronics)

**Figure 26.1**
*Shopzilla is one of many comparison-shopping sites you can find online.*

# Buying Online

The procedure for shopping at most online stores is fairly standard—you find the product you want, check out the product details and what other consumers have to say about it, click a button to order the product or place it in your shopping cart, and check out by entering your payment and shipping information. Figure 26.2 pretty much captures the online shopping experience, except for the part when you have to enter your credit card and shipping information. Most dedicated shopping sites make finding and ordering items very intuitive.

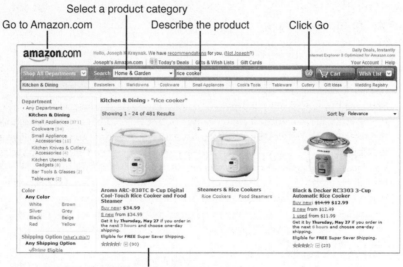

**Figure 26.2**

*You can search for specific products on Amazon.com.*

After you've successfully placed your order, Amazon sends you a confirmation e-mail describing what you ordered, the price of each item, the shipping cost, and your grand total.

# Booking Travel Reservations Online

If you do any traveling, whether for business or pleasure, you can often save considerable amounts of money by serving as your own travel agent and booking your reservations online. Several companies offer one-stop shopping for airline tickets, hotel and motel accommodations, and car rental. Visit the following sites to see what they have to offer:

- Kayak (www.kayak.com)
- Expedia (www.expedia.com)
- Orbitz (www.orbitz.com)
- Yahoo! Travel (travel.yahoo.com)

- Travelocity (www.travelocity.com)
- Hotwire (www.hotwire.com)
- Priceline (www.priceline.com)

Don't stop at simply making reservations online. Plenty of websites offer free information and resources on just about any destination you can imagine. You can go online and check Eurorail routes and schedules and buy your Eurorail pass online, visit museum websites to plan which exhibits you'd like to see, explore an area's hottest attractions to figure out what you'd like to do, find the best restaurants and entertainment, and much more.

> **INSIDE TIP**
>
> Some websites specialize in providing information about your preferred mode of travel. For example, Hobo Traveler (www.hobotraveler.com) can show you how to travel around the world even if you have no travel budget to speak of. If you're looking to trim your travel budget by staying in lower-priced accommodations, visit Hostels.com (www.hostels.com), where you can obtain information about hostels located in just about every country. You can also find sites that specialize in timeshare rentals, cruises, and other special travel opportunities.

# Buying and Selling on eBay

Even if you've never placed a bid or purchased anything on eBay, you've probably heard about it. eBay bills itself as "The World's Marketplace," where its eager community of online sellers and buyers from all around the world gather to buy, sell, and trade products every day. When most people think of eBay, however, they think "online auction," and even though eBay now has its own eBay Stores, it still serves primarily as an online auction.

In the following sections, I step you through the process of buying and selling stuff on eBay, including how you pay for items you buy and collect money for items you sell.

## Buying Stuff on eBay

Most people get their first taste of eBay by bidding on and eventually purchasing an item. The process is very similar to buying a product on Amazon.com or from any online store, except that you set the maximum price you're willing to pay for an item. In the following sections, I step you through the process of buying something on eBay. (You can also buy some stuff without bidding if the seller enables the Buy It Now option.)

You don't need to be an eBay member to window-shop on eBay. Point your web browser to www.ebay.com. A Search bar appears at the top of the opening page. Click in the Search box and type one or more words to describe what you're looking for. To narrow the search to a specific category of products, open the Categories list and click the desired category. Now click the **Search** button. eBay displays a list of items that match your description, as shown in Figure 26.3.

Describe the product                Click Search

Products that match your search

**Figure 26.3**
*eBay can help you find what you're looking for.*

Before placing a bid on an item, click the item that interests you to display more information about it. Check the product description to determine whether the item looks and sounds like the product you want.

Also click on the seller's feedback score to view information about the person who has listed the product for sale. eBay encourages buyers to rate sellers and provide feedback so that future buyers know how trustworthy or untrustworthy a particular seller may be. You'll also find a link you can click to ask the seller questions about the product or about payment, shipping, or customer service.

Placing a bid is very easy. Click in the **Your maximum bid** box, type your bid amount, and click the **Place bid** button, as shown in Figure 26.4. (Below the Your maximum bid box is the minimum amount you can enter to place a bid. The seller can specify how much each bid must be over the current bid in order to be acceptable.)

Click Watch this item to add it to your Watch list

Type your maximum bid here

Product description

Click Place bid

Information about the seller

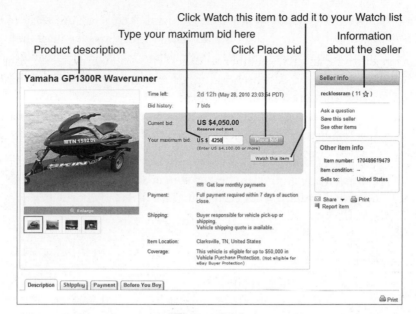

**Figure 26.4**
*You can learn more about the item and the seller and place a bid.*

After you place your bid, eBay refreshes the page to show your bid amount as the high bid (or inform you that other eBay users have already bid higher). In a matter of seconds, someone else can enter a higher bid, so if you really want the item, you'll need to keep a careful watch on the bidding activity. You can click the **Watch this item** button to have eBay add the item to a list of items you're interested in. This makes it easier to follow what you're bidding on.

After you win an auction or choose to Buy It Now, eBay sends you and the seller an e-mail message confirming the transaction. Your e-mail message contains a Pay Now button. Click the **Pay Now** button and follow the onscreen instructions to submit your payment.

**INSIDE TIP**

Most eBay sellers accept PayPal payments, so if you plan to make regular purchases, I strongly recommend that you set up a PayPal account at www. paypal.com. PayPal is an escrow service that protects (hides) your primary account information. You fund your PayPal account from your bank or credit card account and use PayPal to buy products, pay vendors, send money to relatives or friends, and so on. The person you pay never sees your bank account or credit card information. PayPal also protects against fraud and insures you against unauthorized payments from your account.

After you receive the item(s) you purchase, remember to return to eBay to rate and provide feedback to the seller. Not only do these ratings and feedback help other eBay buyers determine whom they can trust, but positive feedback helps sellers become more successful. Sellers often succeed or fail based on their feedback ratings.

## Selling Stuff on eBay

eBay began as a tool to help collectors of Pez dispensers swap dispensers online. From there, it evolved into more of an online flea market, where people would try to sell their collectibles and anything else they no longer wanted to store in their basements or attics. (There's still a lot of that going on.) Now eBay also provides a forum where professional retailers can sell brand-new products.

> **WHOA!**
>
> Before you list an item for sale, do some research to find out the going price of the item or similar items and see how other sellers are marketing these items online. Using other sellers' marketing materials (photos and product descriptions) is a no-no, but existing product listings can give you some ideas of what works and what doesn't.

When you have something for sale, all you have to do is take a photo of it, write a description of it, log on to eBay, and list the item. Keep in mind, however, that eBay charges listing fees, whether or not your item sells. You pay an *insertion fee* to list an item for sale. This fee varies depending on the type of item and the starting bid or reserve price (the lowest bid you'll accept), but it ranges from 25¢ to $2. The *final value fee* is calculated as a percentage of the purchase price (rates vary; check eBay's help system, where you can find a link to learn more about seller fees).

To sell something on eBay, rest the mouse pointer on **Sell** (upper-right corner of the page), click **Sell an Item**, and follow the onscreen instructions as eBay steps you through the process. eBay assists you in determining how much the item you're selling is probably worth, choosing a category for the item, entering a description, uploading photos, specifying the shipping fee, and so on. See Figure 26.5.

After you list an item, you can monitor your auctions to observe the bidding process. When the auction is over, you receive an e-mail message informing you of the winning bid. The buyer then submits the payment, and you package and ship the product.

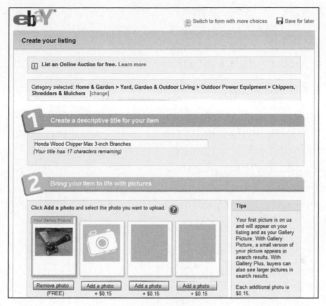

**Figure 26.5**
*eBay makes it easy to list items for sale.*

# Checking Out Craigslist

Another popular (and free) online shopping venue is Craigslist, which is essentially a free online classifieds service. Craigslist members can list products and services for sale (or for free), job openings, positions wanted, rooms for rent, roommates wanted, and so on, just as in a newspaper's classifieds section. Visitors to Craigslist can then e-mail the person who posted the listing to finalize the transactions.

To see what Craigslist has to offer, point your web browser to www.craigslist.org and click the link for your city (or the nearest city). You'll see a screen similar to Figure 26.6 that displays the available listings, grouping them by category. Follow the trail of links to find what you're looking for, and use the online help to find out how to post your own listings.

When you join Craigslist, you enter your e-mail address, but this address does not appear on your listings. All correspondence is handled behind the scenes, so you get to choose the people you pass along your contact information to.

**Figure 26.6**
*Craigslist offers free classifieds for nearly every major city in the world.*

## The Least You Need to Know

- To shop safely online, stick with well-established stores and place orders only on secure websites, indicated by the closed lock in your browser's notification area, until you gain more experience.

- Comparison-shopping sites such as Shopzilla and PriceGrabber can help you track down the best deals.

- Buying something online usually consists of finding what you want, checking the product details, adding the item to your shopping cart, and checking out.

- On eBay you can buy and sell items through an auction, the Buy It Now option, or an eBay Store.

- On Craigslist, you can browse and post ads to sell products and services in your area.

# Touring Message Boards, Mailing Lists, and More

## In This Chapter

- Reading and posting on message boards
- Signing up for mailing lists or newsletters
- Staying up-to-date with RSS news feeds

The Internet enables people to share common interests in slightly less personal ways through message boards, mailing lists, newsletters, and RSS feeds. With message boards, people post messages where anyone (or members only) can read them. On message boards, you can commonly find answers, solutions, guidance, support, and camaraderie without having to know someone's e-mail address or screen name. With mailing lists and newsletters, organizations can keep members posted of the latest news and information, notify members of upcoming events, and call members to action. And with RSS feeds, you can create your own custom resource that updates itself from all your favorite sources of information!

In this chapter, you learn how to stay in the loop with all these powerful communication tools.

## Pulling Up Message Boards on the Web

Many websites have their own message boards (commonly called *discussion groups* or *forums*)—online bulletin boards where people can read and post messages. To access a message board, simply click its link and follow the trail of links until you come upon a list of posted messages, as shown in Figure 27.1. (To keep out the riffraff, many sites require you to register to gain access to their message boards, but it's usually free.)

**INSIDE TIP**

Many online services have their own discussion groups. You can access Google groups at groups.google.com. To access Facebook groups, sign in to Facebook and then click **Groups** (left menu).

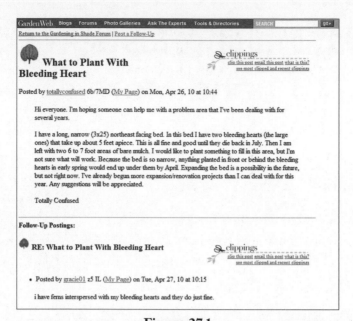

**Figure 27.1**

*A message board enables users to read and post messages.*

To read a message, click the message description or whatever link the site provides for reading the message. You can then reply to the message by posting a response (in most cases) or reply to the originator of the message via e-mail (in some cases). (See Figure 27.2.) You can also choose to start a new discussion by posting your own message. The steps vary depending on the message board, but they're usually fairly intuitive.

**Post a Follow-Up**

**User Name:** joetheimpatien      [If you aren't joetheimpatien, please click here.]

Zone (optional): 5

**Subject of Posting:** RE: Shade in garden!

**Message:**

    I live in the woods, so growing plants in the shade has
    become my specialty. My favorites are bleeding hearts,
    foxfire, hostas, and ferns. In the summer in areas with a
    little more sun, impatiens (especially New Guinea
    impatiens), begonias, and Coleus seem to do well. If you
    have a large area to cover, lilies of the valley are a
    great choice, but they'll quickly take over and crowd out
    the other plants.

**Optional Link URL:**

**Name of the Link:**

    Preview Message

**Figure 27.2**

*Post your reply.*

# Registering for Newsletters and Mailing Lists

Many websites have a huge following and thousands of members and other interested parties. Rather than communicating with members individually, a site often enables members and sometimes even nonmembers to subscribe to its mailing list or newsletter. You typically click a link to subscribe to the site and then enter your name and e-mail address and perhaps some additional information, as shown in Figure 27.3.

**Woodworking Tips Mailing List**

This site is always expanding, and we're always adding new content. We want to keep you up to date and let you know when a new article has been added to the site.

This mailing list is separate from Gregory Paolini's Furniture & Cabinetry mailing list, and caters specifically to you, the woodworking enthusiast! If you are signed up on the Furniture mailing list already, please make sure you sign up for woodworking tips here!

By Subscribing, You will receive an e-mail when ever the "Woodworking Tips" web site is updated.     The information you provide will NEVER be shared or Disclosed

Please provide the following contact information:

|                          |                        |
|-------------------------:|:-----------------------|
| *Name*                   | Joe Kraynak            |
| *City*                   | Laguna Beach           |
| *State/Province*         | CA                     |
| *Country*                | USA                    |
| *email\**                | joe@lagooneyB.com      |
| *How Did You Hear About Us?* | Web search at Google. |

`Submit Form`   `Reset Form`

**Figure 27.3**
*Subscribe to a mailing list.*

In many cases, clicking the **Subscribe** link runs your e-mail program and simply addresses a message from you to the site. To subscribe, you just send the message. Your e-mail address is added to the list, and whenever the next scheduled mass mailing occurs, you receive your copy via e-mail.

When you've had enough, you can unsubscribe from the list. Most legitimate companies insert a message, typically near the bottom of the mail message or newsletter, providing instructions about how to unsubscribe and remove yourself from the mailing list.

**WHOA!**

If you don't completely trust the website you're visiting, don't subscribe to its newsletter or mailing list. Some sites pass your e-mail address to other sites, and you're then inundated with unsolicited messages. Create a separate (free) e-mail account, as discussed in Chapter 21, and use that to register. That will save your primary e-mail account from spam.

# Getting Up-to-the-Minute RSS Feeds

As you're cruising around the web, you might encounter some sites that offer Really Simple Syndication (RSS) feeds. News feeds are typically flagged with an icon with the letters RSS or XML or an icon that looks like radio broadcast waves. With an RSS reader or a web browser that supports RSS, you can subscribe to RSS content and have sites deliver late-breaking news directly to you rather than having to visit the site and poke around for what you want. It's sort of like creating your own custom newspaper that's automatically updated 24/7.

In Internet Explorer, you can subscribe to RSS feeds by pulling up the feed (click the RSS or XML button on the web page offering the feed) and then clicking on the **Subscribe to This Feed** link and clicking **Subscribe**, as shown in Figure 27.4. You can access your feeds at any time by clicking the **Favorites** button and clicking **Feeds**.

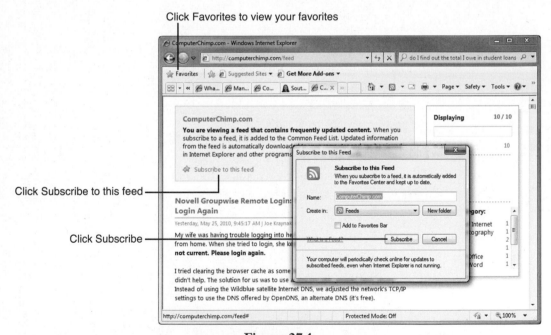

Figure 27.4
*Internet Explorer enables you to subscribe to RSS content on the web.*

**INSIDE TIP**

Google Reader is a web-based RSS feed *aggregator*. In short, an aggregator pulls all the RSS feeds you subscribe to into one easy-to-access area, so you don't have to check websites or feeds individually. Check out Google Reader at www.google.com/reader. To take advantage of it, you need a Google account, as explained in Chapter 20.

## The Least You Need to Know

- Message boards, or discussion groups, are great places to share interests and get help from peers.

- To read a message in a discussion group, click the title of the message.

- Before you start a new discussion, search the group to determine whether the topic is already under discussion and read the discussion so you don't post something someone else already posted.

- You can subscribe to mailing lists and newsletters on the web to have news and notices e-mailed to you.

- With an RSS-enabled web browser or reader app, you can subscribe to content on several websites and have it delivered to a single location.

# Publishing Your Own Web Page or Blog

## In This Chapter

- A sneak peek at the codes behind web pages
- Creating a website without knowing anything about HTML
- Launching your own website for free
- Blogging 101
- Adding YouTube videos to your web pages and blog posts

Surfing the web is nice, but you want more. You want to establish a presence on the web, publish your own stories or poems, place pictures of yourself or your family online, show off your creativity, and communicate your ideas to the world.

Where do you start? Right here. This chapter shows you how to whip up your first web page or blog right online, without having to learn any special programs or deal with any cryptic web page formatting codes (unless you really want to). And because you create the page online, you don't have to worry about publishing your web page when you're done. Quick. Easy.

## Behind the Scenes with a Web Page

Behind every web page is a text document that includes codes for formatting the text, inserting pictures and other media files, and displaying links that point to other pages. This system of codes (commonly referred to as *tags*) is called *HTML* (Hypertext Markup Language).

Most codes are paired. The first code in the pair turns on the formatting, and the second code turns it off. For example, to type a heading such as "Apple Dumplin's Home Page," you use the heading codes like this:

```
<h1>Apple Dumplin's Home Page</h1>
```

The <h1> code tells the web browser to display any text that follows the code as a level-one heading. The </h1> code tells the web browser to turn off the level-one heading format and return to displaying text as normal. Unpaired codes act as commands; for instance, the <img> code inserts a graphic, so <img src='http://www.sample.com/horse.jpg' /> inserts a graphic file named horse.jpg that's stored in the root directory of the website www.sample.com.

# Forget About HTML

A basic introduction to HTML is helpful in understanding how the web works, troubleshooting web page formatting problems, and customizing web pages with fancy enhancements, but don't worry—you don't need a certification in HTML to create your first web page. Many companies have developed specialized programs that make the process of creating a web page as easy as designing and printing a greeting card.

Professional web designers use industrial-strength tools like Dreamweaver to design and create websites. If your website needs are modest, however, you can create and format your web pages right on the web simply by specifying your preferences and using forms to enter your text. The next section shows you just how easy it is to create and publish your own web page online with Google Sites.

**INSIDE TIP**

If you want your own unique domain name with an address like www.yourname.com, a matching e-mail address like bill@yourname.com, and a site with a custom design that's easy to maintain, I recommend starting an account with a web hosting provider—such as Bluehost, HostGator, or GoDaddy.com—and using WordPress to create and maintain your site. (These hosting providers enable you to register a domain name, and they feature numerous tools for creating and maintaining websites and blogs.)

On my website/blog ComputerChimp.com, I've posted a four-part series on how to create a combination website/blog like ComputerChimp.com, using Bluehost, WordPress, and a custom theme called Thesis. The cost is about $80 per year to start and maintain, plus an $87 one-time fee for the Thesis Theme. Check out my tutorial at computerchimp.com/website/make-a-website-starting-with-bluehost.html.

# Creating a Free Website with Google Sites

Here's what you do to publish a simple web page (for free) using Google Sites:

1. Using your web browser, go to **sites.google.com**.

2. If you have a Google account, log in. If you don't have a Google account yet, get one: Click **Create an account now** and follow the onscreen cues to enter your desired e-mail address and password.

3. Click the **Create site** button.

4. Click the template you want to use, as shown in Figure 28.1. (For more templates, click **Browse the gallery for more.**)

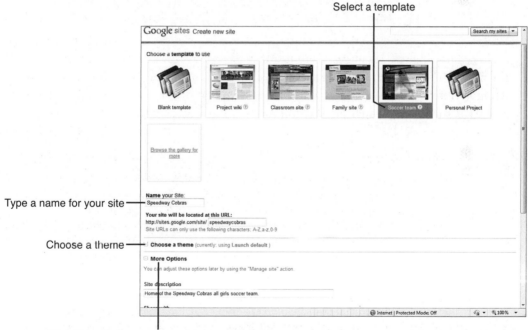

**Figure 28.1**
*Select a template and enter a name for your site.*

5. Click in the **Name your Site** box and type a name for your site. Google Sites automatically assigns your site a URL (address) based on the name you typed. You can edit the address, if desired.

6. Click **More Options**.

7. Click in the Site description box and type a brief description of your site's content.

8. Under Share with, click **Everyone in the world can view this site** or **Only people I specify can view this site**.

9. If your site contains adult-only content, click **This site contains mature content only suitable for adults**.

10. Click in the verification text box and type the verification code that's displayed.

11. Click the **Create site** button. Google Sites creates your website and displays it. The page contains a bunch of placeholder text and graphics you can replace with your own text and graphics. The page also contains links you can click to learn how to replace images, text, and other objects with your own; click one of these links for complete instructions.

## Editing Your Google Site

To edit your site, click the **Edit page** button (upper right). The page appears in edit mode, as shown in Figure 28.2. To replace text, drag over it and then type your own text. You can use the four buttons in the blue toolbar near the top to do the following:

- **Insert:** Insert an image, link, table of contents, subpage listing, Google calendar, Google map, and other objects. (See the following two sections for more about inserting objects, apps, and gadgets on a page.)

- **Format:** Add formatting to create headings; change a paragraph to normal text; add subscripts and superscripts; align text left, right, or center; and more.

- **Table:** Insert and manipulate a table by adding or deleting rows and columns.

- **Layout:** Change the overall page layout—for example, from a three-column layout to a two-column layout, or vice versa.

You can delete or move any of the images or boxed objects on the page. To move an object, hover the mouse pointer over it so that the pointer appears as a four-headed arrow, and then drag and drop the object to the desired location. To delete an object, click it and press the **Delete** key.

The gray toolbar (just above the page) displays buttons for applying standard formatting, such as bold and italic; choosing a type size; creating numbered or bulleted lists; and aligning text left, right, or center. For more about using buttons like these to apply formatting, see Chapter 12.

Undo or redo changes     Add formatting to selected text
Click an object to select it

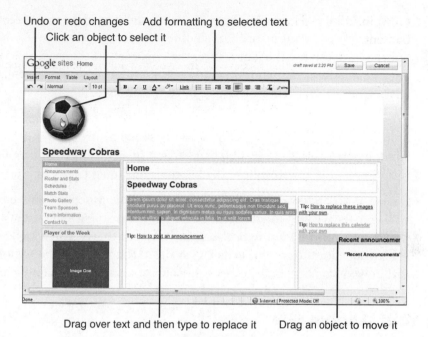

Drag over text and then type to replace it     Drag an object to move it

**Figure 28.2**
*Edit and format text and objects on your site.*

## Inserting Objects and Apps

Using the Insert menu, you can insert a variety of objects and apps (applications) to make your site more feature rich. Click on the page where you want the object or app inserted, and then follow the instructions for the type of object or app you want to insert (this list includes a small selection of available objects and apps):

- **Image:** Click **Insert**, **Image** and use the resulting dialog box to upload an image from your PC or use an image from a specific web address. After the image appears in the Add an Image box, click **OK**. Click the image and use the options below it to select an alignment (left, center, or right), size (small, medium, or large), and word wrap preference (on or off), as shown in Figure 28.3.

- **Video:** Upload the video you want to insert to Google Video or YouTube, and then copy its web address (URL). Click **Insert**, **Video**, **Google Video** or **YouTube**. In the resulting dialog box, right-click in the **Paste the URL** box and click **Paste**. Enter any other preferences and click **Save**.

- **Horizontal line:** Click where you want the horizontal line to appear, and then click **Insert, Horizontal Line**.

- **Google Map:** Click **Insert**, **Map**. In the Search box, type the address of the location you want mapped (including city, state, and zip code) and click **Search**. You can use the controls on the upper left of the map to zoom in or out or pan left, right, up, or down. When the area you want shown appears, click **Select**, enter your preferences in the resulting dialog box, and click **Save**.

- **Picasa Photo:** If you use Picasa to store and manage your digital photos online (see Chapter 31), you can easily insert photos from your online photo albums into a Google Sites web page. Click **Insert**, **Picasa Photo**, use the resulting dialog box to choose the photo to insert, and click **Select**.

- **Picasa Web Slideshow:** If you use Picasa, you can insert an entire photo album to have your Google Site web page display it as a slide show. Copy the web address of the Picasa photo album you want to use. Click **Insert, Picasa Web slideshow**. Right-click the **Paste the URL** box near the top of the resulting dialog box and click **Paste**. Enter your preferences and click **Save**.

Click the image to select it

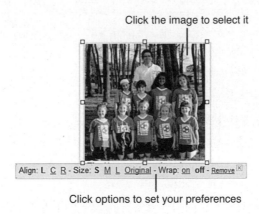

Click options to set your preferences

**Figure 28.3**
*Enter preferences for your image.*

## Inserting Gadgets

Google includes gadgets you can add to your site to improve navigation and add features to your site. To add a gadget, click where you want the gadget inserted; then click the **Insert** menu, scroll down to near the bottom, and click the desired gadget, as shown in Figure 28.4.

A dialog box pops up requesting additional details. For example, the Recent posts gadget displays a list of the most recently published posts, so visitors can quickly find out what's new on your site. When you choose to add the Recent posts gadget, the dialog box prompts you to specify the type of post, post length, number of posts, and so on.

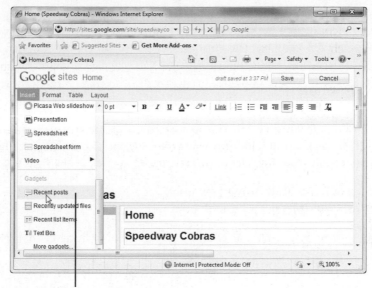

Select the gadget you want to insert

**Figure 28.4**
*Insert a gadget.*

## Saving or Canceling Your Changes

When you're done making changes to your Google site, you have the option to save the changes or cancel them. To save the changes, click the **Save** button (upper right). To cancel changes, click the **Cancel** button (next to the Save button).

# Blogging Your Way to Internet Fame

Relatively recently (sometime in the late 1990s), self-publishing on the web became easier with the introduction of *web logs*, or *blogs* for short. These relatively simple web pages are primarily text based, and you can create and update them by filling out a form. You type a message, comment, or other text and then *post it* to the blog. The most recent posting appears at the top of your blog, followed by prior postings. As your list of posted messages grows, old messages are pushed off the main blog and archived.

The first blogs focused on news and commentary. Bloggers would read an article online and then post a link to the article along with their comments, insights, questions, and sometimes corrections or additional facts concerning the article. Over the years, the scope of blogs has broadened considerably. Now people commonly use blogs to publish their own poetry and fiction; broadcast news stories the mainstream media has overlooked; share business expertise; communicate with family members, friends, and colleagues; promote grassroots movements; keep an online journal; and much more.

> **DEFINITION**
>
> A **blog** (short for **web log**) is a publicly accessible personal journal that enables an individual to voice his or her opinions and insights, keep an online record of experiences, and gather input from others. People also use blogs to share photos with friends and family and set up their own online clubs.

## Launching Your Blog

To start blogging, you need a *blogging platform*—an application that provides the tools you need to post messages to your blog and maintain it. Several developers offer platforms for free and can even host your blog for you. The following steps show you how to launch your own blog using the popular WordPress blogging platform:

1. Run Internet Explorer and go to **wordpress.com**.

2. Click the link to sign up and follow the onscreen instructions to sign up for a WordPress account. When you log in to WordPress, it displays a page that's packed with information and links to other people's blogs.

3. Click the **Register a blog** link. If you don't see the link, click the **My Blogs** link (upper-left corner of the page). The Register a Blog page appears, as shown in Figure 28.5.

4. Click in the **Blog Domain** box and type a name for your blog. This name will be added to the beginning of wordpress.com to create your blog's domain name. You won't be able to change this later, although you can delete the blog later and create a new one.

5. Click in the **Blog Title** box and type the title you want to appear at the top of every page of your blog.

6. If you want to prevent search engines from indexing your blog, click the check box next to the Privacy option to remove the check mark.

7. Click the **Create Blog** button. As long as the domain name you entered is not already in use, WordPress displays a message indicating that the domain name is now yours and showing you the username to use to log in.

**Figure 28.5**
*Register a new WordPress blog for free.*

You can now visit your blog by entering its address (for example, **yourblogname. wordpress.com**) into Internet Explorer, but it consists of only an opening page that contains a welcome message.

To log in to your blog, launch Internet Explorer, type **yourblogname.wordpress. com/wp-admin** in the address box near the top of the window, and press **Enter**. You're already logged in, so this displays the WordPress Dashboard for your blog, as shown in Figure 28.6. However, if you log out and then try to use Internet Explorer to go to **yourblogname.wordpress.com/wp-admin** later, WordPress displays a page prompting you to enter your username and password. When you enter the correct information, WordPress displays the Dashboard, as shown in Figure 28.6.

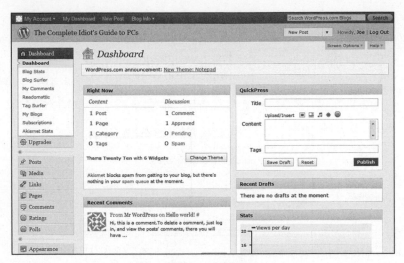

**Figure 28.6**
*The WordPress Dashboard gives you access to the tools you need to post messages and manage your blog.*

## Making Your Blog Your Own

The WordPress Dashboard provides all the tools you need to post content to your blog, redesign it, and manage it:

- **Write a new post:** Writing a post is as easy as typing in a word processing application, as shown in Figure 28.7. Click **Posts** (left menu), **Add New**, and then simply type a title for the post, type and format your content, add a photo or other graphic, and click **Publish**. Posts appear on your opening page with the newest post first.

- **Create a page:** Pages are almost identical to posts, but they're used for static content. In other words, they function more like web pages. Links for the pages you create appear under "Pages" in your blog's navigation bar. To create a page, click **Pages** (left menu), **Add New**, and use the resulting form to create your page.

- **Manage your blog:** The Dashboard contains everything you need to manage your blog, and all of it is accessible through the left menu. You can install WordPress upgrades, create and edit posts and pages, create your own media library with digital graphics and video, approve and reject comments others have posted, check your site statistics, and much more.

- **Give your blog a new look and layout:** Click **Appearance** (left menu) for options to change the theme that controls the look and layout of your blog, add widgets to include new features, change the background and header, and even edit the theme to customize it for your own use.

Type a post or page title      Formatting buttons          Click Publish

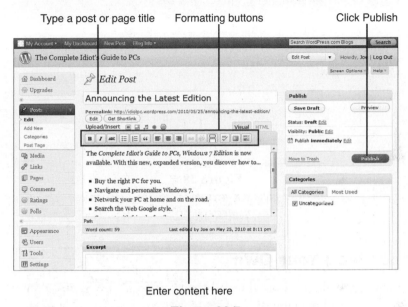

Enter content here

**Figure 28.7**

*Posting content to your blog is as easy as filling out a form and clicking **Publish**.*

**WHOA!**

If you publish a post or page and regret it later, you can delete or edit it. Log in to your blog, click the **Edit** link below Pages or Posts, scroll down to the end of the entry you want to delete, and click **Remove** or click **Edit** to change your entry.

# Embedding a YouTube Video in a Web Page or Blog Post

In Chapter 23, you learned how to watch and share YouTube videos. One of the best ways to share a YouTube video is to include it on a web page or blog. YouTube makes this very easy to accomplish with its *embed* code. The embed code provides a link that pulls the video from YouTube and plays it on a web page. To embed a video in a web page or blog post, here's what you do:

1. Head to YouTube and display the video you want to embed in your web page or post.

2. Click the **<Embed>** button below the video.

3. Enter your preferences, as shown in Figure 28.8.

4. Click in the box that contains the embed code, and then right-click the code and select **Copy**.

5. Open the post or page you want to add the video to and display it in HTML mode. (This works only if you paste the code into the page's or post's HTML.)

6. Right-click where you want the video inserted and click **Paste**.

7. Save your changes. Now whenever someone opens this page or views this post, they'll see a box in which they can click the play button to view the video.

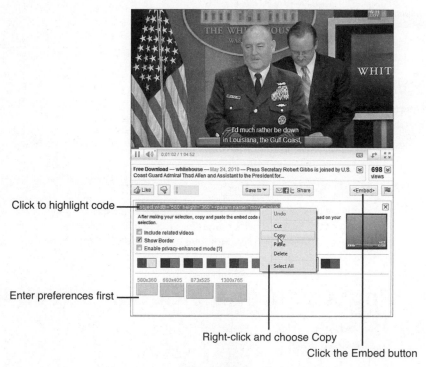

**Figure 28.8**
*Copy and paste the embed code into the HTML for your page or post.*

## The Least You Need to Know

- Hypertext Markup Language (HTML) is a system of codes used to format web pages.
- You don't need to master HTML to create your own attractive web pages.
- Google Sites, at sites.google.com, provides an easy (and free) way to build a website.
- An easy way to establish and maintain a presence on the Internet is to create your own blog.
- You can place a YouTube video on a web page or blog post by copying and pasting the video's embed code into the HTML for the web page or post.

# Protecting Your PC from Viruses and Other Online Threats

## In This Chapter

- Scanning incoming files for viruses and other malware
- Preventing unauthorized access to your PC with a firewall
- Installing Windows 7 security updates
- Managing e-mail more carefully and slowing the flow of spam
- Dodging phishing scams
- Preparing for and recovering from catastrophe

The Internet is a virtual city packed with shopping malls, libraries, community centers, museums, newsstands, meeting rooms, and other valuable offerings. But like any city, the Internet has its dark side—a section of town ruled by vandalism, theft, and other criminal behavior. You want access to all the positive features the Internet offers, but you need to protect your system, data, and confidential information from the riffraff and from viruses and other *malware*. (Malware is short for "malicious software"—any computer code designed to do something bad.)

This chapter shows you how to protect yourself and your PC from various Internet threats.

## Keeping Out Viruses and Other Malware

Picking up a virus on the Internet is like coming home from vacation with some exotic illness. You were having so much fun; how could this happen? And how can you prevent it from happening again? By following a few simple rules:

- Download programs, plug-ins, and add-ons only from reputable and known sites. If you know the company that created the program, go to its web page or FTP server and download the file from there. Most reputable sites regularly scan their systems to detect and eliminate viruses.

- Don't accept copies of a program from another person (for example, by e-mail). Although the program might not have contained a virus when your buddy downloaded it, your buddy's computer could have a virus that infected the program. Ask your friend where he or she got the file and then download the file from its original location.

- If your web browser displays a message indicating that a program it's being asked to download is unsigned or from a questionable source, cancel the download.

- If you receive a file attachment from someone you don't know or from a questionable source, delete the message along with the attachment. Do *not* open it.

- Keep an antivirus program running at all times. Antivirus programs scan any incoming files for viruses and scan your computer regularly to identify viruses before they can damage files. Two of the best antivirus programs around are also free for home users—Avast (www.avast.com) and Microsoft Security Essentials (www.microsoft.com/security_essentials/). All you do is download and install them. Either one runs in the background, constantly monitoring activity and incoming files; warns you when they detect anything suspicious; and provides options for dealing with each incident.

**WHOA!**

If you receive e-mail, you'll eventually receive virus warnings indicating that a nasty new virus is infecting thousands of computers all over the world and wiping out hard drives or stealing confidential information. Most of these warnings are hoaxes, and you should *not* forward the message as it instructs you to do. Check the source of the hoax first. Virus hoaxes are posted at http://home.mcafee.com/virusinfo (open the **View** drop-down menu below Virus Information and click **Hoax**).

# Detecting and Eliminating Spyware

Spyware is unauthorized software that works in the background to collect information about you or what you type (such as usernames and passwords) and transmits the information to another computer. Fortunately, Windows 7 is equipped with Windows Defender to deal with spyware before it has a chance to do much harm.

To access Windows Defender and scan your system for spyware, click **Start** and type **defender** in the **Search programs and files** box. Click **Windows Defender** to run the utility and then click the **Scan** button, as shown in Figure 29.1.

Click Scan

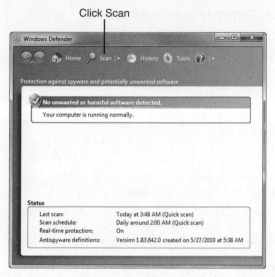

**Figure 29.1**
*You can scan your PC for spyware.*

# Keeping Hackers at Bay with a Firewall

Whenever you're connected to the Internet, you run the risk of having a mischievous hacker break into your system, steal information, and even damage files. Hackers rarely break into home PCs that are connected to the Internet by a dial-up modem (via a phone line), because you typically disconnect when you're done working. If you have a DSL or cable modem connection, which keeps your computer connected to the Internet at all times, consider installing a *firewall* to prevent unauthorized access to your system.

A firewall stands between your PC and the Internet, enabling your PC free access to the Internet but limiting access to your PC from outside sources (including hackers). It does this by monitoring activity between your PC or network (*trusted* network) and the Internet (*untrusted* network). As long as the trusted network initiates contact, the firewall allows the connection. If the untrusted network (another PC on the Internet) initiates contact, the firewall blocks the connection.

If you have two or more computers that share an Internet connection through a router, the best option is to use your router's firewall to limit outside access to your networked computers. If your PC is connecting directly to the Internet through a modem or a Wi-Fi connection (not through a router), turn on the Windows Firewall. If your PC works fine with both firewalls on, you have added protection.

## Configuring Your Router's Firewall

Your router should have come with instructions that show you how to configure it or at least access the configuration settings. In most cases, you can access the configuration settings by running your web browser and then entering the IP address of your router, as shown in Figure 29.2.

After accessing your router's configuration settings, select the Security or Firewall option and enable the firewall, if it's not already enabled. (It's probably already enabled.)

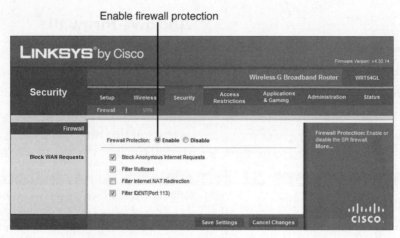

**Figure 29.2**
*Configure your router's firewall and security settings.*

You can have two or more firewalls in place—your router's firewall (hardware based) and Windows Firewall (software based), for example. If you have an Internet security suite, such as a Norton 360 or McAfee Total Protection, you may have a third firewall. Running multiple firewalls is fine but may cause problems, such as preventing your PC from accessing the Internet, specific sites, e-mail, or applications on your computer. If you encounter problems, try disabling the software firewalls one at a time until the problem is resolved. See "Activating or Deactivating the Windows Firewall" later in this chapter.

> **WHOA!**
>
> Your PC should always have at least one firewall running when connecting to the Internet—your router's firewall if you're connecting through a router with firewall protection, or Windows Firewall if you're connecting via a Wi-Fi hotspot or other public network.

## Limiting Access to Your Wireless Network

Restrict access to your network by enabling encryption and entering a passphrase that all computers on the network must use to establish a network connection. (See Chapter 11 for details about setting up a wireless network.)

Check your router's wireless settings to determine whether it has an option to allow the network name to be broadcast. If it does, you can improve security by disabling this option so the router won't broadcast the network name, making your network less visible.

## Activating or Deactivating the Windows Firewall

One of the best ways to protect your computer from break-ins is to install a firewall. A firewall is security software that stands between your computer and the Internet, enabling your computer to freely exchange data with the Internet but blocking access to your computer or network from other users on the Internet.

If you're using a router to connect to the Internet, it probably has its own firewall, which is usually superior to any software firewall, such as the Windows firewall.

Activate both your router's and the Windows firewall. (Check your router documentation to determine how to enable/disable its firewall.) If you run into problems connecting to the Internet, try enabling the router's firewall and disabling the Windows firewall. To turn the Windows firewall on or off, follow these steps:

1. Click **Start**, **Control Panel**.

2. Click **System and Security** and then **Windows Firewall**.

3. Click **Turn Windows Firewall on or off**. Enter your log-on password, if prompted to do so, and click **Yes**.

4. Below Home or work (private) network location settings, click the desired setting: **Turn on Windows Firewall** or **Turn off Windows Firewall (not recommended)**. Click **OK**.

**WHOA!**

Always have at least one firewall running whenever your network is connected to the Internet. For most people, this means all the time.

## Making Exceptions for Certain Programs

A firewall can cause Internet connection problems for some features, including instant messaging, especially when you're trying to share files or videoconference. If you experience a connection problem when Windows Firewall is on, you may need to set up exceptions to allow specific programs free access to the Internet.

To set up an exception, click **Start, Control Panel, System and Security, Allow a program through Windows Firewall** (below Windows Firewall). Click the file or program you want to exempt from Windows Firewall protection, as shown in Figure 29.3, and click **OK**.

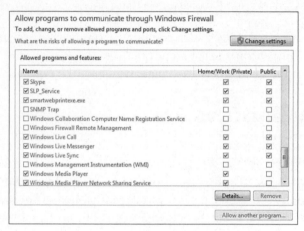

**Figure 29.3**

*Allow a program to bypass Windows Firewall.*

# Securing Your Portable PC in Public Hot Spots

Wi-Fi is great. You can spend the entire day at Starbucks drinking your caffé latte and playing on your Wi-Fi–enabled laptop. Unfortunately, this makes your PC vulnerable to anyone else in the vicinity who may log on to the Wi-Fi network looking to view or steal information either stored on your computer or passing between your computer and the network. Consider a few tips to protect yourself:

- When you're ready to head out, change your network location to Public: Click **Start, Control Panel, Network and Internet, Network and Sharing Center**. Below View your active networks, click your current network location and then click **Public network**.

- Be sure you send and receive your e-mail over a secure connection. If you use a web-based e-mail program, you can usually tell whether the connection is secured by looking at the web-based e-mail services address in your web browser. If it starts with "https" instead of "http," you're on a secure site.

- If you use a separate e-mail account, check with your e-mail service provider to determine whether it offers a secure connection. This is usually referred to as SSL (Secure Socket Layer). You'll need to enter special settings in your e-mail program to send and receive e-mail over these secure connections. Your e-mail service provider can give you detailed instructions.

- Don't lug around sensitive data on your notebook computer. None of the other precautions listed here will protect your data if someone walks off with your computer or steals it out of your car. The only protection is to keep sensitive data at home, although this isn't always practical.

# Updating Windows 7

Microsoft is constantly improving Windows in all sorts of ways and tweaking it to repair security holes. Assuming that you didn't mess with the Windows update feature, Windows automatically downloads updates when your PC is connected to the Internet and installs those updates either automatically or after receiving your okay. If you disabled automatic updates, be sure to check for and install updates regularly to ensure that you have the latest security updates in place.

To check for updates, click **Start**, **All Programs**, **Windows Update**. Click **Check for updates** (on the left). Windows connects to the Internet, checks for updates, and (if it finds any) displays a link showing the number of updates available, as shown in Figure 29.4. Click the link to check out the available updates. You can then choose the updates you want to download and install, and click **OK** to install them.

To enable or disable automatic updates and adjust the feature's settings, click **Start**, **Control Panel**, **System and Security**, **Windows Update**, **Change settings**. The Choose how Windows can install updates screen appears, which allows you to enable or disable automatic updates, choose when Windows checks for updates, and adjust other settings.

Click Check for updates    Click the link for available updates

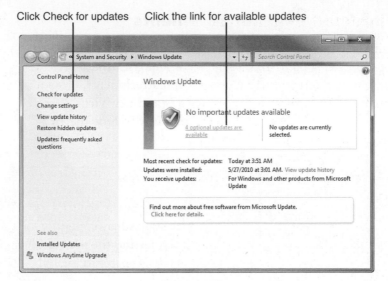

**Figure 29.4**
*Check for Windows updates.*

# Opting for a Standard User Account

Chapter 7 introduces the three types of user accounts: Administrator, Standard, and Guest. An administrator account gives you complete control over your PC, but it also poses a security risk. If other users (or hackers) gain access to your PC when any user is logged on as an administrator, they can cause all sorts of trouble.

Consider creating only one password-protected administrator account and using a standard user account for daily PC use. If someone happens to gain access through the standard user account, he won't be able to change settings, create or delete other user accounts, or damage system files. When you're logged on as a standard user, you can still perform administrative tasks, as long as you know the administrator's password. And if Windows prevents you from performing a specific administrative task, you can switch to your administrator account to proceed with whatever you want to do and then log out when you're done.

# Dealing with E-Mail Threats and Annoyances

Many of the most serious threats to your PC come in the form of e-mail or e-mail attachments. By knowing what to watch out for and what to do or not do, you can steer clear of most problems.

## Avoiding Infected E-Mail Attachments

The cardinal rule for avoiding viral infections from e-mail attachments is this: never open an e-mail attachment unless you know and trust the source. Your antivirus program will scan incoming e-mail messages and attachments, providing you with some protection, but if the attachment contains a brand-new virus your antivirus program doesn't recognize, or the sender figured out a way to hide the virus's true identity, your antivirus program may not catch it.

## Don't Even Preview Junk Mail

You can recognize most junk mail just by looking at the sender's name or the message description, so don't even look at it. Some messages may contain images or other objects that send a message back to the sender, letting the person know that the message arrived and someone looked at it. This tells a spammer that your e-mail address is legitimate.

To avoid looking at junk mail, take the following precautions:

- Turn off your e-mail client's preview pane. Check your e-mail program's help system for details.

- Use your e-mail client's junk mail feature to automatically route suspected spam to the junk mail folder. You can then pick through the junk to find legitimate messages and delete the rest. Later in this chapter, you learn how to deal with junk e-mail (spam).

- Open e-mail only from known and trusted sources, and immediately delete all the rest.

## Avoiding Phishing Scams

Phishing scams are commonly initiated via e-mail. *Phishing* is a fraudulent means of obtaining someone's username and password. The con artist/identity thief sends an e-mail that appears to originate from a bank, credit card company, or other such company warning of a serious issue you must address *right now* by clicking a link and logging into your account. The link takes you to an official-looking site complete with text boxes for entering your username and password. If you enter this sensitive information, the con artist has what he or she needs to log in to your real account.

To avoid falling victim to e-mail phishing scams, take the following precautions:

- Play it safe and go to the website yourself without clicking the e-mail or a link in the message. (You should be able to identify the website from the subject line or the address from which the e-mail originated.) If the website is legitimate and the message did in fact originate from it, you should be able to find something on the website about it; otherwise, it's most likely a scam.

- If your e-mail program features phishing protection, enable it. Check your e-mail program's help system for details.

- Be aware that most legitimate companies do not send alarming e-mail messages with links to click to resolve issues. If you receive such a message, it's probably not from the source it claims to come from.

- Mouse over the link and look in the status bar at the bottom of the window to see the address the link will take you to. Chances are, the link indicates one destination while the address takes you somewhere else entirely. This is a sure sign of a phishing scam.

- If you think the e-mail message is legitimate, head to the company's website to obtain legitimate contact information, and then contact the company to verify that someone at the company sent the message.

- If you determine that an e-mail message is fraudulent, report it to the legitimate company from which it supposedly originated so the company can take action.

Phishing scams are most common but not exclusive to e-mail. Con artists may try to obtain login information in chat rooms, via instant messaging programs, and in social networking venues (including Facebook). A good rule of thumb is this: provide sensitive information only if *you* initiated contact.

## Avoiding, Filtering, and Blocking Spam

*Spam* is unsolicited, unwanted e-mail—junk mail. When you first get an e-mail account, you receive very little spam. The spam starts to flow when you post your e-mail address on the web or sign up for free offers with companies that pass your e-mail address to others. Once your e-mail address lands on a spam list as a legitimate address, the spam is almost impossible to stop. When it comes to spam, an ounce of prevention is worth a kilo of cure. Here are a few tips for preventing spam:

- Don't use your primary e-mail address to register for anything on or off the web. Get a free e-mail account from Gmail, Yahoo!, or Hotmail and use this disposable e-mail address to register for stuff. If you start receiving too much junk e-mail, you can dump the address and use a different one.

- If you receive a spam message, don't reply to it. Replying verifies your e-mail address to the spammer and encourages more spam.

- Don't put your primary e-mail address on the web—for example on your website or blog. Spammers scan the web for e-mail addresses.

If you're receiving an overwhelming amount of spam, try the following solutions to slow the flow:

- Log in to your Internet service provider's website to find out whether it uses a spam blocker and whether you can configure it to make it more aggressive in identifying spam.

- If you have the e-mail account through a hosting provider (a business that hosts your website), log in to your account to find out about available options.

- Purchase and install a spam blocker of your own. You can find plenty of good spam filters/blockers out there, including SPAMfighter (www.spamfighter.com), ChoiceMail (www.digiportal.com), and Spameater Pro (www.spameaterpro.com), to name a few.

Most newer e-mail programs offer some sort of spam protection (perhaps in the form of a Junk Mail folder) and enable you to enter settings to make the program more or less aggressive in identifying spam. In addition, you can usually create lists of safe senders and blocked senders and block e-mail from certain domains or countries. Search your e-mail program's help system for "spam" to determine what, if any, spam protection features are available.

# Checking Your Browser's Security Settings

Your web browser has its own security guard on duty that checks incoming files for potential threats. If you try to enter information such as a credit card number on a form that's not secure, the web browser displays a warning message asking if you want to continue. If a site attempts to install a program on your PC, your browser displays a confirmation dialog box or a warning near the top of the window asking for permission to download and install the program.

With most browsers, the default security settings are fine, but they may be a little on the aggressive side, warning you too much. In any event, checking your browser's security settings is usually a good idea, just in case your browser has a setting you'd like to change. To check security settings in Internet Explorer, click **Tools**, **Internet Options**, and then the **Security** tab.

If you use a browser other than Internet Explorer, check the browser's help system for information on how to enter your security preferences. All browsers have security features, although they all handle them a little differently.

## The Least You Need to Know

- To protect your PC against viruses, purchase and install a good antivirus program, and keep it updated with the latest virus definitions.
- To prevent unauthorized access to your PC, enable the Windows firewall or configure your router's firewall settings.
- Update Windows 7 regularly to ensure that you have the latest security updates installed.
- Log in to a standard user account for your daily activities to limit access to your PC in case a hacker breaks in and takes control of it.
- To avoid potential virus infections from e-mail attachments, install an antivirus program and open attachments only from trusted sources.

# Going Digital with Music, Photos, and Video

Although you may think your food processor is the most versatile tool in your home, your PC has it beat. With the right software and accessories, your PC can moonlight as a powerful jukebox, photo lab, and video studio.

The chapters in Part 5 introduce you to the most popular home-based computer gadgets. Here you learn how to download and play music clips from the Internet, burn your own custom music CDs, transfer music to a portable MP3 player, snap and print photos, edit your home movies, and burn your movies to DVDs. Part 5 takes you from tech weenie to tech wizard in just a few short chapters.

# Playing, Growing, and Managing Your Music Collection

## In This Chapter

- Playing music on your PC
- Copying tracks from CDs and creating your own playlists
- Producing your own audio CDs
- Purchasing music online
- Copying music to a portable music player

If you thought the move from LPs to CDs was impressive (if you're old enough to even remember that!), you're going to love the latest in audio and video technology. With your PC, a *CD drive*, a sound card, and a decent set of speakers, you can create your own computerized jukebox that can play hundreds of your favorite songs. With an Internet connection, you can download music to add to your collection. With a portable music player, you can take your favorite tunes wherever you go. And if you have a recordable disc drive, you can even "burn" your own custom CDs and play them on any CD player!

This chapter shows you how to do all this and more with Windows Media Player.

## Digital Music Basics

Digital music is music stored in files rather than as grooves on the surface of vinyl records. Recordings on audio CDs, computers, and digital music players (MP3 players) are all forms of digital music. Digital music offers several advantages:

- You can create your own custom mixes and burn them to CDs.
- You can copy music to a portable digital audio player and take it with you wherever you go.
- You have less clutter than you do with CDs.

- You can buy and listen to only the songs you like instead of having to buy an entire CD.

- You can buy and download music and listen to it right now instead of waiting for CDs to arrive in the mail.

- You don't need to worry about scratches rendering your favorite CDs useless.

## Digital Players, Rippers, and Burners

One of the complications of digital music is that different devices store and play music in different, often incompatible formats. For example, CDs store music in a format that most portable digital players can't play. Fortunately, various programs can handle the required format conversions for you:

- A *digital music player* plays audio in one or more digital formats. The player may be a program on your PC, such as Windows Media Player, or a portable digital music player, often referred to as an MP3 player.

- A *CD ripper* converts audio clips from a CD into a format you can play on your PC or MP3 player.

- A *CD burner* copies digital audio clips from your PC to a recordable CD. You can then play the CD in a standard audio CD player.

## Choosing the Right Recordable Discs

With digital music, you don't need discs unless you plan to burn music to recordable CDs. You can download digital clips, copy them to your MP3 player, and use your MP3 player as the stack of CDs you would otherwise carry around with you or play in your car. On some newer cars, you can plug your MP3 player into the car's sound system. On older cars, you can purchase an adapter that enables you to play recordings from your MP3 player through the car's sound system.

If you want or need to burn music to CDs, however, make sure you purchase CD-R, not CD-RW, discs. You can record to CD-R discs only once, but they're more reflective, making them a better choice for storing digital music. (Some audio CD players have a tough time reading a CD-RW disc.) Also make sure the maximum recording speed of the discs is at least as fast as that of your CD-R drive. If you have a drive that can print labels on the CDs and you want to do that, look for *printable* discs that support the same print technology the drive uses. (For more about the differences in CD drives and discs, check out Chapter 8.)

# Playing, Ripping, and Burning with Windows Media Player

If you insert an audio CD into your PC's disc drive, Windows should display the Audio CD dialog box, prompting you to specify which action you want Windows to perform: **Play Audio CD** (with Windows Media Player), **Rip Music from CD** (with Windows Media Player), **Open Folder to View Files** (in Windows Explorer), or perform another action with some other audio program that's installed on your PC. To start listening to the CD, click one of the options for playing it. (The audio CD may begin to play automatically when you insert the CD, depending on how your system is configured.)

If Windows Media Player starts playing the CD, you'll see a small window like the one in Figure 30.1. This is how Windows media player appears in Now Playing mode, a streamlined version of Media Player. To see Windows Media Player in its full glory, click the **Switch to Library** button. (You can switch back by clicking the **Switch to Now Playing** button in the lower-right corner of the Library window.)

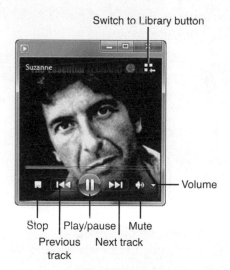

**Figure 30.1**
*Windows Media Player in Now Playing mode.*

## Ripping Tracks from CDs

Playing an audio CD makes your PC little more than an overpriced CD player. To make your PC a *superior* overpriced CD player, record your favorite audio clips to your PC's hard drive as files. This provides you with a virtual jukebox, which you can program to play only the songs you want to hear in the order you want to hear them. It also allows you to copy the clips to your MP3 player, but we'll get to that later.

1. Establish a connection to the Internet, if possible. If your PC is connected to the Internet, Media Player can automatically download the title of the album, the name of the artist, and track titles for most CDs so you don't have to enter this information manually.

2. Run Windows Media Player by selecting **Start**, **All Programs**, **Windows Media Player**.

3. Insert a CD that has one or more tracks you want to record into your PC's CD player. Media Player displays a list of the tracks stored on the CD, as shown in Figure 30.2, with all tracks on the CD selected.

4. (Optional) Click the check box next to each track you do *not* want to record to remove the check mark from the box.

Click Rip CD

Click the check box next to a track to omit it

**Figure 30.2**
*Windows Media Player makes it easy to copy individual tracks from a CD.*

5. Click **Rip CD**. Media Player begins ripping the selected tracks from the CD and displays its progress.

6. When Media Player is done ripping the selected tracks, eject the CD.

To play the tracks you just ripped from the CD, click **Music** (in the navigation bar on the left) and scroll down to the album you just ripped, as shown in Figure 30.3. To play the entire album, double-click it. To start playing at a particular track, double-click the track.

**Figure 30.3**

*Play tracks ripped from the CD.*

## Creating a Playlist

With Media Player, you can mix tracks from various CDs and downloads by creating *playlists*. Here's how:

1. Click **Create Playlist**, type a name for the playlist, and press **Enter**.

2. In the list pane (on the left), below Music, click **Album**. A collection of ripped CDs appears on the right.

3. Double-click an album that contains tracks you want to add to your playlist.

4. Select the tracks you want to add to your playlist.

5. Drag and drop any one of the selected tracks onto the name of the new playlist, as shown in Figure 30.4.

Drag selected tracks here          Select tracks

Figure 30.4

*Drag and drop the audio tracks you recorded to your playlist.*

6. Repeat steps 2 to 5 to add tracks to your playlist from other CDs.

7. Click the name of the playlist.

8. Drag items up or down in the list to rearrange the tracks in the desired order.

To play your clips, click the clip you want to start playing and then click Media Player's **Play** button (near the bottom of the window). Media Player plays the selected song and then the remaining songs in your playlist.

## Burning an Audio CD

You can burn a CD, a playlist, or a new collection of audio tracks to a CD. Take the following steps:

1. Click the **Burn** tab (upper right).

2. Click the **Burn Options** button (below and to the right of the Burn tab) and click **Audio CD**.

3. Insert a blank CD-R disc into your CD drive. (If the AutoPlay dialog box appears, close it.)

4. If the burn list contains tracks from a previous session, click the **Clear list** button to remove the tracks.

5. Select the album, artist, or playlist that contains tracks you want to burn to the CD.

6. Drag the tracks from the details pane (center) to the list pane (right) and drop them in place. (You can drag individual tracks or an entire album or playlist. If you drag more tracks than will fit on the CD, Media Player creates a new list for another CD.)

7. To change the order of tracks in the burn list, drag a track up or down. To remove a track from the burn list, right-click the track and click **Remove from list**.

8. When you're ready to burn the CD, click **Start burn**, as shown in Figure 30.5.

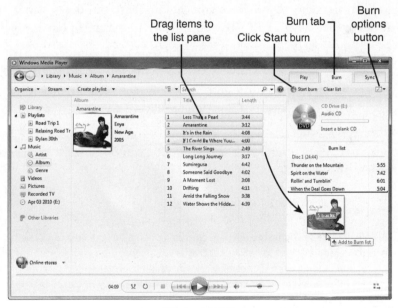

**Figure 30.5**
*Burn an audio CD.*

# Downloading Music from the Web

The web is buzzing with companies that sell downloadable music, audio books, and other digital audio. You can go to any number of online music stores and pack your shopping cart with tracks for under a buck each. You might even be able to legally pick up a few tracks for free. You can then burn the tracks to CDs, copy them to your MP3 player, and add them to your PC's growing audio library.

Keep in mind that downloading and "sharing" music without paying for it (unless you're downloading a free promotional track) is against the law.

Downloading any file is pretty easy. You click a link and follow the onscreen instructions to tell your browser where to save the file. However, before you can download audio clips, you have to find some tunes that are worth downloading. The following sites are popular online stores where you can purchase individual tracks:

- iTunes (www.apple.com/itunes) is the home of one of the most popular music stores on the Internet. Here you can download and install a free copy of iTunes so you can listen to your favorite tunes, preview recent releases, and purchase and download quality clips online for less than $1 per tune.

- Rhapsody (www.rhapsody.com) is where the creators of RealPlayer host their own online music store. Here you can purchase and download individual tracks to play on your RealPlayer, transfer to portable players, or burn to CDs.

- Yahoo! Music (new.music.yahoo.com) is one of the most popular online music sites, featuring Internet radio stations. If the station is playing a song you like, you can jump to the online store, order it, download it, add it to your playlist, and transfer it to your portable music player or burn it to a CD.

- AOL Music Now (music.aol.com) features on-demand Internet radio and customizable, commercial-free listening; you can order individual tracks online for less than a buck.

> **WHOA!**
>
> Before you start purchasing audio recordings online, be sure you can play them in Windows Media Player (or whatever player you use) and on your portable music player. Recordings from iTunes play only on an iPod, and the iPod can't play tunes that you download from Rhapsody. Most sites have a link you can click to learn which portable players and programs are compatible with the service.

As soon as you find a clip you want to download, simply click its link to play it. When your PC is finished downloading the clip, it should run your MP3 player, which typically starts playing the clip. If the clip doesn't start, click the **Play** button.

# Copying Music to a Portable Music Player

Building a huge music library on your PC is cool, but your PC may be a bit too bulky to carry around in certain situations. How do you take your music collection (or at least a portion of it) on the road? The easiest and lightest way is to purchase a portable music player, often called an MP3 player. Portable music players come equipped with enough storage to hold gobs of music. Typically, you can rip tracks from CDs or download them from various sources on the Internet and then transfer (copy) them to your player.

Portable music players are usually equipped with the software you need to transfer clips from your PC to your player. Many of the music stores discussed earlier in this chapter also offer free software that can handle the file transfers. However, this software may not enable you to rip music from the CDs you already own. An alternative is to use Windows Media Player or Apple iTunes to perform both jobs. This assumes, of course, that you have a portable music player one of these programs supports. If you don't, you may need to purchase additional software.

The process of transferring clips to your player is fairly straightforward. The following steps show you how to copy files from your PC to your portable music player using Windows Media Player. If you're using other software, the steps should be similar:

1. Connect your portable music player to your PC as instructed in the player's documentation, and turn it on.

2. Run Windows Media Player, as explained earlier in this chapter.

3. Click the **Sync** tab. A pane appears on the right, instructing you to drag tracks into the pane to add them to the Sync list. (If your portable music player or a drive letter for it does not appear, Windows Media Player may not support your player.)

4. Use the navigation pane (left) and the details pane (center) to display tracks you want to copy to your portable music player.

5. Drag and drop one of the selected tracks into the Sync pane (on the right).

6. Repeat steps 4 and 5 to copy any remaining tracks to the Sync pane.

7. Click the **Start Sync** button (near the bottom of the Sync pane).

8. When the sync is complete, exit Media Player and disconnect your portable music player as instructed in its documentation.

## The Least You Need to Know

- To play an audio CD, insert it into your PC's CD-ROM drive. When a dialog box pops up asking what you want to do, click **Play Audio CD** and click **OK**.
- To run Windows Media Player, click **Start**, **All Programs**, **Windows Media Player**.
- To copy all the tracks from an audio CD to the Windows Media Library, run Windows Media Player, insert the audio CD, and click **Start Rip**.
- To create a new playlist in Media Player, click **Create playlist**, type a name for the playlist, and press **Enter**. Drag and drop tracks over the name of the new playlist to add them to the playlist.
- To burn an audio CD, run Media Player, click the **Burn** tab, drag and drop albums and/or tracks into the Burn pane, and then click **Start burn**.
- To transfer music to a portable music player, run Media Player, click the **Sync** tab, drag and drop albums and tracks into the Sync pane, and then click **Start sync**.

# Snapping, Enhancing, and Sharing Digital Photos

## In This Chapter

- Snapping shots with a digital camera
- Making your photos look their best
- Sharing your photos online
- Sending digital photos via e-mail

With a digital camera, you get instant gratification. Right after you take a picture, you can check out the results on the LCD display and delete the photo and retake it if it didn't turn out right. You can plug your camera into a TV set and view the picture, or connect your camera to your computer and print the photo. In addition, digital photography enables you to e-mail photos to your friends and relatives, post them on your website or blog or an online photo album, and pack them away on CDs or DVDs. Perhaps best of all, you can airbrush out any imperfections before sharing your photos.

In this chapter, you learn the basics of digital photography, including how to take photographs, enhance your photographs with digital imaging software, share photos online in places like Facebook, and print and e-mail photos.

## Taking Digital Snapshots

Digital cameras are modeled off standard 35mm cameras, so snapping a picture is easy: you just point and shoot. If the camera has an autofocus feature, you may need to hold down the button halfway to focus the camera and then press down all the way to snap the shot.

Before you snap too many pictures, check the following camera settings:

- **Resolution, image size, or megapixels:** Most cameras enable you to adjust the size and quality of the image. If you plan to print the photos, choose a higher setting. If you're going to e-mail the photos or place them on a web page, a setting of 640×480 pixels is usually sufficient. Larger images are higher quality, but they're also larger files, requiring more storage space and taking longer to transfer on the Internet.

- **Mode or environment:** Many cameras feature an assortment of modes or environments that automatically adjust the camera settings for different types of photos—for example, parties, landscapes, sporting events, daytime or nighttime portraits, and so on.

- **Flash:** In most cases, leave the flash setting on Auto. If you're taking all your pictures outside, turn off the flash. For backlit scenes, turn on the flash, if this option is available on your camera.

- **Exposure:** Many cameras enable you to bump the exposure up or down for very dark, very light, or high-contrast subjects. (When you're first starting out, you may want to leave this setting alone.)

- **Date imprint:** Some cameras can add a date imprint to your photos so you can later tell the date you snapped them. If you find the date imprint more annoying than helpful, turn it off.

Some digital cameras can capture audio and short video clips as well as take photographs. Check your camera's documentation to determine any additional features it may have.

The procedure for checking the camera settings varies from one digital camera to another. Some cameras have two buttons: one for changing to a feature (such as flash, image quality, timer, and audio) and another for changing the settings. You change to the desired feature (for instance, flash) and then press the other button to change the setting (for instance, Autoflash or Flash On).

**INSIDE TIP**

Carry an extra memory card and battery with you … especially the battery. Most digital cameras use a lot of battery power, especially when you're using the flash.

# Getting Windows Live Photo Gallery

You can find numerous programs for managing and editing your photos and converting them into slide shows with background music or other audio. Your digital camera or even your printer may have come with its own photo-management software. You can also pick up free software on the web, such as Google's Picasa (picasa.google.com), or use free online photo-editing and sharing services, such as Flickr (www.flickr.com) and Photobucket (www.photobucket.com). I use Picasa for photo management and editing.

If you want to stick with a Microsoft product that has the look and feel of Windows 7, a good choice is Windows Live Photo Gallery. You can download it from download.live.com. I use Photo Gallery throughout this chapter to illustrate common photo-editing and management tasks. I use Windows Live Movie Maker (explore.live.com/windows-live-movie-maker) to transform my photos into DVD slide shows, as explained in Chapter 32, but you can use Windows DVD Maker instead, as explained near the end of this chapter.

After installing Photo Gallery, you can run it by selecting **Start**, **All Programs**, **Windows Live**, **Windows Live Photo Gallery**.

# Managing and Editing Your Photos

You have a bunch of photos on your camera. Now what? How do you transfer those photos to your PC, organize them, and edit them to improve their quality? The following sections answer all of these questions by showing you how to perform these essential tasks with Windows Live Photo Gallery.

## Transferring Photos from Camera to PC

To transfer the images from your camera to your PC, connect the cable to your camera and to the specified port on your PC, and turn on the camera. (Most cameras connect to a PC via a USB cable.) Windows should detect the camera and display a dialog box, like the one shown in Figure 31.1, prompting you to select the program you want to use to import photos from the camera to your PC.

**NOTE**

Many new printers and some PCs, especially portable PCs, are equipped with memory card readers. Instead of connecting the camera to your PC with a cable, you remove the memory card from your camera and plug it into the memory card slot on the PC or printer. The memory card reader typically appears as another storage drive on your computer.

**Figure 31.1**
*Choose the program to use to import photos from the camera to your PC.*

If Windows does not detect the camera, try running your photo-management program and clicking the button to import photos. If you're using Windows Live Photo Gallery to import images, here's what you do:

1. Click **Start, All Programs, Windows Live, Windows Live Photo Gallery**.

2. Connect your digital camera to your PC and turn on the camera.

3. Click **File, Import from camera or scanner**. Photo Gallery displays a list of sources from which you can import photos. (Your camera may appear as a drive letter rather than a camera.)

4. Click the icon for your camera and then click **Import**. The Import Photos and Videos dialog box appears with **Review, organize, and group items to import** selected by default.

5. Click **Next**. All photos on the camera are selected and grouped by date taken, as shown in Figure 31.2. Unless you specify otherwise, each group will be saved to a different folder.

6. (Optional) Click the check box next to a group to deselect it so it won't be imported. To deselect specific photos in a group, click the group and then click the check box next to each photo to remove the check mark next to it.

7. (Optional) Click **Enter a name** next to a group and type a name for the folder in which you want the photos stored. (To import all the photos into the same folder, give all folders the same name.)

8. (Optional) Click **Add tags** and type words that will help you locate the photos later.

9. Click **Import**. Photo Gallery starts importing the photos and displays its progress. You can click **Erase** after importing to have the photos removed from the camera when Photo Gallery has finished.

Click and type a name for the group

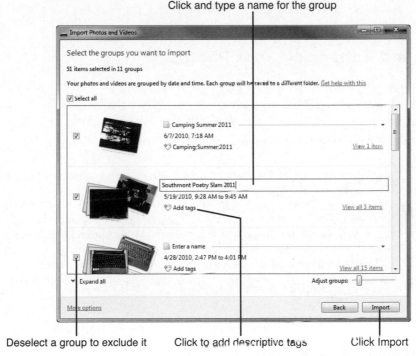

Deselect a group to exclude it        Click to add descriptive tags        Click Import

**Figure 31.2**
*Import photos into your photo-management program.*

## Copying Photos to a Recordable CD

After you transfer the photos to your computer's hard drive, consider copying them to a CD for safekeeping, just in case anything bad happens to your hard drive. Be sure to label the CD with a title and date so you can tell what's on it.

Later in this chapter, you learn how to transform a collection of photos into a slide show complete with background music and burn it to a recordable DVD so you can play it in most TV DVD players. If you simply want to copy the photos to a disc for safekeeping or share them with someone else, for viewing on a PC, here's what you do:

1. In Windows Live Photo Gallery, select the photos you want to copy to a CD.

2. Open the **Make** menu and click **Burn a data CD**. Photo Gallery prompts you to load a recordable CD.

3. Insert a recordable CD into your PC's CD-R drive.

4. Type a descriptive name for the disk, choose how you want to use it, click **Next**, and follow the onscreen cues to complete the operation. Windows formats the CD, and Photo Gallery copies the selected photos to the CD.

## Editing and Enhancing Your Photos

Most photo-management programs include their own photo-editing tools. After you retrieve the images from your camera, you can adjust the brightness, color, and contrast of an image, as well as crop it, flip it, resize it, and perform other digital photo gymnastics.

**WHOA!**

Before making changes to an original photo, check your program's help system to determine how it saves changes. Some programs create a backup copy of the original file, so you end up with two copies—the original and the changed photo. Others save your changes so you can revert to the original later. Some programs provide no way for you to go back to the original. The safest way to proceed is to use the program's File, Save As command to create your own backup copy.

To edit a photo in Photo Gallery, double-click the photo. The photo appears, as shown in Figure 31.3. You can then click the icon for the desired quick fix:

- **Auto adjust:** Automatically adjusts color and contrast so you don't have to mess with it.

- **Adjust exposure:** Enables you to adjust the brightness and contrast, correct for shadows, and mute or accentuate highlights.

- **Adjust color:** Allows you to adjust the color temperature (drag left for more blue, right for more yellow and red), tint, and saturation.

- **Straighten photo:** Allows you to straighten a photo by dragging a slider left or right to pivot the photo around its center point.

- **Crop photo:** Enables you to choose a preset crop or drag a box to define the area you want included in the photo. (Anything outside the box will be cropped out.)

- **Adjust detail:** Allows you to sharpen the photo or reduce "noise."

- **Fix red eye:** Corrects red-eye problems. Click this option and then drag a small box around each red eye you want to repair.

- **Black and white effects:** Enables you to convert a color photo into various black-and-white renditions.

**Figure 31.3**
*With digital photo-editing tools, you can enhance your photos.*

## Resizing Your Photos

Before you share photos via e-mail or on the web, you may want to make the photo files smaller so that they consume less storage space and transfer faster over the Internet.

To make a smaller copy of a photo, right-click the photo in Photo Gallery (not in photo edit mode) and click **Resize**. Open the **Select a size** drop-down list, click the desired size, and then click **Resize and Save**, as shown in Figure 31.4. Photo Gallery resizes the photo and saves it.

Select a smaller size

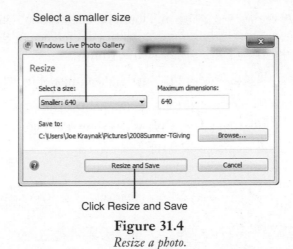

Click Resize and Save

**Figure 31.4**
*Resize a photo.*

# Sharing Your Photos on the Internet

One of the best features of digital cameras is that they create graphic files you can immediately use on web pages and in e-mail messages. You don't have to scan the picture after taking it, because it's already in a digital format.

You can share photos via the Internet in the following ways:

- Insert or attach photos to an outgoing e-mail message, as explained in Chapter 21. You can e-mail photos directly from Photo Gallery by selecting the photos you want to e-mail and then clicking the **E-mail** button and composing and sending the message.

- Upload photos to an online photo album. You can upload photos to Facebook, Flickr, Photobucket, and other social networking and photo-sharing sites. If you're using Windows Live Photo Gallery, check out the options on the Publish menu. The More Services option allows you to publish photos to Flickr and movies to YouTube, and install plug-ins for publishing photos directly from Photo Gallery to other sites, including Facebook.

You can upload photos directly from your PC to Facebook, without the help of Photo Gallery. Here's what you do:

1. Log in to Facebook and click **Photos** (in the left menu).

2. Click **+ Upload Photos**. Facebook prompts you to create a new photo album.

3. Complete the form to enter an album name, location (where the photos were taken), and description; choose a Privacy preference to determine who can look at the photos; and click **Create Album**.

4. If prompted to install the Uploader add-on, install it.

5. Use the resulting screen to choose the photos you want to upload into the new photo album and click **Upload**, as shown in Figure 31.5. (Facebook offers a basic uploader if this doesn't work.)

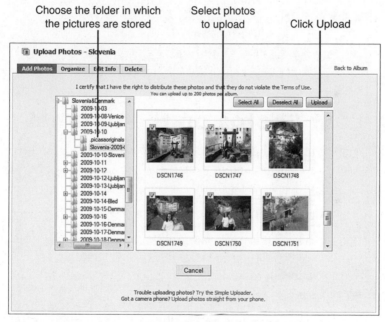

**Figure 31.5**
*Upload photos to Facebook.*

# Creating a Photo Slide Show and Burning It to a DVD

In Chapter 32, I show you how to transform a collection of photos and video clips into a slide show complete with musical accompaniment and burn it to a DVD that you can watch on TV or share with friends and family. I recommend that you use Windows Live Movie Maker (a free download from Microsoft) to perform this magic. Movie Maker has features that enable you to make a really cool movie.

If you're in a hurry and need something more basic, consider using Windows DVD Maker instead. Windows DVD Maker, included as a part of Windows 7, is a little less feature rich. It doesn't allow you to add video clips (photos and music only), and you can't insert text slides between groups of photos as you can in Windows Live Movie Maker. Nevertheless, Windows DVD Maker is an excellent program that suits most users' needs.

You can run Windows DVD Maker directly from Photo Gallery. Simply select the photos you want to burn to the DVD, and then click **Make**, **Burn a DVD**. Windows runs Windows DVD Maker and adds the selected photos to the list of photos to be burned to the DVD, as shown in Figure 31.6.

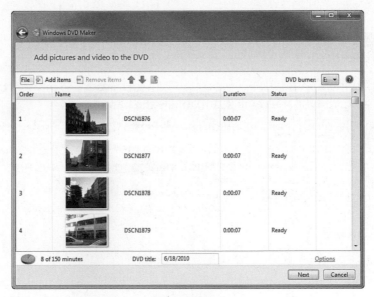

**Figure 31.6**
*Burn your photos to a DVD to create a slide show.*

Click **Next** and use the options on the resulting screen to select a menu style, edit the text on the menu, customize the menu, and add slide show features—add background music, adjust the time each slide appears, and control the transitions between slides. Click **Change Slide Show** to save your preferences. You can then click **Preview** (near the top) to play the slide show and make sure everything is just right before you burn it to a disc.

When you're ready to burn the slide show to a disc, click **OK** to end the preview (if it's still playing). Insert a blank DVD-R into your PC's recordable DVD drive, and then click the **Burn** button. Depending on the number, size, and quality of the photos; the amount of music; and the performance of your PC, Windows DVD Maker can take quite a while to produce the video and burn it to the disc.

> **INSIDE TIP**
>
> If you use something other than Windows Live Photo Gallery to manage and edit your photos, you can still use Windows DVD Maker to create a slide show and burn it to a DVD. Simply run DVD Maker as a standalone program: **Start**, **All Programs**, **Windows DVD Maker**. Click the **+ Add items** button to add the digital photos stored on your PC to the slide show, and then proceed as described earlier.

## The Least You Need to Know

- Download and install Windows Live Photo Gallery at download.live.com.
- To transfer photos from your digital camera to your PC, connect the camera to the PC, turn on the camera, and follow the onscreen cues.
- Double-click a photo in Windows Live Photo Gallery to display it in edit mode.
- To transform a collection of photos into a movie, select the photos in Windows Live Photo Gallery, open the **Make** menu, and click **Burn a DVD**.

# Playing and Making DVDs

## In This Chapter

- Watching DVDs on your PC ... like TV!
- Buying a digital camcorder
- Transferring video from your camcorder, memory card reader, CD, or DVD to your PC
- Transferring old videotapes to your PC
- Creating your own DVD movies with collections of photos and videos
- Adding musical accompaniment to your DVD movie

Your PC is your own digital film studio, where you can watch DVD movies (even Blu-ray, if your PC is properly equipped); edit, manage, and share your own video clips; and even make DVD movies to watch on TV and share with family and friends. This chapter shows you how.

## Playing DVDs on Your PC

If your PC has a DVD drive, it probably came equipped with its own DVD video player—the software required to show movies on the "big" screen. If it didn't, Windows Media Player can handle the job. Insert the DVD. If Windows prompts you to choose the DVD player you want to use, click **Play DVD Movie using Windows Media Player**. Media Player begins to play the movie. You can use the controls at the bottom of the screen to stop, pause, play, skip forward or back, or access the DVD menu, as shown in Figure 32.1.

If you change to full-screen mode, the controls at the bottom of the screen disappear when you stop moving the mouse. To bring the controls back into view, simply move the mouse.

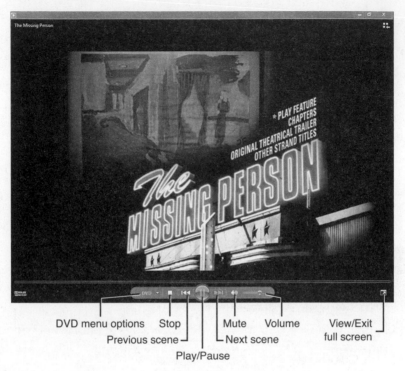

**Figure 32.1**
*Windows Media Player plays a DVD movie.*

# Transferring Video to Your PC

The procedure for transferring video from a digital camera or camcorder, a memory card reader, or a disc (CD or DVD) is relatively easy, because you're merely transferring a file from one device to the other.

Your camcorder probably came with its own video transfer/editing program, and chances are pretty good that it's better than Windows Live Movie Maker. If you don't have a specialized program or simply need to transfer video from a memory card reader, CD, or DVD, you can use Windows Live Movie Maker to perform the transfer.

**WHOA!**

To use Windows Live Movie Maker, Windows Live Photo Gallery must also be installed on your PC. You can pick up a free copy of both programs at download. live.com.

To transfer video from a digital camera or camcorder, a memory card reader, or a disc (CD or DVD) using Windows Live Movie Maker, here's what you do:

1. Connect the device to your PC, if it's not already connected, and turn it on.

2. Click **Start**, **All Programs**, **Windows Live**, **Windows Live Movie Maker**.

3. Click the **Movie Maker** menu button (to the left of the Home tab) and click **Import from device**. A dialog box appears, indicating "Photos and videos will be imported into Windows Live Photo Gallery."

4. Click **OK**. A list of devices you may be able to import video from appears.

5. Click the device that contains the video and click **Import**. The Import Photos and Videos dialog box appears, indicating the number of new photos and videos found on the device.

6. Click **Next**. All videos and any photos on the device are selected and grouped by date taken, as shown in Figure 32.2. Unless you specify otherwise, each group will be saved to a different folder.

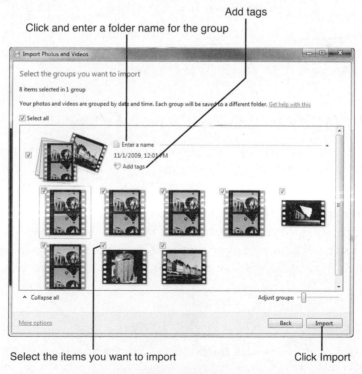

**Figure 32.2**
*Import video into Movie Maker.*

7. (Optional) Click the check box next to a group to deselect it so it won't be imported. To deselect specific videos or photos in a group, click the group and then click the check box next to each item to remove the check mark next to it.

8. (Optional) Click **Enter a name** next to a group and type a name for the folder in which you want the videos or photos stored. (To import all the items into the same folder, give all folders the same name.)

9. (Optional) Click **Add tags** and type words that will help you locate the items later.

10. Click **Import**. Movie Maker starts importing the videos and photos and displays its progress. You can click **Erase** after importing to have the items removed from the device (if possible) when the transfer is complete.

# Converting Old Tapes into Digital Video

If you already have an analog camcorder and/or old camcorder or VHS tapes, consider adding a video capture device to your PC. You have several options here. The most convenient is to purchase an external unit that connects to your PC's USB or FireWire (IEEE-1394) port, or into a circuit board that comes with the unit. Figure 32.3 shows Diamond's One Touch DVD Creator, which can capture from analog camcorders and VCRs.

**Figure 32.3**
*An analog-to-digital converter lets you connect a camcorder or VCR to your PC.*
(Courtesy of Diamond Multimedia.)

Video capture boards and external units have special ports that let you connect your camcorder to your PC. They typically capture video at a rate of 15 or more frames per second (fps) (30 fps is better), and they do a fairly good job of converting your analog clips into a digital format. If you're looking for a way to convert your collection of old camcorder or VHS tapes into a digital format and store them on DVDs, this is the way to go.

To transfer video from an analog camcorder or VCR to your PC, you must connect your analog-to-digital converter to your PC and connect the camcorder or VCR to the converter. In the case of an external converter, you connect it to the PC with a USB or FireWire cable. You use a composite or S-Video cable to connect the camcorder or VCR to the converter:

- **Composite video** combines the color and brightness data in a single signal, resulting in a lower-quality display. A composite cable typically has three RCA connectors: yellow (video), red (right audio), and white (left audio).

- **S-video** divides the video into two signals—one for color and one for brightness—generating a high-quality image. An S-video cable has a male connector with four pins that plugs into a female connector.

- **Audio jacks** carry the audio portion of the recording. Most analog-to-digital converters have two audio jacks: right (red) and left (white). However, most cameras have a single audio output jack. You can connect the audio output jack on the camera to either the left or right audio-input jack on the converter.

Figure 32.4 shows a schematic drawing of the connections for Pinnacle System's Video Transfer unit. Note that the camcorder or VCR provides the input (at the top of the diagram). The bottom of the diagram shows a single connection from the USB port on the converter to the PC to which you'll be recording the video.

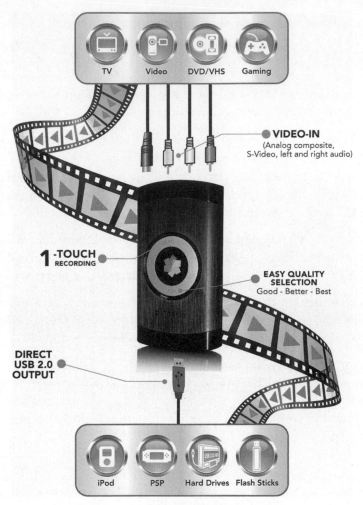

**Figure 32.4**

*An analog-to-digital converter receives input from the analog camcorder or VCR and converts it into a digital stream that can be recorded on a PC.*

(Courtesy of Pinnacle Systems, Inc.)

Your digital camcorder or video capture device probably came with its own program for recording and editing your video footage. Most of these programs are similar and follow the same overall procedure for recording video. Here's a quick overview of the process:

1. Connect your camcorder or VCR to your PC through the converter, as instructed in the previous section.

2. Use your camcorder or VCR controls to play the video to the point at which you want to start transferring the video to your PC.

3. Run your video transfer/conversion program.

4. Start playing the video and immediately click the **Start Record** button in your video transfer program to start capturing the video, as shown in Figure 32.5.

5. When you're ready to stop recording, click the **Stop Record** button in your video transfer program. Depending on the length of the video, the video transfer program may chop the recording into separate files to make them more manageable.

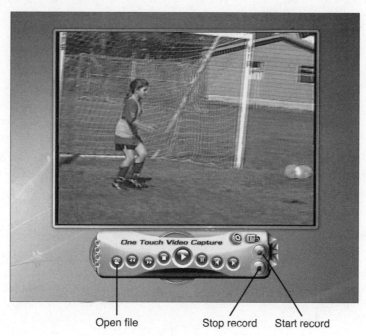

Open file          Stop record    Start record

**Figure 32.5**
*Transfer video to your PC.*

To find out where your video transfer program stores the video files, click the button to open a file. Jot down the location for future reference.

> **NOTE**
>
> If your analog converter does not include its own software (a highly unlikely scenario), Windows Live Movie Maker may be able to transfer video from the analog device.

# Converting Your Photos and Videos into a DVD Slide Show

You can transform a collection of photos and/or videos into a slide show and burn it to a DVD so you or anyone else can view your photos on a TV equipped with a standard DVD player. To make your DVD even more engaging, you can add music tracks that play in the background. (See Chapter 30 for details about digital music.)

One of the best tools for transforming a collection of photos into a slide show DVD with musical accompaniment is Windows Live Movie Maker. (Picasa also has a Movie Maker.)

## First Things First

Before creating a movie, correct any photos that are too dark, are too light, have red-eye problems, or just don't look right for some reason. (See Chapter 31 for details on photo editing.) If your photos look bad, your movie will look bad, too. Also rotate any images as necessary to display them in the proper orientation. (Movie Maker can rotate the photos for you, but you're better off having them look just as you want them to appear in the movie before you begin.)

> **INSIDE TIP**
>
> You can start your movie from Windows Live Photo Gallery and then skip the next section on adding photos and videos. Select the photos and videos you want to include in your movie, open the **Make** menu, and click **Make a Movie**. Photo Gallery runs Movie Maker and adds the selected photos and videos.

## Adding Photos and Videos to Create a Movie

To start making the movie using Windows Live Movie Maker, take the following steps:

1. Click **Start, All Programs, Windows Live, Windows Live Movie Maker**.

2. Click the **Home** tab and click **Add videos and photos**.

3. Change to the folder that contains the photos and/or videos you want to include in your movie, select all the items you want to include, and click **Open**. Movie Maker adds the selected items to your movie, as shown in Figure 32.6.

4. (Optional) To move an item, drag and drop it where you want it to appear in the movie. To remove an item, right-click it and click **Remove**.

**Figure 32.6**
*Photos and videos in Movie Maker.*

After choosing the photos and videos to include in your movie and arranging them in the order you want, you can have Movie Maker do the rest, and you can skip the rest of this chapter. Just click the **Home** tab and click **Auto Movie** to have Movie Maker create a movie for you. Auto Movie adds a title slide, credits, and transitions. All you need to do is add background music (assuming that you want background music).

## Adding a Title, Credits, and Captions

To give your movie a professional touch, consider adding a title slide and credits. (You can add a title slide at the beginning to introduce the movie or between sections to transition from one series of related photos and videos to another.) You can also add captions to your photos and videos. Click the **Home** tab and then add the desired text object:

- **Title:** Click the slide before which you want the title slide to appear, type the desired text, and then use the options near the top of the screen to format the title slide and specify the time it remains onscreen, as shown in Figure 32.7.

- **Caption:** Click the photo you want to caption, click **Caption**, type the desired text, and use the options near the top of the screen to format the caption.

- **Credits:** Click the slide after which you want the credits to appear, type the names of the people you want to credit (pressing **Enter** after each name), and then use the options near the top of the screen to format the credits and specify the amount of time to display the credits.

To change the background color for a title or credit slide, click the slide, click the **Edit** tab, open the **Background color** list, and click the desired color.

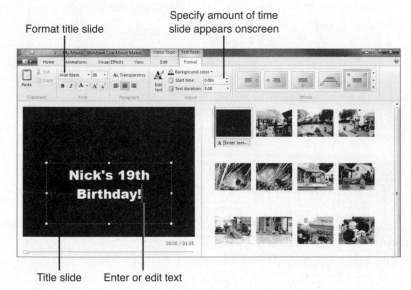

**Figure 32.7**
*Add a title slide.*

## Controlling Slide Transitions

To add cool, smooth transitions between slides, right-click anywhere in the collection of photos and click **Select all**, click the **Animations** tab, and select the Transition and Pan and zoom options you want to use. It's tough to tell what each option does, so choose an option and then play a portion of your movie to see the effect in action. (See "Previewing Your Movie," later in this chapter.)

## Adding Background Music

Audiences love background music, if you choose the right selections. You can use music you ripped from CDs or downloaded from the Internet. See Chapter 30 for more about working with digital music.

Once you have some audio clips stored in one or more folders on your computer's hard drive, you can import them into Movie Maker and add them to your movie:

1. Click the slide where you want the audio track to begin playing.

2. On the Home tab, click the musical note icon above Add music.

3. Change to the folder that contains the audio track you want to include in your movie, select the track, and click **Open**. Movie Maker imports the selected track and displays a green bar above the photos indicating that photos will be displayed during the track, as shown in Figure 32.8.

4. Repeat Steps 2 and 3 to add tracks.

5. (Optional) Move a track by dragging and dropping it where you want it to begin playing. To remove a track, right-click it and select **Remove**.

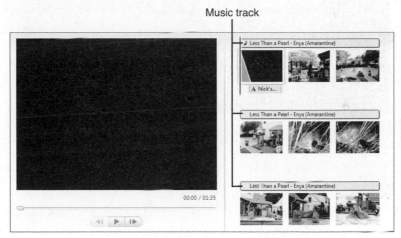

**Figure 32.8**

*Add background music to your movie.*

## Previewing Your Movie

Before burning (recording) your movie to a DVD, preview it to make sure it contains all the photos, videos, and music you want it to include in the order in which you want them to play.

To preview your movie, click the first slide in your show (probably the Title slide, if you added a title to your movie) and then click the **Play** button.

## Saving Your Project

To save your project so you can edit it later, open the **Movie Maker** menu (to the left of the Home tab) and click **Save Project**, or press **Ctrl+S** and then save the file as you would save any file on your PC. This simply saves your project; it doesn't allow you to play the movie on a TV DVD player. To do that, you need to save your project as a *movie*, as discussed in the following section.

## Burning Your Movie to a DVD

To publish your movie to a DVD, your computer must be equipped with a recordable DVD player and you must use DVD-R discs. To burn your movie to a disc, take the following steps:

1. Insert a blank DVD-R in your PC's recordable DVD drive.

2. Open your movie project in Windows Live Movie Maker, if it's not already open.

3. Click the **Home** tab.

4. Click the DVD icon.

5. Choose a folder in which to save the movie, type a name for the movie file, and click **Save**. Movie Maker saves the project as a movie. (This can take quite a bit of time, depending on the movie length and your PC's speed.)

6. Click **Next**. Movie Maker displays a dialog box for creating an opening menu for your movie.

7. Click the desired menu style (on the right) and then click **Customize menu**, use the resulting options to make additional changes, and click **Change Style**. (The Foreground and Background video options are a little misleading; you can use videos or photos for the opening menu, in addition to the photos and videos already included in the movie. You may also want to add a separate music track for the menu.)

8. Click **Menu text**, use the resulting screen to edit and format the opening menu text, and click **Change Text**.

9. Click the **Burn** button. Movie Maker encodes the movie to play on a TV DVD player and burns the movie onto the recordable DVD, which can take quite some time. When the process is complete, Movie Player ejects the disc and offers you the option to make another copy of the DVD or close (exit).

## The Least You Need to Know

- As long as your PC is equipped with a DVD player, Windows Media can use it to play DVD movies on your PC.

- You can connect a digital camcorder directly to your PC via a USB port.

- With an analog-to-digital converter, you can transfer video from old VHS and analog camcorder tapes to your PC.

- You can pick up a free copy of Windows Live Movie Maker at download.live.com.

- To add photos and videos to your movie in Movie Maker, click the **Home** tab, click **Add videos and photos**, use the resulting dialog box to select the photos and videos you want to add, and click **Open**.

- To burn your movie to a DVD in Windows Live Movie Maker, make sure the project is open; then click the **Home** tab, click the DVD icon, and follow the onscreen cues.

# Maintaining and Troubleshooting Your Computer

You don't need to be a mechanic to use a PC, but you should perform some basic maintenance tasks on a regular basis to keep your PC in tip-top condition and running at peak performance.

Part 6 acts as your PC maintenance and upgrade manual. Here you learn how to clean your monitor, keyboard, mouse, printer, and system unit; give your PC a regular tune-up to keep it running at top speed; troubleshoot common PC problems; and prepare for and recover from unavoidable disasters.

# Keeping Your PC Clean

### In This Chapter

- Dusting your computer
- Squeegeeing your monitor
- Scrubbing your mouse
- Keeping your printer shiny and new
- Spin-cleaning your disk drives

One of the best clean-air machines on the market is a computer. The cooling fan constantly sucks in the dusty air and filters out the dust. A monitor acts like a dust magnet, pulling in any airborne particles unfortunate enough to get close to it. And the keyboard and mouse act like vacuum cleaners, sucking crumbs and other debris from your desk.

Unfortunately, the dust and smoke that your computer filters out eventually build up on the mechanical and electrical components inside it. When enough dust and debris collect on your computer and accessories, it's time for a thorough cleaning.

## Tools of the Computer-Cleaning Trade

Before you start cleaning, turn off your computer and any attached devices, and gather the following cleaning equipment:

- **Screwdriver or wrench:** This is for taking the cover off your system unit. (If you don't feel comfortable going inside the system unit, take your computer to a qualified technician for a thorough annual cleaning. It really does get dusty in there.)

- **Computer vacuum:** Yes, there are vacuum cleaners designed especially for computers.

- **Can of compressed air:** You can get this at a computer or electronics store. Compressed air is great for blowing the dust out of tight spots, such as between keyboard keys.

- **Soft brush:** A clean paintbrush with soft bristles will do. Use this to dislodge any stubborn dust the vacuum won't pick up.

- **Toothpick:** This is the only tool you need to clean your mouse.

- **Cotton swabs:** Another good tool for cleaning your mouse, it's great for swabbing down your keyboard, too.

- **Paper towels:** Use these for wiping dust off your equipment and for cleaning the monitor.

- **Alcohol:** This is not the drinking kind; save that for when you're done.

- **Distilled water:** You can get special wipes for your monitor, but paper towels and distilled water do the trick.

**INSIDE TIP**

You've probably seen floppy disk or CD-ROM cleaning kits, but most likely you don't need one. If your drive is having trouble reading disks, buy a cleaning kit and clean it. If it's running smoothly, let it be.

# Vacuuming and Dusting Your Computer

Work from the top down and from the outside in—with the power off and the pieces unplugged.

Start with the monitor. You can use your regular vacuum cleaner for this part; if you have a brush attachment, use it. Run your vacuum hose up and down all the slots at the top and sides of the monitor. This is where most of the dust settles. Work down to the tilt-swivel base and vacuum that, too. You might need a narrow hose extension to reach in there.

Next, vacuum your printer, speakers, and any other devices. If dust is stuck to a device, wipe it off with a damp (not soaking-wet) paper towel.

The system unit comes next. When vacuuming, be sure you vacuum all the ventilation holes and any gaps that allow air to flow into the system unit, including the power button, the DVD drive, open drive bays, and so on.

Now take the cover off the system unit and vacuum any dusty areas. You can't just poke your vacuum hose in there, though. Use only a vacuum designed for computers.

Don't use a DustBuster, your regular vacuum cleaner, or your ShopVac. These can suck components off your circuit boards and can emit enough static electricity to fry a component. A computer vacuum is gentle and grounded. Also be careful not to suck up any loose screws. Before you begin, touch a metal part of the case to discharge any static electricity from your body, and keep your fingers away from the circuit boards.

Dust likes to collect around the fan, ventilation holes, and disk drives. Try to vacuum the fan blades, too. If you can't get the tip of the vacuum between the blades, gently wipe them off with a cotton swab. Some fans have a filter where the fan is mounted. If you're really ambitious, remove the fan (be careful with the wires) and clean the filter.

(Alternatively, take your PC outside and blow the dust out using your can of compressed air. Be careful spraying the air against internal components. Compressed air can be very cold and can cause condensation to form on sensitive electrical components.)

You can use a can of compressed air to blow dust off external peripheral devices as well, such as your keyboard and speakers.

## Cleaning Your Monitor

If you can write "Wash Me" on your monitor with your fingertip, the monitor needs cleaning. Check the documentation that came with your computer or monitor to see if it's okay to use window cleaner on it. The monitor might have an antiglare coating that can be damaged by alcohol- or ammonia-based cleaning solutions. If it's not okay or if you're not sure, use water.

With your monitor turned off and unplugged, spray the window cleaner (or water) on a paper towel, just enough to make it damp; wipe the screen; and wipe with a dry paper towel to remove excess moisture. *Don't* spray window cleaner or any other liquid directly on the monitor; you don't want moisture to seep in.

You can also purchase special antistatic wipes for your monitor. These not only clean your monitor safely, but they also discharge the static electricity to prevent future dust buildup.

If you don't want to spend money on antistatic wipes, wipe your monitor with a *used* dryer sheet. A new dryer sheet might smudge the screen with fabric softener.

# Shaking the Crumbs Out of Your Keyboard

Your keyboard is like a big placemat, catching all the cookie crumbs and other debris that fall off your fingers while you're working. Unlike a placemat, however, the keyboard isn't flat; it's full of nooks and crannies that are perfect hiding spots for crumbs and debris and are nearly impossible to reach to clean. And the suction from a typical vacuum cleaner just isn't strong enough to pull up the dust (although you can try it).

The easiest way I've found to clean a keyboard is to turn it upside down and shake it gently. Repeat two or three times to get out any particles that fall behind the backs of the keys when you flip it over. If you don't like that idea, take your keyboard outside, get your handy-dandy can of compressed air, and blow between the keys.

**NOTE**

Rubbing alcohol is an excellent cleaning solution for most electronic devices because it cleans well and dries quickly. Use it for your keyboard, plastics, and most glass surfaces (except for some monitors). Avoid using it on rubber (for example, the rubber rollers inside a printer), because it tends to dry out the rubber and make it brittle.

For a more thorough cleaning, shut down your computer and disconnect the keyboard. Dampen a cotton swab with rubbing alcohol and gently scrub the keys. Wait for the alcohol to evaporate completely before reconnecting the keyboard and turning on the power.

If you spill a drink on your keyboard, try to save your work and shut down the computer fast but properly. Flip the keyboard over and turn off your computer. If you spilled water, let the keyboard dry out thoroughly. If you spilled something sticky, give your keyboard a bath or shower with lukewarm water. Take the back off the keyboard, but do not flip over the keyboard with the back off, or parts will scurry across your desktop. Let it dry for a couple of days (don't use a blow dryer), and put it back together. If some of the keys are still sticky, clean around them with a cotton swab dipped in rubbing alcohol. If you still have problems, you may have to buy a new keyboard.

# Making Your Mouse Cough Up Hairballs

If you can't get your mouse pointer to move where you want it to, you can usually fix the problem by cleaning the mouse. Most new mice are optical or laser mice and use light to detect motion, so they have no moving parts to clean. I've never had a problem with an optical mouse getting gunked up. The only part you may need to clean are the little raised areas on the bottom of the mouse that come in contact with your desk or mouse pad, because these can get sticky. Simply dab a lint-free cloth in alcohol and gently wipe the pads.

**WHOA!**

Whatever you do, don't allow any cleaning solution or your cleaning cloth to come in contact with your mouse's light sensor, as this could negatively affect its operation.

If you have a mouse with a ball in it (a mechanical mouse), forget about cleaning it. Take the plunge and purchase an optical mouse.

And don't forget to clean your mouse pad or the area of your desk where your mouse scurries about. If the mouse was dirty, there's a good chance it picked up the dirt from your desk or mouse pad.

# Cleaning Your Printer

Printer maintenance varies so widely from one printer to another that I recommend referring to the manual that came with your printer. In some cases, for example, cleaning the print heads means wiping them off with a damp, lint-free cloth; other printers may have a control panel option for cleaning the print heads, and if you touch the print head, you void the warranty.

If you don't have the printer manual, you can usually visit the manufacturer's website and obtain an electronic version of the manual, as explained in Chapter 35. If no manual is available, search the website for general instructions on printer cleaning and maintenance, or try to find a manual for a similar make and model.

**WHOA!**

Toner used in laser printers can be hazardous to your health. Using compressed air to blow toner out of the printer or a standard vacuum cleaner to suck it out can launch a lot of toner dust into the air. You can buy a special toner vacuum, but they're fairly expensive. You're better off hiring out the job to someone who has the right equipment and experience.

Even with these variables, there are a few things the average user can do to keep the printer in peak condition and ensure high-quality output.

When turning off the printer, always use the power button on the printer or press the **Online** button to take the printer offline (don't use the power button on your power strip). This ensures that the print head is moved to its rest position. On inkjet printers, this prevents the print head from drying out.

Avoid touching the print heads unless the manufacturer or a tech support person tells you specifically to do so.

If the ink starts to streak on your printouts (or you have frequent paper jams in a laser printer), see if your printer has an option for cleaning the print heads. If it doesn't, get special printer-cleaner paper from an office supply store and follow the instructions to run the sheet through your printer a few times.

Using a damp cotton cloth, wipe paper dust and any ink off the paper feed rollers. Do not use alcohol. Do not use a paper towel; fibers from the paper towel could stick to the wheels.

# What About the Disk Drives?

Don't bother cleaning your CD or DVD drives unless they're giving you trouble. If one of these drives is having trouble reading a disc, the disc is usually the cause of the problem. Clean the disc and check the bottom of the disc for scratches. If the drive has problems reading every disc you insert, try cleaning the drive using a special drive-cleaning kit. The kit usually consists of a disc with some cleaning solution. You squirt the cleaning solution on the disc, insert it, and remove it, and your job is done.

## The Least You Need to Know

- Vacuum your system, especially around its ventilation holes.
- Wipe the dust off your screen using a paper towel and the cleaning solution recommended by the manufacturer.
- Blow the crumbs out of your keyboard with compressed air.
- To clean your printer, follow your manufacturer's instructions.
- Clean your CD or DVD drive only if it's having trouble reading discs.

# Giving Your PC a Tune-Up

## In This Chapter

- Cleaning up your hard disk
- Repairing hard disk problems
- Doubling your disk space (without installing a new drive)
- Increasing your memory (without installing more RAM)

Over time, you'll notice that your PC has slowed down. Windows takes a little longer to start up, programs that used to snap into action now seem to crawl, scrolling becomes choppy, and your PC locks up more frequently. You might begin to think that you need a new processor, more RAM, a larger hard disk drive, or even a whole new PC.

Before you take such drastic action, work through this chapter to give your PC a tune-up. By clearing useless files from your disk drive, reorganizing files, and reclaiming some of your PC's memory, you can boost your PC's performance and save a lot of money at the same time.

# Eliminating Useless Files

Your hard disk probably contains *temporary files* and backup files that your programs create without telling you. These files can quickly clutter your hard drive, consuming space you need for new programs or new data files you create. You can easily delete most of these files yourself.

The easiest way to clear useless files from your hard drive in Windows is to let the Windows Disk Cleanup utility manage the details:

1. Click **Start, All Programs, Accessories, System Tools, Disk Cleanup**. If your PC has more than one hard drive, Windows prompts you to select the drive you want to clean.

2. If prompted to select a drive, click the arrow to the right of the Drives box, click the desired drive, and click **OK**. The utility scans your PC's hard drive for useless files and displays a list of file types you probably won't ever need, as shown in Figure 34.1.

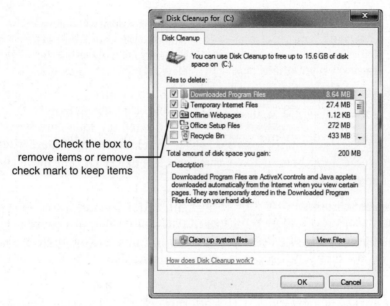

Check the box to remove items or remove check mark to keep items

**Figure 34.1**
*Disk Cleanup can remove useless files from your hard drive.*

3. Check the box next to each file type you want Disk Cleanup to sweep off your PC's hard drive, and uncheck the box next to any items you want to keep.

4. Click **OK** to commence the proceedings. The Cleanup utility removes the files you selected in Step 3.

**DEFINITION**

**Temporary files,** those files that end in .TMP, are files that your programs create but often forget to delete. You can safely delete them to make more room on your PC.

For a more thorough and aggressive cleaning, perform Steps 1 and 2 and then click the **Clean up system files** button. Windows displays a Disk Cleanup dialog box, sort of like the one shown in Figure 34.1, but this one has a More Options tab. Click the **More Options** tab, and then click the **Clean up** button under Programs and Features or System Restore and Shadow Copies to clear additional items from the disk. Confirm you're sure you want to delete by clicking **Delete**.

> **INSIDE TIP**
>
> You can clear temporary Internet files off your hard drive without having to perform a full disk cleanup. In Internet Explorer, click **Tools**, **Internet Options**. Under Browsing history, click **Delete**; use the resulting options to choose the items you want to delete, or click the **Delete All** button to delete everything.

Disk Cleanup does not remove copies of old digital photos you never look at, video clips you never watch, or music clips you never listen to. These are the items that really gobble up hard drive space in a hurry. Track down the folders where these files are stored and delete them or move them to CDs or DVDs. For more about managing files and folders, skip back to Chapter 8.

While you're at it, open your e-mail program and delete any e-mail messages you no longer need, including copies of messages you sent. When you delete e-mail messages, some e-mail programs stick the deleted messages in a separate folder (usually called Deleted Items). Be sure to delete the messages from that folder, too.

> **NOTE**
>
> Disk Cleanup can dump your Recycle Bin and open up a lot of disk space. If you already did this, that's fine, but know that you can dump the Recycle Bin at any time. Just be sure it doesn't contain something you might need. Open the Recycle Bin by double-clicking its icon on the desktop, and scroll down the list of deleted files to be sure you don't need anything in the Bin. If you find a file you might need, drag it onto the Windows desktop for safekeeping, or right-click the file and select **Restore** to restore the file to its original location. Then click the **Empty the Recycle Bin** button.

# Checking for and Repairing Damaged Files

Windows comes with a utility called ScanDisk that can test a disk, repair most problems on it, and refresh it if needed. What kind of problems? ScanDisk can find defective storage areas on a disk, retrieve any recoverable data, and block those areas to prevent your PC from using them. ScanDisk can also find and delete misplaced (usually useless) file fragments that might be causing your PC to crash.

Run ScanDisk regularly, at least once every month, and whenever your PC seems to be acting up and crashing for no apparent reason.

To run ScanDisk, follow these steps:

1. Click **Start**, **Computer**.

2. Right-click the icon for the drive you want to scan and click **Properties**.

3. Click the **Tools** tab and (under Error-Checking) click the **Check now** button. The Check Disk Local Disk dialog box appears, as shown in Figure 34.2.

**Figure 34.2**
*ScanDisk can repair most disk problems.*

4. Click the check box next to **Automatically fix file system errors**.

5. To check for bad areas on the disk, click the check box next to **Scan for and attempt recovery of bad sectors**. Checking this option tells ScanDisk to do a thorough job, which might take several hours; turn on this option only if you don't plan to use your PC for a while.

6. When you're ready to begin the scan, click **Start**. ScanDisk either automatically starts to scan the drive or displays a message indicating that it will scan the drive the next time you restart Windows.

# Defragmenting Files

Whenever you delete a file from your hard disk, you leave a space where another file can be stored. When you save a file, your PC stores as much of the file as possible in that empty space and stores the rest of the file in other empty spaces. The file is then said to be *fragmented*, because its parts are stored in different locations on the disk. This slows down your disk drive and makes it more likely that your PC will lose track of a portion of the file or the entire file. Every month or so, run Windows Disk Defragmenter to determine the fragmentation percent and defragment your files, if necessary.

Before you start Disk Defragmenter, it's a good idea to disable any power-management utilities that might interfere with Defragmenter and any antivirus programs you're using. It's also a good idea to run Disk Cleanup before defragmenting your drive, as discussed in "Eliminating Useless Files," earlier in this chapter. (See Chapter 6 for details on how to configure the Windows power management settings.)

Save and close all open documents and exit any programs currently running. To disable an antivirus program, right-click its icon in the notification area (right end of the taskbar), and click the option to disable the security features or exit the program.

When you're ready to have Disk Defragmenter defragment your files, follow these steps:

1. Click **Start**, **All Programs**, **Accessories**, **System Tools**, **Disk Defragmenter**. Disk Defragmenter appears, as shown in Figure 34.3. You can also run Disk Defragmenter by right-clicking the drive icon and then selecting **Properties**, **Tools**, **Defragment now**.

**Figure 34.3**

*Defragmenter prompts you to select the drive(s) you want to defragment.*

2. If your PC has more than one hard drive, click the icon for the drive you want to defragment.

3. (Optional) Click **Analyze disk** to display the percentage of file fragmentation on the disk and determine whether you need to defragment the disk.

4. When you're ready for Defragmenter to start working, click the **Defragment disk** button. Defragmenter starts defragmenting the files on the disk.

Wait until the defragmentation is complete. It's best to leave your PC alone during the process. Otherwise, you might change a file and cause Defragmenter to start over. Don't run any programs or play any PC games. When defragmentation is complete, Defragmenter displays a message telling you so.

Another issue that can significantly slow down your PC is having numerous programs and processes running in the background. Many programs install automatic update options, for example, that frequently check for updates on the Internet and download and install updates without notifying you. You can use the Windows System Configuration Utility to choose which programs are allowed to run on startup. See Chapter 35 for details.

**WHOA!**

I recommend avoiding any registry "fixes" that optimize your system. I've had registry optimizers severely mess up my system. If you choose to try the registry fixes, make a system restore point first, as explained in Chapter 35.

## The Least You Need to Know

- Clear temporary files; unused photos, videos, and music files; old e-mail messages; and temporary Internet files from your hard disk, and don't forget to dump the Recycle Bin.

- To avoid system crashes and lost files, run ScanDisk at least once a month and whenever your PC is frequently locking up.

- To increase performance and prevent data loss, run Disk Defragmenter at least once a month.

# PC Problems: Preparation and Troubleshooting

## In This Chapter

- Preparing for a possible crisis
- Sniffing out the cause of a problem
- Restoring your PC to a time when it worked right
- Identifying rogue programs and other troublesome software
- Recovering safely when your PC locks up

Your PC can be quite moody. One day, all the components run fine and all tasks proceed without a glitch. The next day, your mouse pointer won't budge, your printer refuses to print a document, Windows locks up, your PC refuses to connect to the Internet, or valuable documents simply disappear.

In this chapter, I help you prepare in advance so you can recover from serious problems, and I reveal troubleshooting techniques that can help you track down the solutions to nearly any PC issue without having to call a technician.

This chapter won't transform you into a professional PC technician, but with a little practice and a lot of patience, you should be able to solve the most common problems and even help your friends with their PC woes.

## Backing Up and Restoring Files

Your PC's hard drive may be very reliable, but it's not totally immune to virus attacks, hardware malfunctions, or human error. Because of this, you should back up all the files on your PC, or at least the files you can't reasonably recover without a backup—data files, e-mail messages and addresses, digital photos, your video or music collection, and so on.

I recommend purchasing an external hard drive for your PC and backing up all your irreplaceable files to the external hard drive at least once a week. If you go on a trip, take the backups with you and leave the originals at home, or vice versa. (If you don't have an external hard drive, you can back up files to recordable CDs or DVDs or an internal hard drive.)

## Backing Up Files

Take the following steps to back up files with Windows Backup's recommended settings:

1.  Click **Start**, **All Programs**, **Maintenance**, **Backup and Restore**.

2.  Under Backup, do one of the following:

    *   If this is the first time you're running Windows Backup and Restore, click **Set up backup** and then proceed to Step 3 to enter your backup settings.

    *   If you already entered your backup settings and want to use those same settings, click **Back up now**.

    *   If you already entered your backup settings and want to use different settings, click **Change settings** and proceed with Step 3.

3.  Click the drive you want to use to store your backup files and click **Next**. (I recommend backing up to recordable DVDs or a removable hard drive so you can store your backup in a safe location away from your PC.)

4.  When asked "What do you want to back up?" do one of the following:

    *   Click **Let Windows choose (recommended)** and click **Next** so Windows can decide which files to back up—all data files saved in libraries, on the desktop, or in Windows default folders. Windows also creates a system image that you can use to restore your PC if it stops working.

    *   Click **Let me choose**, use the resulting dialog box to choose the folders and files you want included in the backup, and click **Next**. (Use this option if you store your data files in folders outside the Windows libraries and default folders—for example, in a folder named C:\Data.)

5.  Click **Save settings and run backup**. (You can stop the backup operation at any time by clicking **View Details** and then clicking **Stop backup** and **Stop backup** again to confirm.)

If you choose to select what to back up, selecting items is the only tricky part. If you click the check box next to a drive or folder that's not expanded (in other words, you can't see the folders below the drive letter or the subfolders below a folder), you select everything on the drive or in the folder. To select specific folders or files, first click the arrow to the left of the drive letter or folder in which the items are stored. This expands the listing for the selected file or folder. You can then select individual files or folders, as shown in Figure 35.1.

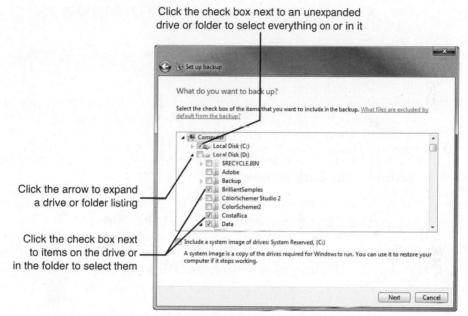

Click the check box next to an unexpanded drive or folder to select everything on or in it

Click the arrow to expand a drive or folder listing

Click the check box next to items on the drive or in the folder to select them

**Figure 35.1**
*Select disk drives, folders, and files to back up.*

As you modify files included in your backup, Windows either adds those files to your backup the next time you perform a backup or automatically backs up files according to the schedule settings. This ensures that you have up-to-date backups.

## Restoring Files

If disaster strikes and you lose valuable files, you can restore your files from your backups.

**WHOA!**

Before restoring files, make sure they're really gone. Backup files tend to be older than the originals, and you usually don't want to replace a new file with an older version. Windows will warn you if you're about to replace a file with a file of the same name and ask you to confirm.

To restore folders or files from your backups, here's what you do:

1. Click **Start**, **All Programs**, **Maintenance**, **Backup and Restore**.

2. Click **Restore my files**. The Restore Files dialog box appears.

3. Click one of the following options:

   • **Search**, to search your backups for specific files and folders.

   • **Browse for files**, to selectively restore specific files within one or more folders.

   • **Browse for folders**, to selectively restore one or more folders and their entire contents.

4. Follow the onscreen cues to find and select the file(s) and/or folder(s) you want to restore and add them to the list of items you want restored.

5. (Optional) Repeat Steps 3 and 4 to select additional files and folders.

6. Click **Next**. Windows prompts you to choose the location where you want to restore the items.

7. Click **In the original location** or choose **In the following location**, and then click the **Browse** button and choose the disk drive and folder in which to restore the items.

8. Click **Restore**.

## Creating a System Image

Windows enables you to create a system image, which essentially clones the hard drive on which Windows is installed. If that drive ever stops working, you can then restore the system image, in its entirety, to return your PC to the time when the system image was created. This returns Windows 7 and all your programs installed on that drive. (You can't selectively restore items from a system image.)

**WHOA!**

Store the system image on a separate disk drive. If the original drive stops working, your system image will be of no use. You can store the system image on another hard drive or on DVDs.

To create a system image, click **Start**, **All Programs**, **Maintenance**, **Backup and Restore**. In the left column, click **Create a system image**. Click the drive on which to store the system image and click **Next**. Choose the drives you want to include and click **Next**. Click **Start backup**.

If your PC's system files are damaged to the point of rendering your PC inoperable, you can recover by restoring the system image to your PC. (If the hard drive on which the system files are stored is not working, you must replace the hard drive first. The hard drive must be the same size or larger than the original drive.) Do one of the following:

- If your PC is working and you can access the Control Panel or you want to restore your system image to another Windows 7 PC, click **Start**, **Control Panel**, **System and Security**, **Action Center**, **Recovery**, **Advanced recovery methods**. Click **Use a system image you created earlier to recover your computer**, and then follow the onscreen cues to complete the operation.

- If you can't access the Control Panel and you don't have a Windows installation or system repair disc, restart your computer and keep tapping the **F8** key to start Windows in Safe mode. On the Advanced Boot Options screen, use the arrow keys to highlight **Repair your computer**, and press **Enter**. Select a keyboard layout and click **Next**. Select a username, type the password, and click **OK**. On the System Recovery Options menu, click **System Image Recovery** and then follow the instructions.

# Creating and Using a System Repair Disc

Viruses or other malware can attack system files and bring your Windows PC to its knees. One way to protect your PC is to prepare for the worst by creating a system repair disc and backing up your files. This section shows you how to create a system repair disc. The following section shows you how to back up and restore files.

To create a system repair disc, click **Start**, **All Programs**, **Maintenance**, **Create a System Repair Disc**. If you have more than one disc drive, open the **Drive** menu and click the drive you want to use. Insert a blank disc into the drive and click **Create disc**. When Windows has completed the disc, it displays a message instructing you to label the disc. Eject the disc, label it as instructed, click **Close**, and then click **OK**.

To use the repair disc, here's what you do:

1. Insert the repair disc into your PC's disc drive.

2. Restart your PC using your PC's power button and watch the screen carefully; it should display a message telling you to press a certain key to access the boot menu. (If you don't see such a message, check your PC's manual to determine how to boot from the disc drive.)

3. Press the designated key and then choose the option to boot from the disc drive instead of the hard drive.

4. Choose your language settings and click **Next**.

5. Choose the desired recovery option and click **Next**.

6. Follow the onscreen instructions to repair or restore your system.

# Troubleshooting Problems

When you run into a problem that doesn't have an obvious solution, the best course of action is inaction—that is, don't do anything. If you're fidgeting to do something, take a walk or grab a snack. Doing the wrong thing can often make the problem worse. After you've calmed down a little, come back and work through this list:

- **Are there any onscreen messages?** Look at the monitor for any messages that indicate a problem.

- **Is everything plugged in and turned on?** Turn off everything and check the connections. Don't assume that just because something looks connected, it is. Wiggle all the plugs.

- **When did the problem start?** Did you install a new program? Did you enter a command? Did you add a new device?

- **Is the problem limited to one program?** If you have the same problem in every program, the problem is probably caused by your PC or Windows. If the problem occurs in only one program, focus on that program.

- **When did you have the file last?** If you lost a file, it probably didn't get sucked into a black hole. It's probably somewhere on your disk, in a separate folder. Chapter 8 reveals several tricks for tracking down lost or misplaced files.

- **Realize that it's probably not the PC, and it's probably not a virus.** The problem is usually in the software—Windows or one of your programs. Of the problems that people blame on PC viruses or the PC itself, 95 percent are actually bugs in the software or problems with specific device drivers (the instructions that tell your PC and Windows how to use the device). Only about 5 percent prove to be caused by viruses.

**INSIDE TIP**

Keep a running log of the changes you make to your system. Every time you install a new device or new software, install updates, or change settings, jot down the date and what you did. It takes a little extra time, but it enables you to retrace your steps later. You may also want to check out a free tool called Belarc Advisor (belarc.com/free_download.html), which creates a detailed profile of your installed software and hardware and displays the results in your web browser. It's a good idea to print an update every quarter.

## Enlisting the Assistance of a Windows Troubleshooter

Windows has a collection of troubleshooters that can help you track down the cause of common issues and resolve them. To run a troubleshooter, click **Start, Control Panel**, and (below System and Security) click **Find and fix problems**. Click the link for the program or feature group that's giving you problems (for example, **Programs, Network and Internet**, or **System and Security**) and then click the specific item. This launches the troubleshooter for that item. Click **Next** and then follow the troubleshooter's lead, as shown in Figure 35.2.

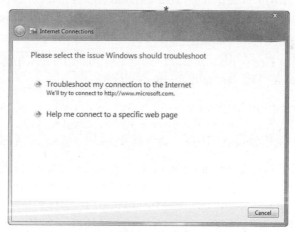

**Figure 35.2**
*The Windows troubleshooters can help track down problems and resolve issues.*

## Searching for Solutions Online

If you can connect to the Internet and access the web, you can often find solutions to common PC problems simply by using your favorite search engine, such as Google or Yahoo!. Run your web browser, access the search engine, type a description of the problem, and press **Enter**. The search likely returns a bunch of links to pages that may or may not contain the solution to the problem you're experiencing.

If Windows or one of your applications displays a specific error message, jot down the message and then enter it as your search phrase enclosed in quotes—for example, "Network Path Not Found".

## Checking the Manufacturer's Website

Every PC hardware and software company has a website and almost always provides technical support, software or driver updates, and online forums where you can find help. If you have an inkling that a particular hardware device or program is causing problems, head directly to the manufacturer's website. Often the manufacturer's website will not appear near the top of the search results when you search for a specific problem, but it will pop up immediately when you search the manufacturer's website.

If you can't find the answer on the website, you can usually find contact information, a contact form, or a link to online technical support. Chapter 5 shows you how to find website addresses and contact information for numerous PC, component, and software manufacturers.

## Getting Remote Assistance

Chapter 5 shows you how to use the Windows 7 Remote Assistance feature to obtain help from a friend or relative over the Internet. Many manufacturers also have their own remote assistance programs and technology that enable technicians to take control of your PC and help you resolve issues. Be sure to check the manufacturer's website for a link to live technical support.

# Thank Goodness for System Restore!

Windows includes a nifty utility called System Restore that can help you return your PC's settings to an earlier time when everything was working properly. System Restore monitors your PC, and when you install a program or a new peripheral device or component, it creates a *restore point* and saves the current settings to your PC's hard drive. System Restore also creates a weekly restore point, just in case something goes wrong that's not a result of something you installed. If you install a program or change a setting in Windows that causes problems, you can run System Restore and pick the desired restore point.

> **INSIDE TIP**
>
> When you return to a restore point, you don't lose any of the work you've done since that restore point. For example, if you made changes to a Word document, those are safe. However, if you installed a device or a program after Windows created the restore point, you'll probably need to reinstall it after you complete the restoration.

## Restore System Using a Restore Point

To return Windows to a previous state using one of the restore points it created, take the following steps:

1. Click **Start, All Programs, Accessories, System Tools, System Restore**. The System Restore window appears.

2. Click **Next**. System Restore displays available restore points. A list of recent restore points appears, as shown in Figure 35.3.

3. Click the desired restore point, click **Next,** and follow the onscreen instructions to complete the operation. Windows restarts your PC as part of the restoration process.

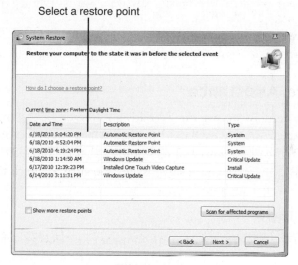

Select a restore point

**Figure 35.3**

*System Restore enables you to return your system to an earlier time.*

After System Restore restarts your PC, it displays a message indicating that you can undo the restoration. Cancel out of this window and test a few of the applications you normally use, to be sure the restoration didn't mess up your system. If the restoration made things worse instead of better, you can run System Restore again and undo the restoration.

## Create a Restore Point

If you plan to change any system settings in Windows, delete device drivers, or install applications, run System Restore and create your own restore point before you begin. If something goes wrong, you can immediately return your PC to its previous condition.

1. Click **Start, Control Panel, System and Security, System**.

2. Click **System protection** (left column). The System Properties dialog box appears.

3. Click **Create** (near the bottom of the dialog box).

4. Type a name for the restore point and click **Create**.

# Identifying Troublesome Software

Although Windows is responsible for its fair share of problems, applications, drivers, and other software are often responsible. Windows provides a couple utilities for helping track down problems with other software—Task Manager and the System Configuration Utility.

**NOTE**

Don't assume that the programs you run are the only programs running on your PC. Many programs that you install or that came already installed on your PC run in the background. You won't see buttons for them on the Windows taskbar or even in the system tray, but they're running just the same and can cause conflicts with Windows and your other programs. They can also consume processor and memory resources.

## Using Task Manager

Task Manager is most useful for identifying programs that have locked up or are "Not Responding." To run Task Manager, do one of the following:

- Click **Start**, type **task manager**, and then click **View running processes with Task Manager**.

- Press **Ctrl+Alt+Del** and click **Start Task Manager**. (This comes in handy when Windows is locked up and you can't open the Start menu.)

In either case, Task Manager appears, as shown in Figure 35.4, displaying a list of applications running on your PC. If an application is shown as "Not Responding," you can exit the application, although you may lose any recent changes to what you were working on in that application. To exit the application, click its name, click **End Task**, and then confirm your request.

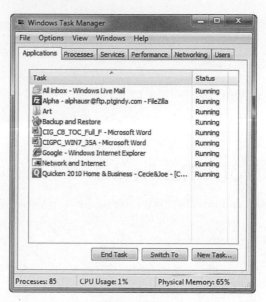

**Figure 35.4**

*Task Manager displays all the applications and processes running on your PC.*

If your PC is running very slowly, you can also use Task Manager to help identify the problem. Click the **Processes** tab and check the CPU and Memory columns, which show the percentage of resources the process is using. (The number in the CPU column is most important.) If the number is consistently high for a program (over, say, 50), you may need to do some additional troubleshooting to find out why it's so high.

## Troubleshooting with the System Configuration Utility

The System Configuration utility enables you to disable programs that automatically run when Windows starts. You can disable most of the programs to prevent them from running and then enable each program to identify the one that's causing problems.

To determine which programs are running on startup and to pick and choose which programs you want to run, perform a diagnostic startup:

1. Click **Start**, type **system con**, and click **System Configuration** (near the top of the Start menu).

2. Click the **Services** tab and click **Hide all Microsoft services**, as shown in Figure 35.5. By hiding Microsoft services, you avoid accidentally disabling a service that's critical for the operation of Windows.

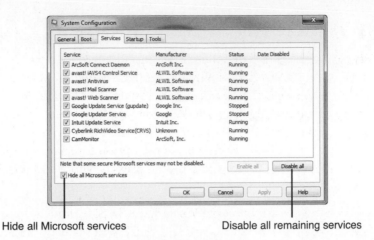

Hide all Microsoft services    Disable all remaining services

**Figure 35.5**
*System Configuration enables you to safely disable programs and services that might cause problems.*

3. Click the check box next to each *service* you don't want Windows to run on startup, being careful not to disable services that are crucial for securing your computer, such as antivirus services. (You can click the **Disable all** button and enable the items you do want Windows to run on startup.)

4. Click the **Startup** tab. A list of all the background programs that run on startup appears.

5. Click the check box next to each *program* you don't want Windows to run on startup, being careful not to disable programs that are crucial for securing your computer, such as antivirus services. (You can click the **Disable All** button and enable the programs you do want Windows to run on startup.)

6. Click **OK**. The System Configuration dialog box appears, prompting you to restart your computer.

7. Exit any currently running programs and click the **Restart** button. Windows restarts. A message appears in the lower-right corner of the screen, reminding you that you blocked some programs.

If the problem is no longer present, you now know that one of the services or programs you disabled is causing the problem and you can enable one or two services and programs at a time to narrow the list of possibilities. If the problem is still present, run the System Configuration utility again, disable more startup programs, and restart your PC. Using this strategy, you can focus on the program or service that's causing the problem.

# Starting Windows in Safe Mode

Windows typically starts in Safe mode if you install a wrong device driver (especially a wrong video or mouse driver). In Safe mode, "Safe Mode" appears at each corner of the desktop. In most cases, you can simply restart Windows to have it load the previous driver. If, upon restarting, the Windows desktop is not visible or you cannot use the mouse, restart your PC and keep tapping the **F8** key every second or so until you see the Safe Mode screen. Then choose the option for starting Windows in Safe mode. (You have to be quick with the F8 key—press it before you see the Windows screen.)

Windows loads a standard mouse and video driver in Safe mode so you can see what you're doing and use the mouse to point and click. This enables you to install a different or updated driver, uninstall a program you just installed, or change settings back to what they were before you encountered problems.

## The Least You Need to Know

- Be prepared for trouble before it strikes by backing up valuable files, creating a system image, and creating a system repair disc.
- To access the Windows troubleshooters, click **Start**, **Control Panel**, **Find and fix problems** under System and Security.
- Use System Restore to return your PC to an earlier time when it was working properly.
- If a program stops responding or Windows freezes up, press **Ctrl+Alt+Del**, click **Start Task Manager**, and end any programs that are "Not Responding."
- Use the System Configuration utility to troubleshoot problems caused by programs that run in the background.
- Don't go into shock when Windows starts in Safe mode. Shutting down and restarting your PC usually corrects the problem.

# Index

# D